The A'
Guide to Nineteenth
Century America

DAVID M. PAINE

Website: davidmpaineauthor.blogspot.com

Twitter: @davidpaine1005

ISBN 10: 1536863971
ISBN 13: 978-1536863970

Edited by Julie Webb
Cover and Interior Design by Victor Rook

Cover Images:
Front: Thomas Jefferson, Gibson Girl, Abraham Lincoln
Back: Andrew Jackson, Chief Garfield
Background: The Assault on Chapultepec Castle, Mexico City

Dedicated to my late mother, Margaret Whittemore Paine, who taught me a love of history.

TABLE OF CONTENTS

FOREWORD

The Industrial Revolution. Edgar Allen Poe. The War of 1812. The Gay '90s. The Trail of Tears. The Transcontinental Railroad. Mark Twain. The Gibson Girl. Thomas Jefferson. The Depression of 1837. The first baseball and football teams. Jacksonian Democracy. Thomas Edison and the light bulb. The Mexican-American War. Samuel Gompers and the American Federation of Labor. The Monroe Doctrine.

The liberation of Cuba, and colonization of the Philippines. The Abolitionist Movement. Sears & Roebuck catalogs. John D. Rockefeller and Standard Oil. The election scandal of 1876. Abraham Lincoln and the Civil War.

How many of these names and events do you recognize? Quite a few I'm sure, hopefully most of them. But you may be surprised that they all came before 1900. They are among the many episodes that make the years 1800 to 1900 such a vital period in American history. *The Average Joe's Guide to Nineteenth Century America* was written to help reacquaint you with some important history that you may have forgotten.

You, the Average Joe, are a man (or a woman, let's call you Jo) who finished high school ten or more years ago. You may have gone to college to forward your career. Years later now, you don't remember most of what you learned about American history and you feel a need to recall. You realize, perhaps now you are "grown-up", that history is pretty important after all. With the world in turmoil and America the sole superpower, you want to know how we got here, how we reached our level of power and wealth, and just what sort of a nation we are.

I submit that if you are just now returning to American history, the Nineteenth Century is the place to start. The years 1800 to 1900 include the pivotal events when America was choosing its direction, expanding, fighting to win the West, and fighting the war over slavery. Of course, our birth as a nation during the Revolutionary period (1770-1800) makes for important study. In 1800 America was still like a young child with a new identity, finding its way in the world. The Nineteenth Century is the incredible story of how we became richer, stronger and freer than any nation in history. A hundred years is a long time, but I think it's wise to learn about the Nineteenth Century as a whole. It is when America went through astonishing changes that shaped history, and when we emerged as a major world power.

Now, Dear Joe (or Jo), your life is focused on work, career, and family, and you don't have much time to delve into history. You could plunge into one of several 900-page, comprehensive volumes covering 350 years of American history. Most of them are written by great scholars who provide vital details to help you interpret events. These works focus on key people and events, but they may not provide enough context to truly grasp how one event connects to another.

Or you can get up close and personal with particular episodes in American history, and choose among an abundance of bestsellers written on a wide range of topics and figures from history. While it is true that there is something deeply satisfying about digging into a great story, where do you start? There are a dozen books written for general readers on the Civil War alone in the last ten years, and hundreds written since the war ended. Then, having learned the whole story on your chosen topic and used all your spare time for a week or two, you are missing the continuity of overall American history, how one event links to the next.

Maybe you could buy one of the easy-history 101 books. They will run you through the past step-by-step, spoon-feeding you in a way that insults your intelligence or leaves you feeling empty, like a fast-food meal. You will learn the basic facts, but you won't get a real sense of the people or the times.

Or you could just give up.

Where does the Average Joe find a relatively short and concise book that covers this essential period in history, and that puts the right amount of detail into context and in a way that tells the full story?

You hold it in your hands. This book will get you up to speed on the most significant one hundred years in American history.

I have always considered history one of the most important subjects a person can learn. After many years of reading, talking with friends and experts, discussing American history, and learning what most historians consider to be the pivotal figures and events, I have a good idea what the Average Joe would like to know. My goal in writing this book is to present the facts needed to come to your own conclusions, and get a well-rounded, balanced perspective on our history.

I want to bring continuity to American history and make the Nineteenth Century come alive and seem less of an abstraction or historical artifact. Americans then were ordinary people, struggling with real questions and dreams, and caught up in sweeping economic and cultural changes under the leadership of strong men – and also some weak men. In the Average Joe's Guide, I highlight the major names, places, and events and I include enough detail to make it a realistic story, but not so much detail you get inundated. History succeeds when it flows, when one event leads logically to the next, and the reader can climb aboard the train of the past and relate it to his present.

There is a large gap in most Americans' understanding of our history and heritage, and this gap usually gets filled with myths, distortions, and outright lies. We need a more accurate and honest relationship with our past. I want to fill this need for you, the Average Joe. I want to empower you to be the best citizen you can be. History illuminates the present. After all, if you don't understand where you came from, you have little idea where you need to go.

DAVID PAINE

THE AVERAGE JOE'S GUIDE TO NINETEENTH CENTURY AMERICA

INTRODUCTION – THE UNITED STATES IN 1800

The United States of America was still a new nation in 1800. The Spirit of 1776 and the heroic days of the Revolution were still fresh in many minds. The US Constitution, the great turning point in our early history, was just 13 years old. America's first leaders, our Founding Fathers, were men whose accomplishments in the Revolution made them famous, and natural choices to lead the young republic. George Washington (1731-1799) had saved the United States as both Commander of the Continental Army and then President of the Constitutional Convention. He went on to serve two terms as our first president, from 1789 to 1797.

President Washington's authority was essential in keeping America on an even keel through some minor crises during his time in office. He knew the nation was still fragile, and kept us out of foreign wars. Together with Alexander Hamilton, Secretary of the Treasury, he established a financial system through the First Bank of the United States. In 1794 he put down the Whiskey Rebellion in western Pennsylvania when protestors threatened and intimidated agents collecting the federal whiskey tax, one of the US's only means of raising revenue. As important as anything else he did was stepping down, his decision not to run for a third term, which would have been the will of the people. In fact, Washington's influence was so strong that he could have overturned the rule of law and proclaimed himself King. His example of a two-term limit set a precedent that, except in the case of Franklin Roosevelt, has been observed by every president since. Washington retired to his farm at Mount Vernon, Virginia, and died in 1799, as much the victim of the malpractice of blood-letting as of illness.

Washington was succeeded by Vice President John Adams (1735-1826) of Massachusetts, another revolutionary famous for leading the Continental Congress. Two political parties had evolved by now, making the presidential election a real contest. Adams and Secretary Alexander Hamilton led the Federalist Party, while Thomas Jefferson and John Madison led the Democratic-Republican Party. According to the law at the time, the president and vice president did not run together on the same ticket. The vice president was the runner-up vote winner, and since Thomas Jefferson came in second in the balloting, he served as Adams' vice president.

This obviously made for tricky politics and even worse government. Adams and Jefferson fought almost constantly and were enemies by the end of Adams' term in office. Meanwhile, Jefferson's party was winning the battle of public opinion, and he defeated Adams in the election of 1800 to become our third president.

Now what about the American people in 1800? History shows that entropy is a powerful force; the tendency of things to fall apart had nearly destroyed the United States in the years of the Articles of Confederation, before the Constitution. Individual states were arguing and taxing each other's commerce, and the federal government was nearly powerless. But the people adapted fairly quickly to the more powerful central government under the Constitution, and voter participation (limited though it was to men who held property) was very high. America was predominantly agricultural. More than 90 percent of Americans farmed or lived in the countryside, and in 1800 there were only five cities with a population of more than 10,000: New York, Philadelphia, Baltimore, Boston, and Charleston.

American industry, like the people, was primarily geared towards agriculture. Iron forges turned out mostly farm implements and guns, and not much machinery; horses pulled all the wagons, and steam was just being harnessed to power boats. The US had an effective postal service, thanks to our first Postmaster Benjamin Franklin (who is better known for countless other achievements), but mail delivery between cities was only as fast as the road conditions between them. Railroads and trains were still thirty years away. As in other countries, the cities were the bases of power where government, banking, fine crafts, and international trade took place, and the eastern financial centers steadily eclipsed the power and influence of the Virginia and Carolina planters.

Compared to other nations, Americans had a high standard living. As an agrarian economy most families were self-sufficient, not wage-earners. Nearly every household had a rifle, a treasured possession much more costly in those days than now. Americans grew plenty of food and there was land for farming and to expand the cities. Pioneers were pushing the western frontier far across the Appalachian Mountains into the Ohio and Mississippi River valleys, with thousands to follow them. The average white American could read, in spite of not having much that we would recognize as a public school system, since he or she was taught at home, at church, and at work. Civic engagement was as participatory as a person wanted it to be; when issues were hot, such as during election seasons, people were tuned in. Otherwise, they just wanted to be left alone—not very different from how we live now.

In 1800, two problems that later exploded on the nation were not yet heavy on the typical American's mind. First, the American Indians. They had fought bloody wars against the British and the colonists in the 1700s, but by 1800 most were living across the Appalachian Mountains and were not immediate threats. The "Five Civilized Tribes" (see Chapter Two) held large areas of land in the Southeast, and were adopting the white man's language, clothing, farming, and construction.

Second, slavery. There were now over a million black slaves in America, and while most Americans both South and

North knew the slavery question would eventually need to be settled, a compromise embodied in the Constitution had laid the issue to rest for the time being. Under terms of the compromise, Congress could not abolish the Atlantic slave trade until 1808 (which came to happen), and the slave states could not fully count slaves for the purpose of representation in Congress. The Northern states steadily abolished slavery, the last state being New Jersey in 1804. But within the South, in cities like New Orleans, Richmond, Atlanta, and Charleston, slaves were sold at auctions like livestock.

After the Revolution, the United States expanded from the original 13 to 16 states. New states added prior to 1800 included Vermont, Kentucky, and Tennessee, the latter two formed from territory given up by the state of Virginia. In the first two decades after 1800, westward expansion brought statehood to Ohio, Louisiana, Indiana, Alabama, Illinois, and Mississippi, bringing the total number of states to 22 in 1819.

CHAPTER ONE—EARLY EXPANSION, JEFFERSONIAN DEMOCRACY, AND THE WAR OF 1812

THE PRESIDENCY OF THOMAS JEFFERSON

The Nineteenth Century in America essentially begins in 1801 with high hopes for the presidency of Thomas Jefferson (1743-1826). Jefferson had served as both George Washington's Secretary of State and John Adams' Vice President, and was best known at the time as author of the Declaration of Independence in 1776. In the late 1790s Jefferson became the leader of the new Democratic-Republican Party, which was formed in opposition to the prevailing Federalists led by President Adams and Secretary of the Treasury Alexander Hamilton. Until this time, America had no organized political parties; however, Jefferson and his allies (including James Madison, a driving intellectual force at the Constitutional Convention) opposed the Federalists' style of strong, central government, and Hamilton's Bank of the United States. His politics usually favored small government and the highest possible liberty for the individual, with minimal responsibilities required of the federal government. Jefferson was highly anti-British and until the Louisiana Purchase (more below) he sympathized with the French Revolution in spite of its repressive, bloody violence.

President Jefferson's first accomplishment was to win a series of small wars against the Barbary Pirates in 1803 and

1805. The Barbary Pirates were Arabs operating out of North African ports in Tunis, Morocco, Algiers, and Tripoli, who attacked merchant ships in the Mediterranean, stealing cargo and holding crews for ransom. Until Jefferson, American leaders, like the British, bought protection from the pirates by paying them tribute. Pasha Yusuf Karamanli of Tripoli demanded that Jefferson pay tribute of $225,000, but Jefferson refused to pay any further, proclaiming "Millions for defense but not one cent for tribute."[1] He made war on the Pasha with a naval blockade and later a land campaign from Tunis to Libya. In May 1805, two squadrons of heavy frigates took control of Tripoli harbor, while US Marines leading a force of Greek and Arab mercenaries attacked the fortress of Derne. Victory was complete, and Hamlet Karamanli, brother of Yusuf, was installed on the throne. The line "From the Halls of Montezuma to the shores of Tripoli" from the Marine Corps' anthem refers to the Marines first engagement as a fighting force. But as we shall see, Jefferson's determination to protect America did not last long; his weaknesses as Commander in Chief led indirectly to the War of 1812.

Thomas Jefferson in 1805, by Rembrandt Peale

President Jefferson also placed a new emphasis on transportation. He expanded public works by building new roads and canals, continuing work begun by George Washington, focusing on projects too large for the small corporations of the time. Treasury Secretary Albert Gallatin prepared (but could not execute) a ten-year, $20 million plan to build and lend money for bridge and road construction. It's important to note that this plan did not entail a new agency or any expansion of government as we would see today; its main purpose was only to complete a project that would benefit commerce.

Jefferson was not a military man, but he can be credited with establishing the United States Military Academy at West Point, New York, in 1801. The Academy had very loose standards for curriculum and for cadets—they ranged in age from 10 to 37 years —until Superintendent Colonel Sylvanus Thayer took over in 1817. Thayer set strict disciplinary and academic standards, emphasizing engineering, military strategy and theory, and a code of personal honor. From this time forward, West Point graduates were the finest officers in America and ranked among the best in the world.

THE LOUISIANA PURCHASE AND THE CORPS OF DISCOVERY

Thomas Jefferson's vision of America was not the nation we have become. He saw a relatively small nation comprised mostly of farmers, where power was held as closely to the local level as possible—not a major world power with a huge bureaucracy divided into myriad functions and exercising control over most of the national economy. But this did not stop him from taking advantage of an opportunity to expand the nation with the biggest real estate deal in history.

Until 1803, Spain controlled Louisiana, the vast area west of the Mississippi River and north of New Spain (Mexico, which was much larger at the time). Louisiana extended north in a roughly V-shaped territory from New Orleans and modern Louisiana to the Oregon Territory on the Continental Divide (near the border between modern Idaho and Montana) and Canada on the north. It contained as much land as the United States east of the Mississippi. But Spain abruptly transferred Louisiana to France in a deal with Emperor Napoleon, gaining only a small kingdom in Italy. In its short-sightedness, Spain agreed with the French argument that France would form "a wall of brass forever impenetrable to the combined efforts of England and America."[2]

The French surely wanted the strategic advantage of holding this territory, uncharted though it was. American trappers and settlers had been crossing the Mississippi and living in Louisiana territory for years, yet Spain had done nothing to stop them. In 1800 over half a million Americans lived west of the Appalachian Mountains, and it was inevitable that more settlers would cross the big river. About this same time, pressure was building from French colonists living in New Orleans to go north and settle the area themselves.

The transfer from Spain to France worried President Jefferson, who believed Napoleon would try to rebuild a North American empire. The Mississippi River carried three-eighths of American goods to port in New Orleans, so French expansion would also threaten American commerce. Even before Louisiana transferred to France, Jefferson wrote to his minister in Paris, Robert Livingstone, that "The day that France takes possession of New Orleans…seals the union of two countries who in conjunction can maintain exclusive possession of the ocean. From that moment we must marry ourselves to the British fleet and nation."[3]

However, once France did acquire Louisiana, Jefferson chose to bargain for and buy the port of New Orleans. Surprisingly, the French offered to sell not just the city but all the land just gained from Spain. As it turned out, Emperor Napoleon and his minister Talleyrand had just lost many men to fighting and disease in the colony of Haiti, and were content to be relieved of the land north of Louisiana. And, perhaps, the French grasped the futility of holding the land against the new rising power across the Atlantic.

In what became known as the Louisiana Purchase of 1803, for just $15 million, or three cents per acre, the United States added 828,000 square miles and doubled its territory. Inflated to 2015 dollars, the payment would be $233 million—even now the Louisiana Purchase would be a tremendous bargain. On December 20, 1803, the French prefect in New Orleans surrendered Louisiana to American officials.

United States Acquisitions in the Nineteenth Century

Most of the land had never been explored, but it was now open for settlement. Jefferson had a great interest in geography (among his many other interests and obsessions), and had studied all the available maps of North America to capitalize on this grand acquisition. Soon after the Purchase, he sent his personal secretary Meriwether Lewis and Captain William Clark upon a two-and-a-half-year expedition to the new territory, with the mission "to explore the Missouri river, & such principal streams of it, as, by its course and communication with the waters of the Pacific Ocean, whether the Columbia, Oregon, Colorado, or any other river may offer the most direct & practicable water communication across this continent for the purposes of commerce". Jefferson also emphasized the need to "Treat (the natives) in the most friendly and conciliatory manner…and allay all jealousies as to the object of your journey…."

The Lewis and Clark Expedition is one of history's great adventures. In May 1804 their troop of 45 men, called the Corps of Discovery, embarked on a courageous journey over 8,000 miles that took two years and four months. They left from Pittsburgh and headed west on the Ohio River, briefly up the Mississippi to St. Louis, and then northwest over a thousand miles on the Missouri. Near modern Bismarck, North Dakota, they were joined by a French trader and his Shoshone wife, Sacagawea, who became invaluable guides and interpreters for the rest of the journey. After wintering there, it took all the warm months of 1805 to cross Montana and the Continental Divide at the Bitterroot Mountains, travel on western rivers to the Columbia River, and reach the Pacific coast at Fort Clatsop. In 1806 they retraced their steps, then separated in two groups, with Clark taking a southerly route to explore trails known by Sacagawea. Lewis and his men took their original route, and fought with Blackfeet Indians trying to steal their horses, killing two. They had been given up for dead when they arrived in St. Louis on September 23, 1806, but they only lost one man to a burst appendix.

Lewis and Clark mapped unexplored rivers and mountains, and brought back a wealth of knowledge about two dozen American Indian tribes they encountered, the geography and resources, the birds, animals, forests, and other scientific information valuable at the time. They did not find a continuous waterway to the Pacific Ocean, as Jefferson hoped, but they located an Indian trail that led from the upper end of the Missouri River to the Columbia River which then ran to the Pacific Ocean. Most important, their journey taught them the tremendous challenge of crossing the varying landscapes, and helped future settlers understand the difficulties they would face when traversing the continent.

MARBURY VS. MADISON

In 1803, a relatively minor case before the Supreme Court had far-reaching consequences which are still being debated today. The Court under Chief Justice John Marshall took a case from William Marbury, who demanded his commission (office) as

Justice of the Peace in Washington, DC, from Secretary of State James Madison. Former President Adams had ordered Marbury's commission but failed to actually deliver it before leaving the White House in 1801. Marbury was suing Madison in the Supreme Court according to his right as stated under the Judiciary Act of 1789.

Justice Marshall and the Court ruled unanimously that the Judiciary Act was unconstitutional, since in actuality it was an attempt to amend Section III of the Constitution, which describes the judicial power of the United States. Although Marbury had a legal right to his commission, there were other means to get it and he did not have the right, after all, to bring his case to the Supreme Court.[4]

All this sounds rather humdrum, but it established a very important legal precedent. By invalidating the Judiciary Act the Court was asserting its right to judicial review over all laws passed by Congress. By extension, the ruling declared the Court's sole authority to decide on the constitutionality of any law, and the meaning of the Constitution itself.

Having established the Supreme Court's authority to conduct judicial review, Justice Marshall applied it to other decisions. In 1819, his Court ruled the state of New Hampshire had no power to make Dartmouth College a public institution, thus strengthening private property rights. In McCulloch v. Maryland, the Court rejected Maryland's attempt to tax the Second Bank of the United States, affirming the Constitutional clause giving the government authority to use all means "necessary and proper" to execute its designated powers. Any Average Joe who has followed Supreme Court cases for the last thirty years or more understands how this authority has shaped current law and political practice. Cases involving school desegregation, abortion, and gun rights have been brought to the Court by plaintiffs wanting to test the validity of law.

AARON BURR

Aaron Burr (1756-1836) is an infamous name in American history. Burr was an ambitious man, and served as Jefferson's first vice president, but neither Jefferson nor the Federalists trusted his character. Burr's enemies combined against him and nominated George Clinton for vice president in Jefferson's second term. Burr's only remaining base of support now came from New York City. With his political career nearly ruined, Burr fixed his revenge on Alexander Hamilton, Washington's secretary of the Treasury. On July 11, 1804, Burr faced Hamilton in a duel on the cliffs of Weehawken, New Jersey, overlooking the Hudson River, and killed him.

Burr did not reckon on Hamilton's popularity and now found himself a hated man, even in the city. In 1805 Burr moved to Louisiana where he made bold plans for a new career, outside of the United States. In 1806 he raised a small force of 80 men and engaged in a conspiracy with Mexico to overthrow Spanish rule, which would also give him control of his own new territory in modern-day Texas. His accomplice was an Army officer named James Wilkinson, who soon betrayed him for violating the Neutrality Act. As evidence against Burr, Wilkinson provided a letter that he had doctored to hide the extent of his own role in the affair. Burr was captured in Alabama and put on trial for high treason, but he was acquitted in part due to Wilkinson's damaged testimony. Burr left in disgrace for England but he returned in 1812 to work in New York as a lawyer.

JEFFERSON'S SECOND ADMINISTRATION

As America expanded, cities on the eastern seaboard grew much larger. By 1800, New York City had surpassed Philadelphia and Boston as the largest city and center of commerce and banking. In 1801 the nation's capital moved from New York to Washington, District of Columbia, which had begun construction under the supervision of a French architect named Pierre L'Enfant. The North was now clearly the center of manufacturing and industry, which drove the growth of all the urban areas. The South, with a longer growing season and with low crop-picking costs from slave labor, concentrated on agriculture, although it operated large ports in Charleston and New Orleans. Under-development of Southern manufacturing thus became an important factor influencing sectional trade and national politics up through the Civil War.

Jefferson's greatest weakness as president was in dealing with tensions stemming from the war between England and France. Jefferson's philosophy of minimal government now failed him, since America lacked the military muscle to adequately protect itself. France under its new emperor Napoleon Bonaparte had enacted the Continental System, which embargoed all British goods from areas that France controlled. Britain then proclaimed its own Order of Council, under which they claimed the right to impound any ship, even from a neutral country, that was suspected of aiding the French. Jefferson favored the French side of the conflict and forced passage through Congress of the Non-Importation Act, an embargo of shipping to England. The British, whose navy was stronger than the French in the open oceans, started pressuring American shipping; any innocent merchant vessel was liable to be stopped and stripped of its crew members if the British cruiser was short of men. In 1807, the British *HMS Leopard* attacked and boarded the *USS Chesapeake* in full view of the shore of Norfolk, Virginia, taking four prisoners from the crew.

British raids on shipping were a step short of war, and a blow to American pride. Since his victory over the Barbary Pirates, Jefferson had done little to build the navy, except to construct hundreds of small, unseaworthy gunboats for coastal defense. Although armed with one cannon, these small boats rocked so much with the waves that the crew couldn't aim the gun. With no real military option against the British, Jefferson's next step was the Embargo Act of 1807, which was a futile and pathetic attempt at neutrality between the French and the British. The practical effect of the embargo was to force most American ships to stay in harbor. As could be predicted the Embargo Act was a huge failure that ruined trade and angered Northern shipping and citizens. The government reversed it with another Act in 1809, as Jefferson was leaving office at his lowest ebb in public opinion. The British continued boarding American ships, and they "impressed" many American seamen into British naval service with the charge of being English deserters.

13

THE WAR OF 1812 AND THE CREEK WAR

President Jefferson's successor in 1809 was another Virginian, his protégé James Madison (1751-1836), the famous leader of the Constitutional Convention of 1787, and a co-author (with George Mason) of the Bill of Rights. But President Madison was a weak executive, and like Jefferson he failed to stop the British assault on American ships. Madison let the situation fester during his first term as president. America's humiliation mounted, year by year, and we drifted into war for lack of the will to address the root of the problem. Madison was reelected in 1812 but only on the strength of votes from people in the South and the West, who favored expansion and a showdown with Britain—unlike the Northern states, who did not want to provoke the English, so as long as trade continued. On June 18, 1812 Congress declared war on Britain.

Yet President Madison had done almost nothing to prepare for war. It went badly from the start. With urging from Jefferson, Madison wanted to conquer Canada and bring it into the Union. Both men were mistaken in believing the Canadians wanted freedom from the British; many Canadians were former American Loyalists, and Catholic *Quebecois* were frightened of domination by the Protestant church. The regular American army was only 7,000 men, spread across the country, and it relied heavily on militia recruited from the states. New Englanders opposed the war as a threat to commerce, and their state militias refused to join the fight. After marching north into Canada, the militia were worthless as fighting men; there was no discipline in their ranks and they suffered a lingering fear of the British Indian allies. And nearly 40 years after the Revolution, the Army now lacked an experienced officer corps, and the generals were openly ridiculed for their blunders.

There were some bright spots in the war at sea, and on the Great Lakes. Some American ships built during the Federalist period were larger than the British, our naval corps was better disciplined and we had better officers, who were promoted on the basis of merit rather than for their noble birth. In September 1813, Commodore Oliver Perry defeated a superior British force in battle on Lake Erie and became an American hero. Just as significant as Perry's victory, Commodore Thomas Macdonough stopped a British force of 14,000 men marching south from Canada by capturing British naval forces on Lake Champlain. Without their naval supply line, the British retreated to Canada.

However, the US never achieved its objectives in the War of 1812, which were vague in the first place. Britain defeated Napoleon and the French in 1814 and was able to focus on war with the United States. Madison was blind to the danger, and again did nothing to prepare defenses on the American coasts. In August, 5,000 British troops landed in Maryland from Chesapeake Bay, and unopposed, they marched on Washington DC. American politicians, troops, and civilians fled the city; Madison's wife Dolly had the foresight to save George Washington's portrait before abandoning the White House. When the British arrived on August 24, 1814 they casually burned the White House, the Capitol, and the Treasury, and left, as unopposed as they arrived. James and Dolly Madison reunited days later at an inn at Great Falls, Virginia, miles up the Potomac from Washington, and returned in despair to the smoldering capital.

The British were finally defeated weeks later when they attempted to take Baltimore. On the night of September 13-14, American defenders at Fort McHenry in Baltimore Harbor resisted a continuous, heavy bombardment by over a hundred British ships. When the huge American flag was still seen waving the morning after the battle, lawyer Francis Scott Key was moved to write the lyrics to "The Star Spangled Banner," which years later was proclaimed our national anthem.

Before wrapping up history of the War of 1812 we need to discuss the Creek War, for it covered the same years and the climaxes of both wars are intertwined. The Creek Indian tribes who controlled much of Alabama and Georgia were split between the Lower Creek villages friendly to Americans, living along the Chattahoochee River, and hostile Upper Creek villages in central Alabama. The hostile tribes, called the Red Sticks for their red war clubs, were determined not to assimilate with Americans as the Cherokee and others tribes were doing.

In 1811, just prior to the War, Governor of Indiana Territory William Henry Harrison, had defeated Shawnee chief Tecumseh at Tippecanoe River. Tecumseh's mother was Creek, and Tecumseh had travelled south to urge the Creeks to join with him and eradicate the white man. Tecumseh appealed most directly to Red Stick Chiefs Red Eagle and Menawa, threatening to shake the ground if they refused. On December 16, 1811, the earth shook for hundreds of miles from a magnitude 7.5 earthquake with its epicenter at New Madrid, Missouri. The Red Sticks were convinced that Tecumseh had divine power and more warriors joined the Red Stick faction. Red Sticks and other Indian tribes allied themselves with the British, and armed with thousands of British muskets, carbines and pistols they attacked American settlements in Indiana and in Michigan at Mackinaw and Detroit, and sent warriors as far as Canada to attack American soldiers retreating from the invasion.

Red Stick raids against white settlements in Georgia led to a civil war between the Creek factions in 1813. Americans civilians, militia, and friendly Creeks north of Pensacola took refuge in a fort built by Samuel Mims, a prosperous merchant who was part Creek. On August 30 Red Eagle and over 1,000 warriors mounted a surprise attack on Fort Mims and massacred 556 settlers, including 453 women and children. Their bodies were mutilated and hacked to pieces. A dozen soldiers managed to escape through a hole in the stockade wall.

News of the Fort Mims massacre spread throughout America. The Creek threat grew across the Southeast, as Red Eagle recruited tribes who had remained neutral and were now encouraged by Fort Mims, and goaded on by the Spanish in Florida. This is when General Andrew Jackson entered the picture.

Andrew Jackson was a prominent man from Nashville, a judge and former US Senator, who was elected commander of the Tennessee militia in 1802. Earlier, in the War of 1812, Jackson and his militia had nearly joined the fighting but were sent back to Tennessee by regular Army commanders. But after Fort Mims Jackson was given the mission of defeating the

Creeks. About 2,500 militia marched into Alabama and established their base at Fort Strother.

General Jackson's first action was retaliation, by killing 186 Creek warriors in the village of Tallushatchee and taking most of the women and children prisoners. On November 9, 1813, Jackson saved a friendly Creek village at Talladega from destruction by the Red Sticks. But Jackson faced a crisis that winter when many of his troops' one-year enlistments were ending. Down to one small brigade (less than 1,000 men), Jackson resorted to writing an angry letter to Governor William Blount of Tennessee demanding more soldiers.[5] Blount changed course and ordered new enlistments, and 1,000 men met Jackson at Fort Strother in early January 1814.

The largest battle ever fought against American Indians was just ahead for Jackson. His ultimate objective was the Red Stick stronghold at Horseshoe Bend on the Tallapoosa River in east-central Alabama. His militia fought two defensive battles with the Red Sticks at Emuckfaw and at Entachopco, where the Creeks proved their tactical ability to execute attack, but still lost many warriors. Jackson attacked Horseshoe Bend on March 27, sending his militia directly against strong Red Stick barricades while 500 friendly Cherokee warriors crossed the river and attacked from the rear. Over 800 Red Stick warriors were killed at Horseshoe Bend, and Jackson took 350 women and children prisoner, ordering that they be treated humanely. Red Eagle was away during the battle, but he walked in days later and surrendered. Jackson agreed to let him go if he convinced the remaining Red Sticks to quit the fight.

The Creeks formally surrendered on April 20, 1814 and submitted to Jackson's demand for over half their territory, 23 million acres. Red Eagle resumed using his English name, William Weatherford, and retired to a large farm in Alabama. However, Jackson betrayed the friendly Creek leaders by taking their land just as he took the Red Sticks'. Shocked, they protested that US General Pinkney had promised to reward them for their alliance; but Jackson claimed that Pinkney had no authority to make that promise. The Creek Nation was mortally wounded; few American Creeks or other tribes fought for the British for the remainder of the war.

Chief Red Eagle (William Weatherford) Surrenders to Andrew
Jackson

General Jackson then moved south and occupied the
Spanish base in Pensacola, Florida. America was not at war
with Spain; however, Spain had encouraged the Creeks, and
this move also prevented the British from using the area in
their planned assault on New Orleans. On January 8, 1815, in
the last battle of the War of 1812, the British attacked
Jackson's forces in uncharacteristically reckless fashion. The
American line defending New Orleans was a 1,000 yard
earthwork in a bottleneck between a swamp and the
Mississippi River. The British made a frontal assault on open
ground, but the Americans' defensive lines and relentless
musket and cannon fire caused tremendous losses. The British
lost 775 soldiers, either killed or missing, including three
generals, while the Americans lost only 58 wounded and
thirteen killed, from all ranks.

The Treaty of Ghent ended the war on December 24, 1814.
Ironically, the Treaty was signed a month before the Battle of
New Orleans, but the news took weeks to cross the Atlantic.
Just the same, Jackson probably saved New Orleans from being

destroyed. The Treaty returned all borders to their status before the war, required the release of all prisoners, and restored diplomatic relations. The United States had to recognize British sovereignty over Canada, which would now stay free from invasion. The British still held the upper hand in negotiations but decided that they had taught the Americans a lesson. They recognized the United States' claim to the Louisiana Purchase, and both sides agreed to peaceful coexistence inside the wild Oregon Territory, where the only men of European descent were fur traders.

SETTLEMENT WITH SPAIN

By time of the War of 1812, the US had been hungering for Spain's colony of Florida for years. Florida included not just the current American state, but the Gulf coasts of Alabama and Mississippi. At this time, these two states were landlocked, so gaining Florida would put them on the Gulf and complete American possession of the entire southeastern continent. In 1810 the US annexed the land north of New Orleans and the Mississippi River, making it part of the Louisiana Territory. In May 1812, President Madison authorized annexation of the Mobile District, the stretch of land between Louisiana and the Perdido River including Mobile Bay. The Spanish commander in Mobile surrendered without resistance in 1813, and this land was added to the Mississippi Territory. Pensacola and Florida remained in Spanish possession, for now.

As described earlier, Spanish-American relations were tense after Spain helped the Creeks resist settlers during the Creek War. Andrew Jackson occupied Pensacola in November 1814, before the Battle of New Orleans. Seminole Indians in Florida, helped by the British, continued attacking settlements in Georgia and Alabama; so in 1818 Andrew Jackson entered central, Spanish-held Florida, marching down the Apalachicola River and breaking Indian resistance. Jackson then turned west to Pensacola and took the city after a short siege.

Florida by now had become a burden to Spain, who could not afford to send troops or support its colonists. The Spanish were already fighting revolutions in Central and South America and had to give up the oldest European colony in North America, with the oldest city, St. Augustine. In 1819, the Adams-Onis Treaty was negotiated by President Monroe's Secretary of State John Quincy Adams and Spanish Foreign Minister Luis de Onis y Gonzalez Vara. The US did not buy Florida, but did agree to pay $5 million in legal claims against Spain. The Treaty solved the Florida issue—and another pressing matter with Spain as well.

The US and Spain had been disputing the western edge of the Louisiana Purchase with New Spain. Adams-Onis set the western border along a zig-zag line on the map (refer to page 9). Beginning at the Gulf of Mexico at the mouth of the Sabine River, the border went north to the Red River, then west to 100 degrees longitude, north to the Arkansas River, and west to the Pacific on the 42nd parallel. The southern section was to become the eastern border of Texas. The 42nd parallel remains the northern border of California, Nevada, and Utah. After the Mexican Revolution of 1821, New Spain became Mexico.

CHAPTER TWO—1820 TO 1844: GOOD FEELINGS, AND JACKSONIAN DEMOCRACY

MONROE AND THE ERA OF GOOD FEELINGS

The presidency of James Monroe (the years 1817 to 1825) has been called the "Era of Good Feelings." Americans were free of the threat of British invasion, and many leaders hoped the Missouri Compromise in 1820 would put the slavery issue to rest for a while. There was also more political peace, since the Democratic-Republican Party had apparently finished off the Federalist party of John Adams and his allies.

President James Monroe (1758-1831) is known for proclaiming the Monroe Doctrine in 1823. The doctrine was a foreign policy declaration that further efforts by European nations to interfere with states in North or South America would be viewed as acts of aggression, requiring an American response. In a message to Congress, Monroe stated "The American continents, by the free and independent condition which they have assumed and maintain, are henceforth not to be considered as subjects for future colonization by any European powers." The Monroe Doctrine was also an expression of American exceptionalism, justified by a new type of government that "has been achieved by the loss of so much blood and treasure, and matured by the wisdom of [its] most enlightened citizens." The doctrine was in part the creation of John Quincy Adams, son of John Adams and Monroe's Secretary of State, who also succeeded him as president.[6]

Aside from asserting an American sphere of influence, the Monroe Doctrine was an idealistic statement that new governments should be free to realize their own destinies, without fear of foreign interference. Since 1810 nations in South America had been winning independence from Spain, and the Monroe Doctrine reflected a very realistic concern that European powers would attempt to re-colonize them. In Europe, the "Quadruple Alliance" of France, Austria, Russia, and Prussia were suppressing democratic movements across the Continent, and Ferdinand of Spain pressed for their help in regaining his lost colonies. President Monroe first exercised his doctrine when he warned Russia, which was threatening to extend its Alaskan claims south into the Oregon Territory. In 1824, Russia backed off and agreed to limit settlement to the latitude at 54 degrees, 40 minutes north.[7]

James Monroe

President Monroe, like Presidents Jefferson and Madison, was a Virginian and a slaveholder, and like them he was ambivalent toward slavery. He kept his slaves, but also knew slavery would have to end, and tried to plan for that time. One of Monroe's solutions to the problem was to resettle freed blacks in Africa, through the American Colonization Society. During his administration, the first black settlers colonized their new nation of Liberia on the Atlantic coast of Africa, and named their capital Monrovia after the president.

The "Era of Good Feelings" ended with Monroe's presidency in 1824, when the Democratic-Republican Party split into factions reflecting sectional antagonisms between the East and newer areas in the South and across the Appalachian Mountains. The election of 1824 started out as a scramble between four men: Andrew Jackson, John Quincy Adams, Henry Clay of Kentucky, and William Crawford. Clay soon left the race and threw his support to Adams. Andrew Jackson won the most electoral votes but not with a majority, and with just a narrow popular vote plurality. According to the Twelfth Amendment, the election had to be decided in the US House of Representatives. There, Jackson lost to Adams. Henry Clay was Speaker of the House, and after Adams won the decision he appointed Clay his Secretary of State.

As president from 1825 to 1829, John Quincy Adams (1767-1848, the son of John Adams) could claim no great accomplishments. This was in part because he had few crucial issues to contend with, and also because Congress was controlled by his enemies, including a faction supporting Andrew Jackson. The Adams administration completed the Cumberland Road, also called the National Road (eventually Route 40) west to the Ohio River. American companies with federal and state support built some of the world's largest canals; most significant was the Erie Canal, completed in 1825, a 360-mile connection between the Hudson River in upstate New York and Lake Erie. Projects like this enabled commerce in finished goods and raw resources to be shipped more quickly between the East and Midwest, compared to the slow travel on roads across the Appalachian Mountains. Other canal projects included the Chesapeake and Ohio, the Chesapeake and Delaware, the Louisville and Portland, and connections between the Great Lakes and the Ohio River system. Steam-engine pioneer Robert Fulton had ran the world's first successful steamship line between New York City and Albany in 1807. Within twenty years, 200 steamships were travelling all major American rivers.

Adams' economic policy was protectionist to benefit northern manufacturers, like the Republicans of the later 1800s; he enacted the Tariff of 1828, which was hated by southern plantation farmers and called the "Tariff of Abominations." After losing reelection in 1828, Adams returned to Massachusetts. But in 1831 he returned to Washington, this time as a mere Representative of his district, and served until 1848, denouncing slavery and arguing the *Amistad* case before the Supreme Court. He was the only person ever to serve in Congress after being president.[8]

John Quincy Adams in the mid-1840s

THE MISSOURI COMPROMISE

At the national level, tensions started building between North and South, and they were reflected in presidential elections and in Congressional votes involving the spread of slavery. The issue first came to a head when Missouri was ready to enter the Union and Northern Senators opposed Missouri's entry as a slave state. At the time there were 11 slave states and 11 "free" states; admitting Missouri as a slave state would tip the Senate balance of power towards slavery, giving the South 24 votes to the North's 22 votes. However, slavery had long been practiced in the territory and abolishing it was a tough proposition. In the first of many heated Senate debates to come, a compromise was struck where Missouri would keep slavery and the state of Maine would break off from Massachusetts and be admitted as a new state, balancing the number of northern vs. southern votes. To make the deal more acceptable to the North, the Missouri Compromise held that in the future, slavery would not be permitted in any new state north of a line drawn west of the southern border of Missouri (the latitude 36 degrees and 30 minutes North, or 36 and a half degrees).

The Missouri Compromise of 1820 achieved temporary peace regarding slavery, but the battle lines for the Civil War were clearly drawn. It took another 40 years of debate and rancor for the sectional divide over slavery to cause secession and lead to war.

POPULATION GROWTH & IMMIGRATION

The American population grew quickly throughout the early 1800s. Large families and rising hopes led to high birth rates and a near doubling of the US population from 5.4 million in 1800 to 9.6 million in 1820. In 1840 the population more than doubled again to approximately 21 million.

America also grew with a new influx of European immigrants. Nations in Europe were going through upheavals and still suffering the financial burdens of wars between France and the rest of the continent. Extremely cold winters ruined their harvests; tax burdens were oppressive to the average person. News of the better life in America, where taxes were almost non-existent, where there was no state church to impose tithes, where wages were much higher, and there was no conscription, censorship, or legal class distinctions, inspired hundreds of thousands to flee to America. For many years, immigration to America was simple and cheap. Immigrants needed no papers, and passage on a ship crossing the Atlantic cost only 10 English Pounds. There was no resentment of immigrants, at least until a financial panic in 1819 caused a crisis in manufacturing and employment.[9] Settlement and westward expansion meant prosperity for millions of Americans, such that for decades to come Americans had the world's highest standard of living. Territories entered the Union as states in a steady stream, with the population boosted by high birth rates and immigration.

In the 1820s, the first generation of American patriots, who had fought the Revolution, written the Constitution, and led the early Republic were passing away. One significant date was the 50th anniversary of the Declaration of Independence, July 4, 1826. This date was especially remarkable as on this day not one but two of our Founding Fathers and former presidents died, John Adams and Thomas Jefferson. After George Washington left office they had become political adversaries, but later in life they reconciled and died as friends. The last words from John Adams on that day were, "Thomas Jefferson survives!"

JACKSONIAN DEMOCRACY

Andrew Jackson (1767-1845), the hero of the Creek War and the Battle of New Orleans, was a famously temperamental man. With little justification he was furious at his defeat in 1824 and charged that a corrupt deal had cost him the White House. After calming down, he developed a four-year campaign to undermine Adams and win the presidency in the election of 1828. Two political parties contended again in 1828, after the Democratic-Republican Party split into the Democrats and the National Republicans, later called the Whig Party. Jackson ran in 1828 as a Democrat and won decisively against John Quincy Adams.

Andrew Jackson's eight-year reign as president, 1829 to 1837, is one of the major turning points in American history. Jackson was the first president born of humble origins, in the western Carolina frontier, and his common touch and popularity resulted in decades of political dominance by Democrats. He was a fierce patriot, a nationalist, and a believer in majority rule. When he was a teenager, a British officer struck Jackson with a sword, scarring his face and hand, and this experience inspired his hatred for royalty and tyranny over the common man. He was a determined populist; very tellingly, he invited the citizens of Washington to the White House for his inaugural celebration, causing chaos and insult to those accustomed to the normal decorum of the occasion.

As the leader of the new Democratic Party, Jackson governed with direct appeals to the people. His federal government found ways to loosen central power and push it closer to the local level; his officials targeted graft in the Washington bureaucracy; and his policies allowed the economy to expand and boom. His philosophy of government was primarily to protect the Union at all costs in order to advance the interests of the ordinary citizen.

Jackson did not initially act to cut the import tariff. Tariffs were an important source of income for the federal government, and Jackson wanted (and succeeded) to eliminate the government debt. (From 1789 to 1909, tariffs provided the largest share of federal revenue in all but nine years.) In this period of industrial growth, protective tariffs also helped new businesses overcome competition from European competitors. Because the North exported more and imported less than the South, tariffs tended to greatly benefit the northern states.

Import tariffs rose higher, including the "Tariff of Abominations". Southerners and their representatives in Congress objected to the high prices that they now paid for goods. Southern states relied on cotton and tobacco exports, and they feared retaliatory tariffs from their European customers. In spite of his coming from the slave state of Tennessee and being a slaveholder (and a brutal one at that), President Jackson had little sympathy for Southern sectional interests. South Carolina's "Ordnance of Nullification" outraged Jackson, who stayed firm on the tariffs. In a famous exchange at the annual Jefferson Birthday Dinner in 1830, Robert Hayne of South Carolina toasted, "The Union of the States, and the Sovereignty of the States." Jackson then stood up and, staring at Hayne, toasted "Our Union: It must be preserved."

In 1832, South Carolina refused to accept a compromise law that would reduce tariffs. Vice President John C. Calhoun helped his home state assemble a constitutional convention where they discussed secession, and pronounced the Tariff Law to be illegal under the Constitution. In February 1833, President Jackson forced Calhoun to resign, but South Carolina then elected Calhoun as a Senator to fight against the tariff and the federal government. In an alarming move, they mobilized the state militia to surround federal sites near Charleston Harbor. Jackson was livid, and threatened to hang Calhoun.

President Jackson issued his Nullification Proclamation, which stated "The power to annul a law of the United States, assumed by one state, is incompatible with the existence of the Union, contradicted expressly by the letter of the Constitution…and destructive of the great object for which it was formed." Later, Jackson ordered commander of the army, General Winfield Scott, to reinforce forts at the mouth of Charleston Harbor and put a fleet of warships inside the harbor.

Senator Henry Clay

The impasse was resolved when Senator Henry Clay of Kentucky (former Speaker of the House) proposed a new compromise tariff to bring the tariff down from near 30 percent to 20 percent. Senators Daniel Webster of Massachusetts and Thomas Hart Benton of Missouri, two leaders with long careers in the antebellum period (pre-Civil War), demanded that South Carolina submit and withdraw its militia from the harbor as a prerequisite for further negotiation. In the end, South Carolina cancelled its Nullification Law and the tariffs were reduced even further. The mighty Andrew Jackson was ready to fight but then forced to deal, even when he held a likely advantage. But his resolve prevented a secession that might have spread across the South.

THE PANIC OF 1837

Jackson's democratic philosophy and vision of government also meant protecting average citizens from the large eastern banks, whose stocks he believed were held mostly by foreigners. His most important domestic action was vetoing a bill to renew the charter of the Second Bank of the United States in 1832.[10] Jackson easily won reelection that year, and in 1833 he removed all U.S. deposits from the Bank, after firing two Secretaries of the Treasury who would not cooperate. This led to the creation of local and state banks across the western states to accept federal deposits. Jackson deposited funds in these rickety new banks in spite of their having no requirements for financial reserves. This led to over-lending, which in turn resulted in speculative deals sweeping over the western states and territories. The new banks boomed, but they were heading for a crash.

In 1836, Jackson tried to curtail this with the "Specie Circular," an executive order requiring that federal land purchases be paid only in specie, i.e. gold or silver coins, what we call precious metals today, rather than bank notes. (Before the Civil War, there was no paper money. The only currency was gold and silver coins, or bank notes between institutions.) However, the small western banks did not have the necessary specie for new land or to exchange for notes they had already issued, so the speculative bubble collapsed. The eastern banks called in their loans to the small banks causing most of them to collapse and the speculative land deals to default. Banks across the nation stopped making payments and thousands of banks and companies went bankrupt. Many thousands of Americans lost their land. Bank notes were nearly worthless; food riots broke out in several cities. Thus happened the Panic of 1837, America's first financial depression. It took the American economy five years for to recover.

THE INDIAN REMOVAL ACT AND THE TRAIL OF TEARS

In 1830, after nearly 40 years of non-intervention or neglect, and horrific losses to smallpox and other European diseases for which they had no immunity, American Indians were under pressure again from white settlers moving into their territories. The federal government was now forced to decide the Indians' claims to land. Some of these cases went as far as the US Supreme Court, as with a case where the Court denied the state of Georgia the right to control the Cherokee territory. Soon after 1830, the government undertook responsibility for the relocation for entire Indian nations from the Southeast.

White Americans were now picturing a nation that extended to the Pacific, regardless of Indian interference. As historian Michael H. Hunt describes it, "This transcontinental drive played out in a series of contested borderlands, marked in varying degrees of by cultural mixing, economic exchange, open conflict, and the politics of accommodation."[11] As president, Andrew Jackson was one of the least accommodating. Jackson's most controversial policies dealt with American Indian tribes, especially the "Five Civilized Tribes" of the Southeast. These tribes included the Cherokee, the Chickasaw, the Choctaw, the Muscogee-Creek, and the Seminoles, living in nations inside the modern states of Georgia, North Carolina, Alabama, Mississippi, and Florida. White squatters were increasingly moving in, and land speculators were agitating for the chance to take titles. President Jackson complied and helped push through The Indian Removal Act of 1830. The Act authorized the President to buy tribal lands in exchange for lands to the west in the Arkansas and Oklahoma territories, and to forcibly relocate the tribes there.

The Indian Removal Act violated policies established by Presidents Washington and Jefferson which allowed the tribes to keep their homelands as long as they adopted farming and other American habits. Jackson's view was that the tribes were subject to the laws of the states that contained them. The Act was the first important betrayal of agreements with Indian nations, and was heatedly opposed by several northern legislators and missionaries, and most notably by Tennessee Congressman David "Davey" Crockett. But Jackson called them hypocrites, given their own history of driving tribes to extinction.[12]

The five tribes were removed separately, following five different treaties signed over the years 1831 to 1837, treaties which were often disputed by tribe leaders and members. Both state militias and, with the Creek and Cherokee, the US Army forced their removal across the Mississippi River. Following routes overland and on the Mississippi, Tennessee, Arkansas, and Ouachita Rivers, the Indians faced brutal treatment, exposure to freezing temperatures, and starvation rations. One incompetent guide with the Choctaw became lost in the swamps of northern Louisiana. The Seminole tribe in Florida under Chiefs Osceola, Tustenuggee, and others, fought against relocation and kept their resistance up until they wore the Army down, in 1842. Several hundred Seminole stayed in their new domain in the Everglades. The government spent $20 million trying to subdue the Seminole, equal to $490 million today.

The Cherokee in Georgia and North Carolina were the last tribe to be removed. It was left to President Martin Van Buren to enforce the treaty, sending 7,000 troops under General Winfield Scott to evict the Cherokee from their homes. Many were forced out with little notice, and their houses looted. The Army pushed them over a grueling, 1,000-mile route through Tennessee, Kentucky, Illinois, Missouri, and Arkansas. Including all five of the tribes, over 10,000 American Indians died out of about 60,000 who were relocated. The US gained nearly 191 million acres of land at a cost of $70 million in gifts and annuities to the tribes.[13]

Routes taken on the Trail of Tears

ANDREW JACKSON'S LEGACY

Next to Abraham Lincoln, Andrew Jackson is the most important president of the nineteenth century. His legacy is one of extremes: he stood for the common man in both his rhetoric and his executive actions. He squelched the first attempt at secession. He defeated the British and a bloody Indian rebellion in his military campaigns. He forced the feckless Spanish to abandon Florida. He added thousands of square miles of new land to the southeastern states, and he eliminated the federal debt—for the last time in history.

But in his zeal to help ordinary Americans, Andrew Jackson uprooted five entire nations of American Indians who had wanted to live peacefully among whites and already shared many of the same ways of life; he let speculators steal their property and he indirectly caused the deaths of thousands. He betrayed the Creek Indian tribes who helped him defeat the Red Sticks in 1814. His suspicions about a national bank led to America's first national depression. And he magnified the office of President as never before, with uniforms and unprecedented pomp and circumstance. Man of the common people though he claimed to be, Jackson loved and created new perks for the office. He retired to his plantation in Davidson County, Tennessee, the Hermitage, where he held hundreds of slaves who got some of the worst treatment in the South. He died of tuberculosis and edema on June 8, 1845 at age 78.

In most Americans' minds, Jackson's successor President Martin Van Buren (1782-1862) took the blame for both for the Trail of Tears and the Panic of 1837, and he was limited to one term as president. Van Buren was also famous for being a "machine politician", who traded favors for position and built a base of support. He brought that philosophy from New York to the White House, and can be blamed more than most presidents for using the "spoils system," in which government jobs went to political supporters.

Van Buren was the last Jacksonian Democrat. After him, Democratic Party leaders acted for slave interests first, and in later years for secession, and 1840 was the last election year when slavery was not the overriding political issue. The Whig Party now defined itself simply as the opposition to the Democrats, and nominated William Henry Harrison (1773-1841), a frontier governor from Indiana and the hero of the Battle of Tippecanoe in 1811. This combination of traits had won for Jackson, and so it won for the Whigs.

But President Harrison is best remembered for being the first president to die in office, and rather quickly, too. He caught pneumonia delivering his inauguration speech and died a month later, in April 1841.[14] His successor, Vice President John Tyler (1790-1862), is the first president widely acknowledged to be a failure in office. Tyler was a compromise running mate for Harrison, had nothing in common with Whig politics, and was not up to the demands of the top job. After promising his cabinet members that he would support a law for a new bank, he had a sudden change of heart and vetoed it. His Whig cabinet was outraged. Most resigned their offices, and they expelled Harrison from the Whig Party. As John Tyler had only come into office through the death of Harrison, the Whigs dubbed him "His Accidency."

President Tyler strongly favored annexation of the Republic of Texas. At the very end of his term in 1845, Texas was admitted to the Union, becoming the largest state in the US and the only one with history as an independent nation. Florida was admitted as a state the same year.

THE GROWING DIVIDE BETWEEN NORTH AND SOUTH

As the years went by, a split emerged between the Northern and Southern economies. Southern states including Virginia, Maryland, North and South Carolina, Georgia, Kentucky, Tennessee, Alabama, Mississippi, Louisiana, and Delaware all practiced slavery. Their economies relied largely, although to varying degrees, on the value of free labor extracted from enslaved men, women, and children. Prior to the Revolution, indentured servants from Europe had lived in near-slave like conditions across America, but by 1820 slavery of all forms had disappeared in the North, and the only slaves in the South were either African-born or their descendants, or from the Caribbean. While the international slave trade was outlawed by Congress in 1809, the slave trade within the South was still a strong business.

Many Americans today are unaware of the long history of the slavery debate in America, about phasing slavery out or completely abolishing it. These debates did not arise just prior to the Civil War. You, the Average Joe, should understand how the critical debate over slavery started 85 years earlier, with the framing of the United States Constitution.

During the debates at the Constitutional Convention in 1787, slavery, along with the structure of government and the powers of the federal authority, was one of the most contentious issues facing the nation's leaders. Men from the South like Jefferson, George Washington, and James Madison recognized the sin of slavery; they were not oblivious, and were aware of the contradictions between the Constitution's promised freedoms for all men, and how their black slaves were kept in captivity. They saw a future where slavery would die out in America. Several of them released their slaves upon their death.

In drafting the Constitution, our Founding Fathers had to forge a compromise. Today, some civil rights activists are quick to condemn any American leader who held slaves. But in the late 1700s the issue was not so simple, and did not seem as urgent as it later became in the nineteenth century. Slavery had become integral to the Southern way of life and seemed like a normal aspect of running a large farm or plantation. Many Southerners defended it by demonstrating the humane way they treated their own slaves, and in the days before cotton farming slavery may actually have been less brutal. It would take decades for many Americans to work out the difficult moral issues involved, and to either take a firm position against slavery, or to rationalize its continued existence.

You can call this thinking relativistic and not absolute, but history is full of compromises necessary for that time and place. The Founders knew their fellow Southerners were not ready to end slavery. The South at that time, in particular the state of Virginia, was equally as powerful as the northern states, it produced more national leaders, and their representatives in Congress could outnumber the North on a vote related to slavery. Compromise was essential if progress was ever to be made.

This compromise was written into the Constitution with the provision allowing representation in the US House of Representatives. Instead of allowing the slave states full representation based on the number of inhabitants, a slave was only counted as three-fifths of a person. On the surface this appears racist, but the intention was to limit the slavers' power. This provision reduced representation from slave states in the House, and it reinforced the Northern states' political power.

We also need to discuss voting rights at this point. Important changes in voting were happening now that continued through the mid-1800s. The Constitution had allowed the individual states to determine "The Times, Places, and Manners of holding elections for Senators and Representatives," and early in the Republic the states imposed the requirement to hold property for the right to vote. Starting with New Hampshire in 1792, one by one the states removed the property requirement, with North Carolina the last in 1856. Some states did not allow Jews to vote, and this practice finally ended in 1828 when Maryland extended the right to all white men. However, the right to vote still applied only to white men, and black Americans were not eligible for the franchise until the Fifteenth Amendment passed in 1869.

While expanding voter rights was a step toward democracy, it had the negative effect of lowering voter participation. In 1820, 97 percent of eligible voters nationwide turned out to vote, but that percentage fell over time. Clearly, removing the property requirement reduced the number of voters who felt vested in the outcome of an election. Around this same time, states and national political parties began holding conventions to nominate candidates for office. Conventions are exciting but in the nineteenth century they were seldom a democratic process, since party leaders had near complete power to select the party's nominee. In general elections Americans could be given a choice between two men they had no prior role in choosing, regardless of their popularity.

So voting patterns reflected a citizen's region, North or South. The slave population was doubling every 30 years, and made up a third of the Southern population. The stark difference between the two regions revealed a tremendous contradiction in the South's approach to democracy. While the slave states grew dependent on slavery to keep farming costs low, states in the North developed new industries by paying and incentivizing men and women to produce. Accordingly, new manufacturing, iron, and oil industries spread across the North. Textile mills for weaving fabrics, mining in the mountains, ship building in the ports, and craftsmen working with wood, glass, iron and silver were the basis for early American industry, and there was much more industry in the North. Secondary industries that sprouted up in most cities included newspapers, finance, and transportation. Because the South never developed the banks and other financial institutions that rose in the North, Southern farmers and industries had to borrow from northern and English banks.

Because the North built and manufactured it also had to ship its products, and in the early republic much of it went to England. Consequently, for many years businesses and banks in New England and New York had closer connections with our former imperial power than the rest of the country. Northern industry and manufacturing didn't just put Americans to work; they increased labor productivity, which boosted peoples' standard of living. While farming was still the predominant activity in the North, even that activity benefited from the labor of men and women who worked harder when tilling their own land.

The biggest farms in the South produced tobacco, cotton, and fruits, and all relied on slave labor. For two different reasons, cotton became the South's biggest industry. First, demand for cotton fabric had spread across the world since cotton fabric was more comfortable and easier to clean than wool. Second, a new device called the cotton gin radically transformed the task of separating cotton fibers from seeds. Eli Whitney's cotton gin was a simple spinning barrel with barbs attached on the outside; these grabbed the cotton and separated the fibers from the shell and seed as the wheel spun the cotton around to the other side. Cotton farming became much more profitable across the South, and many more slaves were needed to harvest cotton plants and package the fiber for market.

Slaves planting sweet potatoes at the James Hopkinson Plantation (c. 1862)

The Southern states were stuck in a semi-medieval economy. Slavery was not much different from serfdom in the middle ages, and with the concentration on farming there was less industrial innovation, so southern manufacturing fell behind. Only a few cities in the South enjoyed the standard of living that was common in Northern cities. And in those cities, the household slaves had it better than their country cousins. Southern cities were much smaller than cities in the North. At the outbreak of the Civil War there were nine northern cities with populations over 100,000, but the largest city in the Deep South was Richmond, with only 38,000. (St. Louis was by far the largest city in a slave state, and had grown to 160,000).

In time, southern leaders saw their region falling behind and grew defensive about slavery and the need to continue it. South Carolina Senator John C. Calhoun pronounced slavery "a positive good" on the floor of Congress. Even southern pastors and writers joined the cause. They came to refer to slavery as their "peculiar institution," something that they alone practiced down South, which didn't bring harm to anyone outside the South. By contrast, they talked about the moral vices and rampant materialism they saw in the northern cities. They pointed out that the South was a self-contained economy; the business of importing slaves from Africa had ended years ago, and they could breed all the slaves they needed. In fact, almost every southern city now had its own slave auction where slaves were bought and sold, the slave often standing naked and inspected like a horse or a cow. But why should that concern people up North? The South's position was, "We treat our slaves well enough, so mind your own business."

DE TOCQUEVILLE AND ANTEBELLUM AMERICA

The Average Joe realizes that as America grew larger, stronger and richer, we developed a uniquely American culture and society. Developments in the US were intensely watched and envied overseas. Since colonial days Americans had enjoyed the world's highest literacy rate, and by the mid-1820s the average citizen had the highest standard of living. An American worker earned much more than a European, and had the advantage of immense lands to explore and settle. The typical American city worker in 1820 earned more than a dollar a day, and he could save enough for his own 80-acre farm in less than a year. European visitors to America were unhappy with our coarse manners, but they noticed a near total absence of beggars.

News like this was actively promoted abroad where it encouraged a new wave of immigrants. Over 100,000 came to America in 1842, and over 400,000 during 1849, the year of the California Gold Rush. Bad winters in Europe, the revolutions of 1848-1849, and the Irish potato famine all caused more new arrivals. By 1860 there were 4 million foreign-born citizens out of 27 million across the nation.

American prosperity, even with high immigration, was a phenomenon enabled by our republican (representative) government and by our civic freedoms. Our rapid growth got the attention of economists and political scientists. Most important among them was Alexis de Tocqueville of France, who came to America in 1831 to learn about American citizens, our social structure, and our way of life. He summarized his findings in the famous book, *Democracy in America*, which was published in 1835 and is still in print. De Tocqueville observed Americans' concern for equality and participatory democracy, and how closely these related to their personal welfare. He wrote, "It is not the elected magistrate who makes American democracy prosper, but it prospers because the magistrate is elected." As related by historian Paul Johnson:

What made de Tocqueville's account memorable is the way in which he grasped the moral content of America. Coming from a country where the abuse of power by the clergy had made anticlericalism endemic, he was amazed to find a country where it was virtually unknown. He saw, for the first time, Christianity presented not as a totalitarian society but as an unlimited society, a competitive society, intimately wedded to the freedom and market system of the secular world. (De Tocqueville) added: 'Religion...must be regarded as the foremost of the political institutions of the country for if it does not impart a taste for freedom, it facilitates the use of free institutions.'[15]

Not all of de Tocqueville's observations were positive. He deplored the boorish behavior and wild clothing he saw near the frontier, considering it the tasteless gaudiness of people with no traditions to restrain them. His most perceptive comments are just as relevant now as then, that the great danger in America was the potential tyranny of the majority. If American society and government were to lose sight of their republican principles, give in to the mob and deny rights to the minority, we should betray those things that make us a successful experiment in democracy.

Alexis de Tocqueville

Young Americans first learned to read at their churches and from the Bible. De Tocqueville made the connection between religious education, morality, and common enlightenment in America. He said, "Enlightenment, more than anything else, makes [a republic] possible. The Americans are no more virtuous than other people, but they are infinitely more enlightened.... The mass of people who understand public affairs, who are acquainted with laws and precedents, who have a sense of the interests well understood, of the nation, and the faculty to understand them, is greater here than any other place in the world."[16]

In the 1840s, Americans experienced a religious fervor called the Second Great Awakening. With cities growing around them in freedom from state control, millions of citizens testified to their rebirth in church hymns and services, mass baptisms in rivers, and in spiritual writings. Poets, writers, and philosophers expressed their insights and devotion through pamphlets and novels, which for the first time were widely published and read across an entire country. It would not be a mistake to say that this Christian awakening heightened moral awareness of slavery, in the South as well as the North—it even converted quite a few slave-owners into abolitionists.

The new nation also gave birth to a new religion, one that reshaped the American West and is still growing. Joseph Smith founded the Mormon Church around 1820, and for many years it was based in Nauvoo, Illinois. The upstart church tolerated polygamy and held convictions about latter-day saints that were alien to other Christians; they clashed with their neighbors and were forced to leave Illinois. In 1847 Church leader Brigham Young led the Mormons on a long westward trek, across the rivers, the Great Plains and the mountains, to their own "promised land," the Salt Lake valley of northern Utah. They founded Salt Lake City and established the headquarters of the Mormon Church. The Utah Territory became a church-dominated society that, although it welcomed newcomers, resisted outside influences as long as possible.

America by the end of the 1840s was a vast nation, rich in resources, larger than any European nation except Russia, and gaining in wealth and abundance. Though isolated by geography, America's size, economy, and exports made the Old World acknowledge our vital place in world affairs. American leaders and institutions were shaping a new heritage for the people, and influence far beyond our borders. Yet the terrible and divisive issue of slavery was still unresolved, and had to be resolved, if America was to continue as a united nation.

CHAPTER THREE—MANIFEST DESTINY AND THE MEXICAN-AMERICAN WAR

Since 1817, the US Military Academy at West Point had been graduating America's finest Army officers. In 1845, the Navy gained its own, the US Naval Academy in Annapolis, Maryland, replacing a naval training school in Philadelphia. The Naval Academy was located on Chesapeake Bay sixty miles east of Washington, in a perfect place to train midshipmen (cadets) in seamanship and command of a vessel.

By the mid-1840s, most American leaders and political philosophers were talking about Manifest Destiny, the conviction that America's destiny was to cover the continent from the Atlantic to the Pacific. The only lands remaining in the way now were the wild Oregon territory, jointly occupied by British and American frontiersmen, and Mexico.

SAMUEL HOUSTON AND THE WAR FOR TEXAN INDEPENDENCE

You can almost think of Texas and its war for independence as a miniature version of the American Revolution. In each case, there was a land of people who felt no affinity for their sovereign masters, who were mistreated by them, and who rebelled, clumsily at first, before finding a leader who was able to unite and lead them to victory and independence. That leader in Texas was Samuel Houston.

The back story is where you find the difference between the

two. In 1819, before the Mexican war for Independence from Spain in 1821, the United States signed the Adams-Onis Treaty with Spain that recognized the border between eastern Texas and Louisiana. (See Chapter One for reference.) The Mexican province of Coahuila contained Texas, and was sparsely populated until white Americans (Anglos) started settling there. The newcomers never developed strong relations with the capital in Mexico City. Mexico never built a road connecting to Texas; the Anglos were on their own to defend against the warring Comanche, and they held status as second-class citizens. They had to convert to the Roman Catholic Church to attain citizenship, they were discriminated against in the courts, and they could not build Protestant churches, hold office, or own a retail business. The Americans also brought slaves with them, and in spite of Mexico's ban on slavery the government did not stop them. In 1833 Mexico closed Texas to further immigration from America. There were now over 30,000 Anglos in Texas now, and they were getting ready to revolt.

Stephen Austin, a Texan leader and one of its original settlers, went to Mexico City to plead for renewed immigration and was thrown in prison for nearly a year. Austin returned to Texas in December 1834 determined to fight for independence. The Texas Revolution began in June 1835 when rebels under William Travis attacked a Mexican Army garrison at Anahuac. Mexico's initial response was to send 500 troops into Texas. Texans met in San Felipe and issued a declaration of independence on November 7, 1835.

Mexican Dictator and General Antonio Lopez de Santa Anna now brought an army of 5,000 men north to crush them. The rebels were disunited and unable to coordinate. There were two separate groups, each with its own war plan and leader. The faction under Colonel Travis chose to make a stand in San Antonio in south-central Texas, where they turned a mission named the Alamo into a stronghold for a defiant stand against Santa Anna. Americans from the South, especially Tennessee, came pouring into Texas to help the rebels, and the Texans were thrilled to have with them the great American frontiersman, sharpshooter, and former Congressman, Davey Crockett. On March 6, 1836, after 13 days of siege, Santa

Anna's army overwhelmed the 300 defenders in the Alamo, and took no prisoners. Only a handful escaped to the east. But the attack on the Alamo cost the Dictator over 1,000 Mexican lives.

In the Texan capital of Nacogdoches (near the border with Louisiana), the other rebels were sorting out their leadership problems. As destiny would have it, Samuel Houston (1793-1863), a former US Congressman and two-term governor of Tennessee, had been in Texas for the past four years working as a lawyer and as an agent for the US government sent to negotiate with the Comanche and Cherokee tribes. Sam Houston was a complicated man recovering from a troubled past, and he found a new calling in Texan independence.[17] His only military service had been under Andrew Jackson during the Creek War 20 years earlier, but the Texans recognized his qualities of leadership and on February 29, 1836 named him Commander in Chief of the Texas army.

General Houston and a small army of less than 500 were moving west in March 1836 when he heard of the massacre at the Alamo. Houston had tried to recall Colonel Travis from San Antonio, and he now retreated east toward Washington-on-the-Brazos, and sent orders to retreat to Colonel James Fallin and his force of 400 men in Goliad, southeast of San Antonio. But Fallin hesitated until it was too late. Santa Anna captured him and his men, and executed them all.

The fate of Texan independence now lay solely with Sam Houston. News spread of the massacres at the Alamo and Goliad and enraged the Texans. Gathering more volunteers on his retreat, Houston moved to block Santa Anna's army at the Lynchburg ferry crossing over the San Jacinto River, the last point protecting eastern Texas. Santa Anna's forces were now reduced to less than 2,000 men but that was still double the number of rebels.

Sam Houston was enigmatic to both his men and the Mexicans. On April 21, 1836 Houston faced Santa Anna across a field next to the ferry at San Jacinto. He watched as Mexican reinforcements arrived and set up camp, and took a nap to rest. Houston knew the Mexicans were confident and they would attack the next day. He at last ordered a Texan attack at 4:00 in the afternoon, in the middle of the Mexican siesta. Houston's surprise was an incredible one-sided victory, and so complete he begged his men to stop killing the Mexicans. The Alamo and Goliad were avenged. Houston was severely wounded and near death for the second time in his life; he rested under a tree, telling his men to plant seeds of the corn of San Jacinto across Texas.[18]

Santa Anna Surrenders to Sam Houston in San Jacinto

Santa Anna tried to escape dressed as a peasant and was not recognized until his own men greeted him as a fellow prisoner. The Texans held him until he signed agreements known as the Treaties of Velasco, afterwards he was sent to Washington, and finally returned to Mexico in February 1837. The agreements required Mexican forces to evacuate south of the Rio Grande, and the mutual release of prisoners.

Sam Houston was chosen President of the "Lone Star" Republic of Texas and served two terms until its annexation by the United States. He lobbied hard for Texas' entry into the United States, including the lands Texas claimed between the Nueces River and the Rio Grande, though they were disputed by the new Mexican government. He then served as Texas Senator and Governor until the Civil War in 1861, when he resigned office. Houston was a slave owner but, like his mentor Andrew Jackson, the Union came first in his heart.

JAMES POLK AND THE MEXICAN-AMERICAN WAR

America's next great expansion came under President James K. Polk (1795-1849). Elected in 1844 against Whig candidate Henry Clay, Polk was a Democrat with Jacksonian convictions and campaigned with the promise of annexing Texas as a slave state. Most of the nation favored annexation, though the Whigs had misgivings about increasing the pro-slave vote. In his retirement, Andrew Jackson wrote letters supporting annexation. Polk won the election with his appeal for Texas, yet he also benefited from the participation of the abolitionist Liberty Party, which split the anti-slave vote with Henry Clay. The United States admitted Texas into the Union at the very end of Tyler's presidency. President Polk could not claim credit for annexing Texas, but he remained anxious to expand into lands further west, still held by Mexico.[19]

President Polk entered office with the goal of bringing Texas, Oregon, and California into the nation. How he achieved this goal was secondary; he would negotiate, buy, or fight to gain them. Americans were saying that Oregon and California were like ripening fruit, ready to fall, and it was our duty to be there and catch them. In June 1845, the Washington *Union* exclaimed, "Who can arrest the torrent that will pour onward to the West? The road to California will be open to us. Who will stay the march of our western people?" Expansion to the Pacific was inevitable. Polk made this his mission, and his first step was Texas.

During its independence the Republic of Texas had claimed a large territory from Mexico, a panhandle much larger than the Texas panhandle we know today. This disputed land lay between the Nueces and the Rio Grande Rivers in southwest Texas, and extended far north with the Rio Grande as its western border. It included the western half of modern Texas, the eastern half of New Mexico, and a shaft of land in Colorado, Kansas and Wyoming. Texas claimed the land according to the Treaties of Velasco which were signed by defeated General Santa Anna in 1836, but the new Mexican government would not abide by these borders. Mexico could perhaps tolerate the ongoing dispute with the Republic of Texas, but could not accept losing Texas to the United States.

Put very simply, President Polk went to war in 1846, when Mexico rejected the annexation of Texas. The Mexican-American War was controversial, and it still is. The US House of Representatives censured Polk for starting the war in 1847.

However, conflict with Mexico may have been inevitable. The Republic of Texas was over 90 percent American settlers. Sam Houston proclaimed a vision of America expanding all the way to the Pacific, starting with Texas and the Texans, who represented true pioneers and heirs of the Western spirit. Texans expected to join the United States and lobbied Washington and neighboring states hard for their cause. And Mexico seemed unable to recognize a good offer when they had one.

Mexico had been run by unstable governments that were prone to revolution and civil war, ever since winning independence from Spain in 1821. Mexican politics and the people were deeply divided between the wealthy and educated landowners and the peons from the countryside. While calling itself a republic, Mexico was in reality jumping from one tyranny to another, with occasional reform governments, and power was usually shared between strong-men and the Roman Catholic Church. Its reform leaders always failed, and its governments were never stable. Mexico had borrowed money from American and European banks, then later repudiated its debts. The property of foreigners was often destroyed in civil chaos. An independent commission judged the damages to Americans to be $3 million; Mexico at first accepted this judgement but soon stopped making payments. Historians have pointed out that Mexican hostility towards the *Yanquis* gave them their best hope for unifying and overcoming their divisions, even if it meant war.

Mexico broke diplomatic relations in March 1845, after President Polk's inauguration and Texas became a state. In November 1845, Polk offered Mexico payment of $25 million and forgiveness of the debt, in return for the New Mexico and Alta California provinces, and for Mexico's acceptance of the

Rio Grande border. Polk sent Congressman John Slidell on a secret mission to Mexico with the offer but the Mexicans refused to meet him. In another upheaval, Mexican President Jose Joaquin de Herrera was deposed and, succeeded by General Mariano Paredes, an anti-American hardliner. Slidell left Mexico in March 1846, writing that "nothing is to be done with these people, until they shall have been chastised." Mexico stationed troops in the disputed territory between the Rio Grande and Nueces Rivers.[20]

The Mexican-American War broke out in April 1846 at the Texas border after President Polk sent General Zachary Taylor across the Nueces River into the disputed territory. Mexican General Pedro de Ampudia ordered Taylor to leave, and Taylor responded by asking the US Navy to blockade the mouth of the Rio Grande. On April 25, 2,000 Mexican cavalry under General Mariano Arista attacked a 70-man American patrol, killing 11 men and taking the rest prisoner. On May 3, General Arista laid siege to a new earthen fort built by the Americans near Matamoros at the mouth of the Rio Grande. American reinforcements soon arrived at the fort, forcing Arista to withdraw. Taylor's and Arista's forces fought two more battles on May 8 and May 9, resulting in the Mexicans' defeat and causing them to abandon their artillery and supplies.

President Polk asked the US Congress to declare war on May 13, 1846; Mexico had declared a "defensive war" on April 23, and followed this with a formal war declaration on July 7. The American Navy blockaded Mexican ports on the Gulf of Mexico. Commodore John D. Sloat set sail with a fleet from the East coast on a long journey around Cape Horn (between Argentina and the Antarctic) to come up the Pacific coast and take position near the Mexican city of Mazatlán.

After Congress' declaration the war lasted a year and a half, and was fought on several fronts including New Mexico, California, the Pacific coast, northern Mexico, the Gulf Coast, and Mexico City. It began with a campaign from Fort Leavenworth into the disputed Mexican province of New Mexico led by General Stephen W. Kearny, and General Taylor leading his forces across the Rio Grande toward the Mexican city of Monterrey. In New Mexico, the Mexican army was weak and demoralized after years of fighting the Comanche and Apache tribes. General Kearny's small army (1,700 men) took Santa Fe on August 15, without firing a shot. Kearney established a civilian government under John Bent, and headed west to California.

General Santa Anna, the conqueror of the Alamo, was living in exile in Cuba in 1846. In August, he pleaded with Mexico to return to help fight the Americans. But Santa Anna had been in secret negotiations with President Polk to settle the war and sell Mexico's northern provinces to the US. However, once he was back in Mexico Santa Anna reneged on his promise to the Americans and took command of the Mexican Army. He then broke his promise to (new) President Valentin Gomez Farias and declared himself the President of Mexico.

Antonio Lopez de Santa Anna in 1853

American forces had two important advantages throughout the war. First was the officer corps. West Point and the Naval Academy turned out professional soldiers and leaders recruited for their intelligence and military skills, not for their political connections or their wealth. Second, American artillery was far superior; they fired explosive shells, while the Mexicans still used lead or brass cannon balls, which were so slow Americans could see them coming and get out of the way.

On September 19, General Taylor and 2,300 troops laid siege to Monterrey. Mexican forces under General Ampudia numbered about 10,000, but Taylor's assault began with well-coordinated movements that isolated the city. But inside Monterrey, American officers were unprepared for urban combat and sent troops walking openly through the streets where they suffered staggering losses. Texas Rangers, veterans of their war for independence, now advised them to move through houses and on the rooftops to root out Mexican soldiers. This tactic won the battle for the Americans. General Ampudia surrendered on September 24, and his troops were allowed to march out of the city.

In February 1847, General Santa Anna marched north with over 21,000 men to meet General Taylor. After losing many men to desertion, Santa Anna arrived with about 15,000. General Taylor's army united with new troops under General John Wool, for a combined force of about 4,700. The Americans took position in a mountain pass south of Saltillo at Hacienda San Juan de la Buena Vista. On February 23, Santa Anna made a flanking attack on the American left, with a diversionary, frontal assault on the right. Mexican General Julian Juvera's cavalry broke through to the hacienda, but Juvera was turned back by dragoons (light cavalry) and a regiment of Mississippi riflemen under Colonel (and future president of the Confederacy) Jefferson Davis. American artillery including light cannon designed for mobility called "flying artillery" repulsed the Mexicans. Santa Anna retreated to south toward Mexico City on February 25.

Zachary Taylor's role in the war was now nearly finished. President Polk was unhappy with him for letting the Mexicans go at Monterrey, and Taylor displeased him further by refusing to cross the 300 miles of desert to Mexico City. Historians have belittled General Taylor's military skills, indicating how his hesitation came close to losing battles, especially at Buena Vista. On the other hand, he was known for his simple manners—he seldom wore his uniform—and his officers performed brilliantly, saving the day for him. He never lost a battle, even against superior Mexican numbers.[21]

The war in California broke out very differently than the war in Mexico. Just like the Texans, settlers in California had long courted American ambitions. In 1842 US Minister to Mexico Waddy Thompson had suggested trading the Mexican debts in return for Alta (Upper) California, "the richest, the most beautiful, and the healthiest country in the world ... France and England both have had their eyes upon it." Indeed, in 1841 the British Minister had written and urged Britain to establish a colony in Upper California.

In June 1846, before even knowing of Congress' declaration of war, American settlers heard that the Mexicans were planning to expel them, and they seized the government outpost in Sonoma. One settler created the "Bear Flag" which was raised over Sonoma Plaza. On July 2, the Bear Flag Revolt took control of San Francisco with the aid of troops under US Army Captain John C. Fremont, who was exploring the Great Basin region (Nevada and Oregon) when he heard of the outbreak of war.[22] On July 7, US Commodore Sloat's fleet and US Marines arrived from Mazatlán, Mexico, and occupied Monterey, California (not to confuse with Monterrey, Mexico). On July 9 Sloat joined forces with Fremont and replaced the Bear Flag with the American flag.

Sloat returned home and transferred command in California to Commodore Robert F. Stockton. Stockton prepared an assault on Los Angeles (which was still a small city of only 3,000) using Fremont's California Battalion. They landed at San Diego and at San Pedro, and General Jose Castro and Governor Pio Pico soon fled to Sonora. Stockton left Marine Lieutenant Archibald Gillespie in charge of the city, however Gillespie imposed a harsh martial law that inspired rebellion. The *Californios* (Californians of Spanish ancestry) regrouped under Captain Jose Maria Flores and forced Gillespie and his garrison to leave Los Angeles on September 29.

Meanwhile, General Kearney's troops were completing their strenuous, 2,000-mile march west across New Mexico, Arizona, and the Sonoran Desert. In October they met Kit

Carson, a scout from the California Battalion who was carrying word to the East that California was under American control. Kearney asked Carson to join him, sent 200 men back to Santa Fe, and continued west with only about 100 men. They crossed the Colorado River into California in late November. On December 5 they met Gillespie and his men, who explained the current situation in Los Angeles. The next day the Americans were defeated by a force of 150 *Californio* horse-mounted lancers in the Battle of San Pasqual. They set up defensive positions on Mule Hill and were lucky enough to be relieved by Americans sent by Stockton, who had received word of the attack from Kit Carson.

Kearney and Stockton combined forces to attack Captain Flores and the *Californios*. On January 7 1847, they attacked at the San Gabriel River. Superior American artillery forced a Mexican retreat, and the same happened two days later at La Mesa. Casualties were very light, only three dead on each side, but the battles were decisive. Los Angeles returned to American control on January 10, and hostilities in California ceased with the Treaty of Cahuenga, signed January 13 in what is now North Hollywood.

After sailing away from California the Navy and Marines returned to the Pacific coast of Mexico, capturing the major cities of La Paz, Guaymas, and Mazatlán, and destroying Mexican vessels in the Gulf of California. On the Gulf of Mexico, Commodore Matthew C. Perry blockaded the port of Frontera to prevent shipments of arms and supplies to Mexico City and in June 1847, Perry brought an invasion force of 1,000 men up the Grijalva River and took control of San Juan Bautista (now Villahermosa).

In early 1847 President Polk decided to send General Winfield Scott, rather than General Taylor, on the campaign to take Mexico City. On March 9, General Scott and 12,000 men carried out the first major amphibious landing in American history in preparation for the siege of Veracruz. Commodore Perry's fleet bombarded the city on March 24, putting a 30-foot gap in the city walls. Veracruz fell 12 days later. Scott was ready to move inland to Mexico City. About this time American troops started falling sick and dying from yellow fever; tropical diseases ended up killing many more troops than died in combat. General Scott left Veracruz with only about 8,500 healthy troops.

On April 18, General Scott's army flanked Mexican defenders in the Battle of Cerro Gordo, about 60 miles east of Mexico City. The biggest battle of the war so far, General Santa Anna had prepared an ambush with 12,000 Mexican troops. But American Army engineers supervised by Lieutenant Robert E. Lee, future commander of the Confederate Army, built a road to the north where there was none. Men lowered and raised artillery by hand over steep mountain chasms. Once the battle began, Santa Anna was in an indefensible position and was forced to retreat. Over 1,000 Mexicans were killed and 3,000 were captured. American losses were 263 killed and 368 wounded.

The Mexican city of Puebla fell without a fight on May 1, as the citizenry hated Santa Anna. General Scott took three months at Puebla to tend to the ill, gather reinforcements and send troops home whose one-year enlistments had expired. He renewed his campaign on August 7 with an army of 10,700 men. On August 19 on the outskirts of Mexico City Scott overcame a force of 7,000 under General Gabriel Valencia at Contreras, and the next day attacked at Churubusco. The combined Mexican losses were nearly 1,000 killed and 3,000 captured, while General Scott lost nearly 200 dead and 800 wounded.

A small but costly battle from the American perspective came on September 8 at *El Molino del Ray* (King's Mill). Scott sent General William Worth to take the mill, which was being used to forge cannon. Worth was surprised by heavy artillery fire and a counterattack; however, American artillery and reinforcements forced the Mexicans to withdraw. The mill was destroyed but was not worth the price of 116 American dead and 665 wounded.

The final battle of the campaign was the assault on Chapultepec Castle, the last defense of Mexico City. Chapultepec Castle was on a 200-foot hill southeast of the city, and in use at the time as a military academy. Battle began with a day-long artillery barrage on September 12. On September

13, over 3,000 American infantry began their assault, climbing the castle walls with scaling ladders. The Mexicans inside were overwhelmed within an hour. The Americans now moved toward the city via the Belen and San Cosme Causeways. Mexicans defended the Belen gates with cannons, then ran out of ammunition. General Worth's division moved down the San Cosme but were slowed by 1,500 Mexican cavalry. American soldiers and Marines kept advancing over an aqueduct and through a tunnel created by sappers. Two officers, including future General and President Ulysses Grant, mounted light artillery in church bell towers, and fired on Mexican gunners. At six in the afternoon Worth's men broke through the San Cosme Gate, the remaining defenders scattered, and Mexico City was taken. Casualties were high on both sides; 1,230 Americans were killed and 703 wounded, and 1,700 Mexicans killed or wounded.

General Santa Anna escaped with 5,000 men, and though six of his generals were now prisoners he made one final attempt to defeat General Scott by attacking Puebla, thus cutting off the American supply line from the Gulf coast. General Joaquin Rea occupied Puebla on September 14 and was reinforced by Santa Anna a week later. After several assaults on the American garrison inside, which held a convent and a citadel, Santa Anna failed when General Joseph Lane's relief forces arrived from Veracruz. In October the new Mexican government demanded Santa Anna's resignation from the Army. The Mexican-American War was over.

On February 2, 1848, the Treaty of Guadalupe Hidalgo gave America huge territorial gains in the Southwest. The US assumed Mexico's debts and paid Mexico an extra $15 million, a total settlement worth $462 million in 2015 dollars. In addition to assuring Texas' addition to the Union, the Mexican Cession established the Rio Grande as the Texas-Mexico border. Most significant of all, the treaty gave the US over 500,000 square miles of new land in California, Colorado, Utah, Nevada, and most of Arizona and New Mexico, the second largest acquisition after the Louisiana Purchase.

President Polk now offered Spain $100 million for the island of Cuba, but Spain declined.[23] Five years later, Secretary of State William Gadsden arranged the purchase of the lower section of Arizona and New Mexico, nearly 30,000 square miles, for $10 million ($287 million in 2015).

James K. Polk

The Mexican-American War was America's first controversial war. Northerners, like writer Henry David Thoreau, opposed it believing that it was largely fought to bring more slave territory into the Union; and others, including Ulysses Grant, because they thought Mexico was outmatched and being bullied. But at the time, European nations expected Mexico to win the war.[24] Many Mexicans living in Texas wanted to become American citizens (how little has changed). Mexico also proved to be its own worst enemy, by stubbornly refusing to let go of Texas or negotiate the debt. They gave us the rope we hung them with. And after the Treaty, American forces withdrew from Mexico, an act that was unprecedented for a victorious army.

THE OREGON TERRITORY

In contrast to the bloody acquisition of lands from Mexico, securing the Oregon Territory in 1847 was a peaceful affair. The wild, mountainous land between the Pacific and west of the Continental Divide was largely unexplored territory and politically unorganized. In 1818, the US and Great Britain agreed to jointly administer Oregon in peaceful coexistence. There were now about ten times as many American settlers as British, but little conflict between the settlers. The 2,170 mile Oregon Trail, from Independence, Missouri to Oregon City, continually brought more into "the Oregon Country." In 1844, 5,000 Americans made the trip, and pressure was mounting in Congress to take it all from the British.

Expansionists wanted all of Oregon, up to the border with Russian-held Alaska (modern British Columbia). Their rallying cry with presidential candidate Polk was "54' 40" or Fight," a reference to the latitude at the territory's northern edge. Earlier administrations had suggested dividing Oregon at the 49th parallel, continuing the existing border between the US and Canada, but Britain refused. Polk and the expansionists upped the ante by threatening war to gain the extra ground up to 54' 40".The British had lost much of their interest in this northern territory with the declining Oregon fur trade and might not have put up a fight.

However, President Polk and Ambassador to Britain James Buchanan offered a compromise treaty that divided the land along the 49th parallel, west as far as Vancouver Island, which stayed British. The US got what it had wanted from Britain in the first place. In June 1846, Oregon became a new US territory and later became the states of Oregon and Washington, and parts of Montana, Idaho, and Utah.

With the Oregon Territory, Texas, and the lands won and purchased from Mexico, the United States had gained a million square miles, and now included all the states and territories comprising our "Lower 48," stretching from the Atlantic to the Pacific. The dreams of Manifest Destiny were complete.

President Polk is remembered for his territorial expansion in Mexico and in Oregon. Polk should also be remembered for re-establishing an independent US Treasury, with responsibility for managing government funds, with the Second Independent Treasury Act. The Treasury replaced the Second Bank of the United States, which was killed by President Jackson in 1836. Polk's independent Treasury helped prevent inflation and an excessive economic boom during the Mexican-American War.

James K. Polk was not the most likeable man to become president. He was rather humorless, his White House seldom entertained, and he was single-minded in achieving his objectives. But Polk knew where to stop, and not to over-reach, when certain leaders demanded that he take all of Mexico. He was perhaps the most effective one-term president in our history. In 1848, he kept a campaign promise and retired after four years in office. However, Polk was very popular with the people. He went on tour in the South, and died just three months after leaving office, from cholera he probably contracted visiting New Orleans.

MID-CENTURY ARTISTS AND WRITERS

American culture began to flourish in the middle of the nineteenth century. American writers and painters achieved recognition and became popular in London and other European capitals. The "Hudson River School" led by Thomas Cole was a movement of landscape painters who created large and fairly romanticized visions of American wilderness, including the Hudson and the Catskill Mountains of New York, and New England. The best known artist of this school was Frederic Church, who painted Niagara Falls and, later in his career, the Andes Mountains of South America. The most prolific portrait artists of this time were G.P.A. (George) Healy, whose subjects included Henry Clay, Daniel Webster, John C. Calhoun, Pope Pius IX, and all the presidents from John Quincy Adams to Ulysses Grant, and Rembrandt Peale. Peale worked from 1800 to the 1830s and painted several presidents, including two of Thomas Jefferson, the second one showing his less formal side in a fur-collared jacket.

American poets and writers first had international success

in the 1840s. This small book cannot cover them all but a few are important and should be mentioned here. All but one of them lived in New York and Massachusetts. Henry Wadsworth Longfellow (1807-1882) was the most popular American poet of his times. He is best known for *The Song of Hiawatha*, a long, mystical poem devoted to the lives and culture of the Iroquois tribe in the Great Lakes area, and for *Evangeline*, an epic poem about a woman separated from her beloved during the British expulsion of Acadians from eastern Canada to colonial America. Ralph Waldo Emerson (1803-1882) was a friend and contemporary of Longfellow's, and better known as an essayist than a poet. Emerson attended Harvard Divinity School, and led a literary and philosophical movement toward a "transcendental" understanding of man's place in nature. Emerson defended freedom and individualism as the greatest virtues, and often tied them to the American spirit.

Three novelists should be familiar to the Average Joe. Nathaniel Hawthorne (1804-1864) spent most of his life in Massachusetts and wrote intense morality tales about early Americans. His best known work is *The Scarlet Letter*, about the illicit love between a pastor and a young woman in Puritan-era Boston. Herman Melville (1819-1891) of New York is known to those people who read *Moby Dick* during high school, the epic (and often symbolic) story of whalers on a ship commanded by a captain with a blood-lust to find and kill a great white whale. James Fennimore Cooper (1789-1851) wrote a series of five novels about the colonial frontier called The Leatherstocking Tales, with the main character Natty Bumpo, nicknamed Hawkeye. The most famous of them, and twice turned into a Hollywood movie, was *The Last of the Mohicans*.

Edgar Allen Poe's (1809-1849) short life and career had a major and lasting effect on literature. Poe was first known as a literary critic and a poet, and in 1845 he achieved a major success with "The Raven." But he is also known for his macabre short stories, including "The Black Cat', "The Pit and the Pendulum" and "The Fall of the House of Usher". He was highly critical of Longfellow's romantic mysticism, and more popular in Europe than in America. Much of Poe's work dealt with death and morbid obsessions, but also with human love so profound it transcended life, as in "Lenore". He is credited with inventing the detective genre of mystery writing with his short novel *The Murders in the Rue Morgue*. Poe lived in several eastern cities, and died and was buried in Baltimore.[25]

Edgar Allen Poe

While we're on the subject of the arts, a few words about the US Capitol Building. As you recall, the British burned Washington in 1814. At the time, the Capitol was only two buildings with a connection between them. Architect Charles Bullfinch restored them and built a copper dome in the middle. In 1850, Congress expanded with senators and representatives from new states, and two larger chambers designed by architect Thomas U. Walter were built next to the old ones. In 1855, Congress decided the copper dome now looked too small, and Walter began construction on the large, iron dome we know today. It was finished during the Civil War, and the 19-foot statue of Freedom was set on top in December, 1863.

CHAPTER FOUR—THE 1850s: COUNTDOWN TO WAR

The decade before the Civil War was a period of hardening public opinion, weak presidential leadership, and the birth of the Republican Party. Slavery became the overriding political issue in America, dividing the North and the South. During this crucial period, America would either arrange a final disposition with slavery, or defer such action until the issue could no longer be peacefully resolved.

ABOLITIONISM AND THE FIERCE DEBATE OVER SLAVERY

The phrase "Mason-Dixon Line" originated in a border dispute between the Maryland and Pennsylvania colonies in 1767. With the end of slavery in Pennsylvania in 1780, the Mason-Dixon Line became the actual demarcation line between free and slave states. In the mid-1800s the phrase gained extra significance and came to symbolize the cultural boundary between the free North and the slave South. Citizens identified themselves as coming from one side of the Mason-Dixon Line, or the other.

As of 1845, with the addition of Texas and Florida, there were 15 slave states. With the addition of Michigan, Iowa and Wisconsin (in 1837, 1846, and 1848 respectively), there were 15 Free states. American Territories to the west of the established states included the Minnesota Territory, the huge Mexican Cession (with present-day California), the Oregon Territory, and the large, wild territory remaining from the

Louisiana Purchase north of Texas and east of Oregon—the Great Plains. With America expanding westward, the question returned: Will slavery be permitted in the new territories and states? Or should it be confined to the South?

The Missouri Compromise of 1820 had confined slavery to a southern latitude (36 and one half degrees above the equator), but this was now anathema to the Abolitionists. The movement to abolish slavery was born in the North, and grew quickly in the mid-1800s. The average Northerner might have considered slaves and all descendants of Africans as inferior, but they believed slavery was evil and its days were numbered. No other civilized nation practiced slavery. But even in the North, opinions varied widely about how and when to end slavery. Abolitionism was still a hard sell to political moderates.

In the 1840s and 1850s the most ardent group of Abolitionists spoke the loudest; and like twentieth-century activists they learned how to get public attention. With leaders like William Lloyd Garrison and Thomas Wentworth Higginson, and men in Congress like Senators Charles Sumner and Thaddeus Stevens, the "fire-eaters" started newspapers, wrote books and pamphlets, and organized auxiliary chapters agitating for the end of slavery. The most famous book, and still an American classic, is Harriet Beecher Stowe's *Uncle Tom's Cabin*, published in 1852. Abolitionists didn't just talk. Many helped runaway slaves find their way to freedom in the North or Canada. The Underground Railroad was a secret network of homes and carriage routes which aided and sheltered escaped slaves. Harriet Tubman was an escaped slave living in Philadelphia and one of the most successful leaders of the Underground.

Standing above the Abolitionists, in both fame and character, was Frederick Douglass (1818-1895). Douglass was born a slave on the eastern shore of Maryland, where he received reading lessons from his master's wife, until the master made her stop. But he persisted and taught himself, with both the Bible and a schoolbook anthology he found, and was soon teaching other slaves to read. In 1838 he escaped and traveled the Underground Railroad to New York. In his new home of New Bedford, Massachusetts he served as a preacher and joined antislavery organizations, where he spoke of his life as a slave.

These experiences turned Douglass into an eloquent and powerful orator. In 1843 he joined other speakers for the American Anti-Slavery Society's "Hundred Conventions Project," a six-month tour of Northern cities. He published his best known book, the autobiography *Narrative of the Life of Frederick Douglass, an American Slave*, in 1845, which became a best seller and was translated into French and Dutch. In 1847, now living in Rochester, he began his abolitionist newspaper *The North Star* from the basement of the Memorial AME Zion Church. It later merged with another paper to become *Frederick Douglass' Paper*, which he published until 1860.

Frederick Douglass about 1850

Douglass' greatest influence came through his consistent and principled stands against slavery, and for equality. He spoke about inequality in New York's schools and the need for desegregation. Douglass broke with some of the radical abolitionists, including William Lloyd Garrison, who were convinced the Constitution was a racist document, for he understood the document embodied the best anti-slavery compromise possible, and put his faith in the unconstitutionality of slavery. (See Chapter Two for further information.) Douglass was also an early champion of equal rights for women; in 1848 he attended the Seneca Falls Convention, where Elizabeth Cady Stanton passed a resolution asking for women's suffrage.

During the Civil War, Douglass joined the Republican Party, and was instrumental in Lincoln's decisions to issue the Emancipation Proclamation, and allow black soldiers to serve in the Army. Douglass accomplished two things: he demolished the stereotype that a black man could not be educated and show his genius; and he gave the Republican Party the legitimacy it needed in the fight against slavery.[26]

PRESIDENTIAL LEADERSHIP IN THE 1850S - NOT

There is a school of education in recent decades telling us that leaders and politicians have a minor role in shaping history, and that history is really made by ordinary people. What do they mean? They would tell us that sheer economic forces, demographics, and international powers forced the so-called leaders to behave in specific ways in order to hold on to power. I disagree very much—this theory stretches reality out of recognition. As far back as the Egyptians, history shows us a leader's personality, character, and capabilities have been the key to inspiring whole nations and guiding their fates. Can you imagine how France might have turned out had there been no Napoleon Bonaparte? While no leader is immune to economic forces or demographics, he (or she) is put in a position to deal with these factors in their own manner either successfully, or as can be the case, unsuccessfully.

In America, the history of great political leadership in America began with George Washington. Without Washington's determination, clear vision, and ability to rally his troops, the American Revolution would have failed in months, long before the Declaration of Independence in 1776. His calm leadership set an example for future presidents. Following Washington, leaders like Thomas Jefferson, Andrew Jackson, and James Polk left their personal mark, not only on the map of America, but on the people. These men did not just lead political parties, they understood and commanded the attention of the whole nation.[27]

With this insight into how presidential leadership works, you can also see how history pans out in a vacuum of leadership. For this is the story of the 1850s. Three successive presidents, Millard Fillmore, Franklin Pierce, and James Buchanan all failed to exercise leadership in the face of imminent national crisis. Their collective failure to govern with a firm hand, and especially to resolve the issue of slavery in the new states, meant that sectional divisions would continue to build. They hoped to persevere by deferring the problem, kicking the can down the road, much as current US administrations will not deal with the inevitable bankruptcy of our entitlement programs. However, the North-South divide could not be put off forever and tensions reached the boiling point in 1860.

The Whigs won the presidency again in 1848, with a replay of the soldier-nominee strategy that won Harrison the election of 1840. President Zachary Taylor (1784-1850) was a hero from the Mexican-American War and a strong Unionist. Before Taylor took office, Pennsylvania Congressman David Wilmot submitted a bill to the US House to ban slavery in all territories gained by the Mexican Cession (not including Texas). The Wilmot Proviso passed in the House but was defeated in the Senate. It was submitted again in 1847 with the same results, this time resisted by Representative Stephen A. Douglas of Illinois, the same man who would later defend his Senate office against Republican Abraham Lincoln. Taylor had promised not to veto the bill if it passed, but he faced political trouble with Texans demanding a section of New Mexico territory. Northern Whigs were afraid to upset their Southern associates, for fear of losing their Party, but knew that compromise over slavery was hazardous to their careers.

Zachary Taylor, by Joseph Henry Bush

Taylor had potential to be a strong leader, but unfortunately he died from eating spoiled vegetables just sixteen months in office. His vice president and the new President was Millard Fillmore (1800-1874), the last president from the Whig party. President Fillmore talked like an anti-slavery moderate but he played into the hands of slavers by opposing the Wilmot Proviso's demands to limit slavery. Fillmore supported the Compromise of 1850, which was a series of five Congressional Acts dealing with slavery and the new territories. Fillmore underestimated the political battle played out in Congress and in public opinion, and was not renominated in 1852.

Briefly, the Compromise of 1850 included five major provisions:

1. Texas, which had claimed part of the Mexican Cession, surrendered its claim to the New Mexico territory and to

most of the land in the northern panhandle, in return for the Federal government assuming its debt.

2. California was to be admitted as a free state in 1850. This outcome was seldom in doubt since slavery was not practiced in California.
3. Two new Territories created from the Mexican Cession, Utah and New Mexico (encompassing Arizona), were allowed to permit or deny slavery under the principle of popular sovereignty, i.e. the inhabitants would determine their own course of action.
4. The slave trade—but not slavery itself—was banned in the District of Columbia.
5. The Fugitive Slave Act was strengthened to require that residents of Northern states return known runaway slaves, or face prosecution.

, Under the Compromise of 1850, slavers gave up very little and had a foot in the door to spread slavery into New Mexico Territory. Another problem with the Compromise was that it did not reinforce the Missouri Compromise. Trouble was inevitable. Senator Henry Clay was again instrumental in arranging the Compromise. Henry Clay, a Whig from Kentucky and former Speaker of the House, had run for president three times, and is perhaps the most important nineteenth century figure who never became president. His career in law and Congress reached back to the War of 1812, and although he was a slaveholder he was a moderate who influenced leaders North and South regarding the American West. After passage of the Compromise, Clay retired from Congress, exhausted from the struggle.

Aside from these domestic problems, President Fillmore made substantial progress with lands across the Pacific. He can be credited with opening relations with the hermit kingdom of Japan. In 1853, he sent Commodore Matthew Perry on an expedition to Japan to arrange trade, diplomatic relations, and safe harbor for American ships. Hawaii was considered within America's sphere of influence (although not to become a US possession for another 45 years), so Fillmore stopped French emperor Napoleon III from annexing Hawaii with an implicit threat of action if France were to colonize the islands.

Democrat Franklin Pierce (1804-1869) of New Hampshire won election in 1852 as a compromise candidate between northern and southern interests, against a weakening Whig party. Pierce was from the North but he opposed the Abolitionists as a threat to the Union and an infringement on states' rights. As such, he supported the highly divisive Kansas-Nebraska Act of 1854, which repealed the Missouri Compromise. That Compromise had forbidden slavery within lands acquired by the Louisiana Territory north of a line drawn west (latitude 36 and a half degrees) from the southern borders of Kentucky and Virginia, except for the state of Missouri. The Kansas-Nebraska Act changed all that by allowing popular sovereignty to decide whether or not to allow slavery. We will talk about this law, and the fighting that followed, in the next section.

President Pierce's legacy was working with Southern slave owners and causing further polarization within his party. Senator Benton of Missouri said of Pierce, he acts with "undaunted mendacity, moral callosity, and mental obliquity." Pierce's support of Kansas-Nebraska cost him the re-nomination in 1856. But the Democrats did not learn the lesson that slavery had to be contained before it could be ended. In 1856 they nominated an even more wretched candidate, James Buchanan (1791-1868) of Pennsylvania. Buchanan was Polk's Secretary of State, and since then had stayed clear of slavery politics by serving as Ambassador to Great Britain. While he did not aspire to become president, he did not actively discourage it when he returned to America. He was another compromise candidate for office, someone who it was thought could play each side against the other. After accepting the nomination, Buchanan stated about the growing schism in the country: "The object of my administration will be to destroy sectional party, North or South, and to restore harmony to the Union under a national and conservative government."

The trouble was that by this time the Democrats were almost completely identified with slavery. Even northern Democrat candidates for offices had to mollify southern slave interests. President Buchanan suffered from the illusion that nationalism would unite the opposing factions, and he simply stood on the Compromise of 1850 as the government's final word on slavery. Buchanan is quoted as saying, "It is better to bear the ills we have than to fly to others we know not of." In other words, he was no help at all. And at this point, two important events eclipsed any effort that Buchanan could make to achieve national unity: Bleeding Kansas, and the Dred Scott Decision.

BLEEDING KANSAS

Some wars follow an earlier episode of violence, where opposing sides fight a relatively small conflict that foreshadows the major war to come.[28] In 1856, this happened in Kansas. The Kansas-Nebraska Act allowed the two new territories (which were formed by splitting up the large Nebraska Territory) to determine for themselves whether to allow slavery. It was the most hotly debated law in American history at the time.

The Act had started with proposals to organize the Nebraska Territory and locate the intercontinental railroad, until senators from slave states refused to support it unless slavery was permitted. Senator Douglas of Illinois joined with the Southerners in demanding popular sovereignty and pressured President Pierce for his endorsement. Northern senators were outraged that the new law would repeal the Missouri Compromise and newspapers condemned the bill, with the New York Times declaring it was the final straw for northern Democrats. "Anti-Nebraska" rallies were held across America. The sectional division handed a fatal blow to the Whig Party.

The Kansas Territory was the first prospective state west of Missouri and become the test case of the new law. After the Act passed in May 1854, political tensions broke out in a proxy war. Local militias fought bloody skirmishes to control Kansas before it could be admitted as a state. To build the popular vote both pro-slave and anti-slave settlers moved into Kansas, with more slavers gathering in Missouri. When the territorial governor arranged a census to prepare for the vote on slavery, thousands of slavers crossed the border and swamped the polls. The governor tried to invalidate the vote but he backed down, probably fearing for his life. The pro-slave forces established Compton as the new state capitol, and adopted a drastic slave code, even making it a capital offense to aid an escaped slave. Kansas anti-slavers regrouped in 1856, wrote their own constitution and established a separate legislature and capitol in Topeka.

This was the beginning of Bleeding Kansas. Gun-runners from both North and South armed the opposing sides. In May 1856 pro-slavers sacked the anti-slave town of Lawrence and used cannons to destroy the Free State Hotel. The attack motivated the radical New England abolitionist John Brown to retaliate. Brown and his sons slaughtered five slavery supporters in cold blood in the village of Pottawatomie. (In 1858, John Brown was captured raiding guns from the federal armory in Harpers Ferry, Virginia, and hung for treason. Brown's small insurrection at Harpers Ferry had an outsized impact by alarming the South and further polarizing the nation.) By the end of 1856, over 200 people had died in the violence in Kansas, which continued and ran with blood for six more years.

THE DRED SCOTT DECISION

In 1857, the Supreme Court under Chief Justice Roger Taney ruled that a slave named Dred Scott must be returned to his master John Sanford, in Missouri. The case came about after more than ten years of court action by Dred Scott to win his freedom, when his master refused to let him buy freedom outright. The background to the case was complicated by Scott's living with his master as a slave before being leased out for labor in free Illinois, and elsewhere. His years of living in Free states were the basis of Scott's continuing lawsuits, which were partly funded by an officer with the Bank of Missouri.

When Dred Scott's case reached the US Supreme Court it had gained national attention not just for its complexity, but for the underlying argument that a slave living much of his life in Free states was due his own freedom. In previous cases, even southern courts had been known to grant slaves that right. However, the political implications were now perilous. President Buchanan, worried about repercussions from overturning principles of the Fugitive Slave Act, intervened and pressured a member of the Court to vote against Scott. Buchanan had declared just days before at his inauguration that the slavery question would "be speedily and finally settled" by the Supreme Court.

The Court's decision kept Dred Scott a slave to his owner, with the Court's majority opinion that a person of the Negro race had no inherent right to citizenship. By implication, the Court also invalidated the Missouri Compromise, stating the government had no right to control how and where a slaveholder can bring his property, i.e. his slaves. Chief Justice Taney stated unequivocally, "[the black man] has no rights which the white man was bound to respect."

National reaction was swift. It polarized opinion and pushed sides into even greater opposition. Northerners were horrified at the cruelty of the decision, while in the South it was seen as vindication of their way of life. Rather than advance the cause of liberty, the decision had actually pushed it back. Future president Abraham Lincoln claimed the Court was in a conspiracy with the Democrats. The decision also touched off economic trouble, the Panic of 1857, as America was engulfed with uncertainty about whether the entire West would become either slave territory or engulfed in violence, as was happening in Kansas.

THE RISE OF THE REPUBLICAN PARTY

After losing two presidential contests to the Democrats and seeing its influence decline, the Whig party went into a tailspin in the 1850s. Opposition to the Democrats and their indecisive president James Buchanan motivated many in the North. To answer the need for an opposition party, Northern Whigs and younger anti-slave politicians formed the Republican Party in Philadelphia in 1856. In June 1858 they met again in Springfield, Illinois and the star of the convention was Abraham Lincoln. Lincoln's "House Divided" speech on June

16th has been called one the great American speeches, in which he infused eloquence, anger, and the longing for posterity in his attack on slavery. Lincoln stated "A house divided against itself cannot stand. I believe this government cannot endure half slave and half free."

The Average Joe needs no introduction to Abraham Lincoln (1809-1865). Lincoln's reputation as savior of the nation has survived 150 years and several attempts by revisionist historians to diminish him. His intelligence and determination had brought him out of the backwoods of Indiana. He was self-educated, and decided at an early age to break out of life as a laborer. After settling in New Salem, Illinois he entered politics at the state level and served a term as US Congressman in 1847 before returning to Illinois to practice law.

Abraham Lincoln in November 1860

In 1858 Lincoln reentered politics to run for the Senate out of a sense of duty to save the nation. He understood better than most how the South would never comply with attempts to contain slavery. The Southern strategy was to keep pushing for more slave territory and states, through majorities in Congress, and with the US House of Representatives controlled by anti-slave Representatives from the populous northern states, the South needed more slave states to hold their majority in the Senate. Six of the past presidential elections had been won by Democrats, but the South was now worried about losing the election in 1860. Lincoln was not for the immediate abolition of slavery; he expected it to die a slow death, once it was kept under permanent control. The Republican Party was the only possible way to stop the Democrats and keep slavery constrained in the South.

Lincoln's opponent was the incumbent Democrat, Senator Stephen A. Douglas, who had sponsored the Kansas-Nebraska Act. Lincoln and Douglas held a series of public debates which were well attended and covered by the major newspapers. Not only Illinois voters but the rest of the nation understood that the question of slavery and the addition of new slave states was the main focus of their debate.

Everyone knew Lincoln's position, but Douglas was famously ambiguous on the issue. Like President Buchanan, Douglas clung to the illusion that he could satisfy both southern slave interests and northern pressure to abolish slavery at the same time. In the debates, Lincoln exposed Douglas's duplicity by forcing him to admit that popular sovereignty, or the will of the people in a territory or state, must determine whether or not to permit slavery. This answer was unacceptable to the South, and while it allowed Douglas to win the election in Illinois, Lincoln emerged as the leader of the Republican Party.

THE ELECTION OF 1860

Lincoln's speeches spread the political argument against slavery and the moral argument that had been made ever since the Constitution. His fame grew with his legend, as the fateful election of 1860 approached. The frontier boy who was raised in a log cabin and taught himself to read by candlelight, becoming a self-made man with a successful legal career and an entrepreneurial spirit, was an inspiration to millions who wanted to build their own lives by the fruit of their labor, free men and women working on "free soil." There was no room for slave plantations in this vision of the West. Nor was there room for slave labor in the growing industries, primarily based in the North, which meant opportunity for city people, American-born and immigrant alike.

Lincoln became a threat to the South and to slaveholders. Though he wanted only to limit the spread of slavery, the slavers would accept no constraints whatever. Antagonism between North and South was already high after Bleeding Kansas and the Dred Scott decision; Lincoln's ascendance, and leading the Republican Party's opposition to slavery, was abhorrent to them and sure to bring things to a breaking point.

The election of 1860 is still the most important in history. (Although the election of 2016 is looking like a close contender.) The Democratic Party had splintered earlier in the year, when Southern Democrats could not win a party platform permitting slavery in every new territory. In June 1860 they formed the new Southern Democratic Party and nominated pro-slave John C. Breckenridge of Kentucky. The remaining Democrats nominated Senator Stephen Douglas of Illinois, who favored popular sovereignty to decide whether to permit slavery. John Bell of Tennessee entered the race as the last of the Whigs, on a platform that tried to de-emphasize the slavery issue.

Lincoln won 180 for a majority of the 303 Electoral College votes, but only a 40% plurality of the 4.7 million popular vote. Breckenridge won most of the Southern states but only 72 electoral votes. Douglas had the second highest popular vote but only carried the state of Missouri, and Bell won the Southern border-states, Virginia, Kentucky and Tennessee.

After Lincoln defeated Breckenridge, Southern states started seceding from the Union. From the Republican point of view, the question now was whether to accept secession or go to war to keep the Union whole. In his famous speech in Springfield, Lincoln had asked whether the nation could still stand without the slave states, and not many were sure. The events of early 1861 would answer that question.

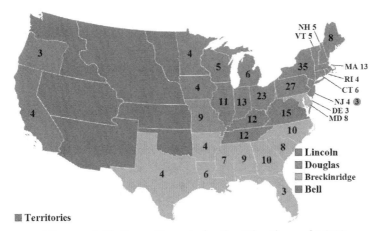

Electoral College Counts in the Election of 1860
(Bell won Virginia, Kentucky, and Tennessee)

CHAPTER FIVE—1861-1865, THE CIVIL WAR

INTRODUCTION

When the Average Joe went to high school, hopefully his teacher told him the Civil War was a pivotal event, if not the central event, in American history. Because it was. Even more than the Revolution or World War II, the Civil War redefined America and the meaning of freedom. The Civil War set us on our current course as a world power. And its deadly toll and massive scale affected the ordinary citizen, the rich, and the poor. This chapter starts by analyzing the cause and impacts of the war and the events leading up to it, then it takes you through the war looking at how the major battles and campaigns were fought. Without using too much military detail, I'm putting special emphasis on Civil War leaders and the most important battles.

Here are a few things you should understand about the Civil War. First, it was a war between the states to settle the divisive question of slavery. The South seceded to keep slavery, and the North fought to maintain the Union. Revisionist historians have argued the South seceded and fought a Northern war of aggression to escape oppressive tariffs and the North's overbearing, economic dominance. They point to the fact that over 90 percent of Southerners owned no slaves and were fighting to preserve their states' rights to live free of federal interference. It is true that Lincoln and the Republicans were not planning to end slavery, and fought the war to restore the Union. High tariffs such as the Morrill Tariff in 1861 hurt southern pocketbooks; and they benefited Northern industry directly and Northerners indirectly, since little tariff-driven federal revenue was spent on Southern projects.

But this line ignores the fact that slavery had been dividing Americans since the Constitution. Slavery was a key factor in Congressional debates, beginning with the Missouri Compromise in 1820. Politicians and officials had identified themselves as pro- or anti-slavery ever since 1850. A small war had just been fought in Kansas over the right to hold slaves. Slavery shook the debate on acquiring land won from Mexico. Abolitionists were calling for war, and newspapers on both sides of the Mason-Dixon Line had been waging a war of words for 20 years. The problem of slavery had dogged the conscience of Americans for over 50 years; and its practice in the South gave rise to an oligarchy of plantation owners who dominated business and the political debate. The Morrill Tariff was not a factor as it didn't become law until March 1861, months after the Deep South states had seceded.

Containing slavery to the South was the immediate issue cause of the Civil War. Rather than accept containment, slavers became even more intransigent in demanding expansion. The Republicans refused to budge and allow any expansion of slavery—and if Lincoln can be faulted on any point it may be this one. He would not accept the Crittenden Compromise, which is described below, and allow the possibility of slavery west of Texas. Slavery would not have been feasible in the New Mexico Territory since the dry soil was wrong for plantation-style farming. Had Lincoln compromised war might have been avoided, and slaves could have been bought out of their slavery, as they were in the British colonies. However, the past ten years had demonstrated the South's stubborn refusal to accept any limits to slavery; some slavers even hoped to bring their slaves to work mines in New Mexico.

Second, in relative terms, the Civil War was by far the biggest American war. In proportion to the overall population, more men were in uniform, fought in combat, and were killed or wounded, than in World War II. The Civil War cost the lives of 620,000 men killed or lost to disease, when our population was less than 30 million. Our dead in World War II were around 405,000 when our population was much larger, about 150 million. We lost over two percent of the entire population during the Civil War. Our population now is over 310 million, so if we lost the same proportion in a war today, we would have well over six million dead. Every soldier lost is a tragedy; but in comparison the United States lost approximately 8,000 men and women in our wars in Iraq and Afghanistan, although many more people from those countries died.

Third, and just as important, by ending slavery and reuniting America the Civil War changed world history. The world we know would be very different today if the war had ended differently. The United States could never have grown as large and powerful if we split into two separate nations, or if slavery had spread to new states, or even continued. And if anyone wonders about the Civil War's impact on the world as a whole, you should know that Europe, Russia, and other advanced nations were closely monitoring the war and sent military observers, to watch its outcome; they knew that America had the potential to shape their own futures. To speculate a little, it is very likely that Germany would have won World War I without American intervention since it seems unlikely that a diminished United States, after losing the Civil War, would have been strong enough to intervene.

So please pay attention, dear Joe. This is the central chapter of American history, and this book. Ignore anyone who says, "History is dead." The Civil War is part of your life, even now.

Note: For the sake of simplification, I will only use the terms North, Northern, and Union, and South, Southern, and Confederate. I will avoid using Federal and Rebel since we have enough terminology to deal with already. Also, during the Civil War most generals were either one-star Brigadier Generals or two-star Major Generals. To keep it simple, in most cases I will only refer to them as "General."

SECESSION AFTER THE 1860 ELECTION

Of the fifteen slave states, eleven would secede from the Union. Seven of them seceded quickly over the winter of 1860-

1861, and the last four states within three months after Lincoln's inauguration on March 4. South Carolina, the home of pro-slavery radicalism, wasted no time. On November 9, 1860 the state assembly voted to assemble an emergency constitutional convention on December 6. On December 20, South Carolina approved an Act of Secession with a statement that the US Constitution allowed them the freedom to leave the Union. States in the Deep South were in constant communication with each other, and soon afterward six other states seceded: Mississippi, Florida, Alabama, Georgia, and Louisiana seceded in January, and Texas on February 1. Texas Governor Sam Houston resigned rather than pledge his allegiance to the Confederacy.

Two efforts were made to prevent war. In December 1860, Senator John Crittenden of Kentucky proposed a compromise consisting of six amendments to the Constitution. The Crittenden Compromise would have guaranteed continued slavery where it was being practiced, guaranteed slavery south of latitude 36 and a half degrees (border of Missouri) straight to the Pacific Ocean, guaranteed it in Washington, DC as long as it was still practiced in Virginia and Maryland, guaranteed financial compensation from Congress to owners of escaped slaves, and it prohibited ANY federal law restricting slavery. The compromise was too generous to slave-owners and unacceptable to Lincoln and the Republicans, and it may very well have led to fighting in the Indian and New Mexico Territories, as happened in Bleeding Kansas. It was voted down in the Senate a week after it was proposed.

The Washington Peace Conference in February 1861 was the last organized attempt to resolve the secession crisis. The Conference was held in the Willard Hotel, not in Congress, and attended by former President John Tyler, 131 former senators, representatives, governors, and cabinet members. After three weeks they recommended a single new amendment; however, it was not much different from the Crittenden Compromise and was also defeated in a vote in the Senate.

The conference was held just as the Deep South states were seceding. The first seven states to secede convened in Montgomery, Alabama on February 4, 1861. The delegates established a new nation, the Confederate States of America (CSA), better known as the Confederacy. They drew up a CSA Constitution which was nearly identical to the original US Constitution, except for explicitly stating that slaves were property of their masters. They also voted Jefferson Davis from Mississippi as their new president. Davis had been in Washington for years, serving as Secretary of War for Franklin Pierce and later as a senator from Mississippi. He was highly respected in the South, but he was humorless and lacked imagination; these traits were to hinder his ability to lead the fledgling nation in peacetime, let alone war.

Southern authorities began seizing federal property such as courts, customs houses, post offices, and arsenals. In January 1861 South Carolina demanded the surrender of all federal property within the state. Major Robert Anderson withdrew local Union forces to Fort Sumter, on an island at the mouth of Charleston Harbor, and waited for instructions from Washington. President Buchanan did almost nothing to help. He sent a supply ship to Sumter which was turned away by Confederate artillery. Buchanan was unwilling to use force and start a war, and punted the choice to incoming President Lincoln.

Lincoln had once hoped not to provoke war. He pleaded strenuously for reconciliation in his first inaugural speech.[29] Yet the situation was at an impasse: neither side was willing to compromise on the expansion of slavery. By this time, all eyes were on Fort Sumter. The South was willing to wait for Lincoln's decision; if he meant to keep it and bring military supplies, they would consider that an attack. On April 6, Lincoln sent a fleet to reinforce and supply Fort Sumter, including 200 troops. On April 12, 1861, Confederate General P.G.T. Beauregard replied by firing on Fort Sumter, taking possession of the fort and 80 federal prisoners the next day.

Fort Sumter was the spark igniting the Civil War. The Confederacy was already recruiting an army, and on April 15, 1861, President Lincoln issued a call for 75,000 volunteers, which was quickly answered by 92,000 recruits. Fighting soon broke out in the border-states between forces loyal to the Union and supporting the Confederacy.

The state of Virginia had perhaps the most agonizing debate over secession. The Virginia Convention convened in Richmond on February 13, 1861, with 152 delegates considering the decision. Unionist delegates were in the majority. The delegates argued the constitutional basis of leaving the Union, often making personal attacks over subversion or disloyalty, and they listened to emissaries from the Confederacy. Secessionists lost the first vote on April 4. The situation changed after Fort Sumter and Lincoln's call for volunteers, and the momentum shifted toward secession. On April 17 the Convention held a new vote, and secession won. Virginia's Governor Henry Wise—who had already ordered the state militia to seize the federal arsenal at Harpers Ferry— proudly announced the vote. However, the 50 counties in mountainous, western Virginia were still loyal to the Union. Farmers there had few slaves and little sympathy for the South, and broke away from Virginia to form their own state. West Virginia entered the Union as a new state in 1863.

Arkansas seceded and joined the Confederacy on May 6. North Carolina, sandwiched between Virginia and South Carolina, seceded on May 20. Tennessee was the only Southern state to put the question to voters in a referendum, and seceded on June 8. These secessions brought the Confederacy to a total of eleven states.

With war imminent, the two "border states" of Missouri and Kentucky declared official neutrality. Missouri had held a constitutional convention rejecting secession.[30] But of course, many Missourians sympathized with the Confederacy. In 1856, pro-slavers from Missouri were primarily responsible for Bleeding Kansas. Thousands of men left Missouri to fight for the Confederacy and as the war expanded there were hundreds of skirmishes in the state between the two sides. The first battle west of the Mississippi happened at Wilson's Creek on August 10, 1861 when the Missouri State Guard, in alliance with the Confederacy, attacked a small Union army near Springfield.

Later in 1861 Confederate forces invaded Kentucky, hoping to sway them into secession; but Kentucky's leaders asked for Union help to drive them out, effectively ending their neutrality. Pro-slavers from both Missouri and Kentucky ended up forming state governments in exile. The Confederacy claimed them as their own, giving them Congressional representation and adding two extra stars to the new Confederate flag.[31]

This left two more slave states on the eastern border between the US and the Confederacy. To prevent secession, the government occupied Baltimore and imposed martial law in Maryland. Little Delaware did not attempt to secede. Citizens in both states had divided loyalties, and regiments of Marylanders joined to fight for the South early in the War. But as the War continued, Missouri and Maryland both sent larger numbers of troops to fight with the Union.[32])

Many American Indian tribes tried to stay neutral during the War. Both the Union and the Confederacy wanted the tribes to help to secure their western territories and sent agents to persuade them to join. Needless to say, the Indians had mixed feelings about joining either side, given their mistreatment and displacement over the years. But several tribes believed the South would keep its freedom, and threw their lot in with them. The Confederacy was able to recruit several American Indian regiments for service in the Indian Territory (Oklahoma), including members of the Choctaw, Chickasaw, Cherokee, Creek and Seminole tribes.

LINCOLN'S ADMINISTRATION AND WARTIME POLITICS

The Union was blessed to have a president with the gifts of Abraham Lincoln. He was a superior politician in the best sense of the word—he knew how to motivate people and gain their cooperation. During the election campaign his opponents and much of the press derided him for being a simple lawyer from Illinois with only one term in Congress years ago. Some Democrats and journalists insulted him for his ungainly looks, calling him an ape or a gorilla. But Lincoln conquered most resistance with his personal charm, intelligence, and humor. Like Davey Crockett, Lincoln was a great story-teller, and used this skill to build alliances.

President Lincoln used some unsavory measures to fight

the war. Assuming his powers as a wartime Commander-in-Chief, Lincoln suspended the legal right to a jury, or *habeas corpus*, and arrested 13,000 people suspected of aiding or sympathizing with the South, many of them in Maryland and others running newspapers in the North. He had 300 newspapers closed during the war. He suffered bouts of depression and insomnia. While he hated slavery, he did not fully believe in the black man's equality, and did not advocate for equal rights as the "Radical Republicans" did (a term we will discuss in the next chapter). Rather, during the war he used slave emancipation as a political weapon to weaken the South, denying slaves their freedom in the border-states that were loyal to the Union. His overarching goal was to save the Union. In an 1862 letter to Horace Greeley, Editor of the New York *Tribune*, Lincoln wrote:

"My paramount object in this struggle is to save the Union, and is not either to save or to destroy slavery. If I could save the Union without freeing any slave I would do it, and if I could save it by freeing all the slaves I would do it; and if I could save it by freeing some and leaving others alone I would also do that. What I do about slavery, and the colored race, I do because I believe it helps to save the Union...."

Lincoln's cabinet included some of the finest men of his time. Secretary of State William H. Seward (1801-1872) was an early member of the Republican Party, a former governor and senator from New York, and very popular in the North. Seward was Lincoln's spokesman during the "Secession Winter" of 1860-1861 and in January he gave a major speech to the Senate urging compromise, and hinting at the possibility of allowing slavery in New Mexico. It is reported that Lincoln liked his speech, but still would not compromise on New Mexico. Seward also asked Lincoln to let Fort Sumter go and not aggravate the border slave states like Virginia, which Lincoln also refused.

After war began, Seward's concerns were to prevent the European nations from supporting the South. Together with Lincoln, he sent a letter to the British ambassador cautioning

Britain not to recognize the Confederacy as a separate nation. Seward succeeded, as both Britain and France declared the South to be "belligerents" by international law, and their boats only allowed to remain in neutral ports for 24 hours. Seward had once hoped for the Republican nomination, and was conflicted about serving in Lincoln's Cabinet, but he learned to respect Lincoln's judgement and executive ability and the two men worked well together.

William H. Seward, photographed by Matthew Brady

Secretary of the Treasury Salmon P. Chase (1808-1873) of Ohio was a staunch abolitionist who had opposed the Compromise of 1850, and a Radical Republican whom Lincoln included in the Cabinet in order to include all elements of the Party. (He also had two Democrat Cabinet members.) Under Secretary Chase, the Treasury issued paper money for the first time and established a national banking system to accept government war bonds. The Treasury sold $500 million in bonds in 1862. The paper money, nicknamed "greenbacks," showed Chase's portrait on the front side in order to further his political career. Chase wanted to run for president in 1864, and three times he threatened to resign, which he knew would damage Lincoln with the Party. The third time, Lincoln was sure to be re-nominated, and he accepted Chase's resignation.

But to soften the blow, Lincoln nominated Chase for the US Supreme Court. In December 1864, Chase replaced the deceased Chief Justice Roger Taney, and served until his own death in 1873.

Secretary of War Edwin Stanton (1814-1869) of Ohio was originally a Democrat who served in Buchanan's Cabinet, and was asked to replace Lincoln's first Secretary of War Simon Cameron in January 1862. Stanton had a very strong role in helping to prepare, plan and direct Union Army movements. Military promotions early in the war were tainted by a political spoils system, and Stanton tamed them to ensure they were based on merit. He worked to create effective railroads, transportation, and telegraph communications across the North. For part of 1862 he functioned as General-in-Chief, which led to him butting heads with General William McClellan during the Peninsula Campaign. Stanton advised Lincoln for the rest of the War, and stayed in his position under Andrew Jackson, until resigning in May 1868.

CONFEDERATE LEADERS, GENERALS, AND ORGANIZATION

By the end of June 1861, the Confederacy was complete and mobilizing for war. They issued a call for 100,000 volunteers from the states. In May they moved their Congress and Capitol to Richmond, Virginia. This move was a strategic mistake because Richmond is only 100 miles from Washington DC; but Virginia was wealthy, populous, and had a heritage as the home of many early presidents. The South was determined to defend Richmond.

President Jefferson Davis (1808-1889) of Mississippi and the new Confederate government began the daunting task of forming an administration while preparing for war. Their challenges were compounded by Davis's weak leadership and poor control of his bureaucracy. Most of his Cabinet members were friends and cronies with limited ability in their areas of control. Petty infighting among them, even social gossip involving their wives, affected government business. Davis and his wife were ostracized by the Virginia aristocrats and ended all official entertainment within a year.

Jefferson Davis

The brightest spot for the South was its military leadership. Even now, 150 years later, Confederate generals and officers are more highly admired than all but a few Union officers. The name Robert E. Lee (1807-1870) can be found throughout the South. Historians and military theorists agree that General Lee's strategic genius nearly won the war for the Confederacy. President Lincoln had even offered Lee command of the Union army before Virginia's secession. Lee's strengths were uncanny; he understood his enemy's next moves, and exploited his defensive advantage in many battles across Virginia. When on the attack he was bold and shrewd, taking evasive and encircling maneuvers around the Union armies, almost always keeping his opponent guessing.

General Thomas J. Jackson (1824-1863), better known as Stonewall Jackson, was General Lee's greatest individual asset. From late 1861 to early 1862 Jackson's army of 17,000 waged a campaign against larger Union armies in the 100-mile long Shenandoah Valley, with Virginia's Appalachian Mountains on the west and the Blue Ridge on the east. Jackson's men moved quickly and stealthily and surprised their enemy, driving them back, thus denying Union troops a line of attack to move south behind Richmond. Lee promoted him in 1862, and Jackson commanded one of Lee's two corps of the Army of Northern Virginia. Jackson's talent was more tactical, with his ability to assess battlefield conditions and give precise and effective orders to his officers. He was a master of surprise and a strict, often brutal disciplinarian with his men.

In spite of their military partnership, Generals Lee and Jackson were different kinds of men. Lee came from a line of plantation owners dating back to the Revolution. With his horsemanship, his gray beard, and his commanding demeanor, Lee looked every bit the southern patrician. Jackson on the other hand was a small man, six feet tall but less than 150 pounds. He came from a humble background, and was a clumsy rider. Jackson's messianic faith in his own righteousness, much more than any dedication to slavery and the Southern cause, was his source of authority over other men. Yet they worked well together because both men adhered to a strict code of honor common to all West Point graduates. In fact, many Confederate officers had been classmates and friends at West Point with the same Union officers they now faced in battle.

Robert E. Lee

Next to Lee and Jackson there are other Confederate names worth the attention of the Average Joe. General James Longstreet was second only to Stonewall Jackson in service to Robert E. Lee, starting as a division leader in Tennessee before serving as a corps commander for General Lee in Virginia. After the war ended, Longstreet went on to serve the Union as a diplomat and administrator. General Joseph E. Johnston's career spanned the entire war, from command of the First Battle of Manassas, to the defense of Atlanta in 1864, to the surrender in 1865. General J.E.B. Stuart was the South's most brilliant cavalry commander. The many roles of the cavalry during the Civil War included charges in advance of infantry formations, rapid attacks behind enemy lines, and reconnaissance to gather intelligence for corps commanders, what commanders called "their eyes and ears." Stuart's horsemen supported General Jackson in the Shenandoah Valley, fought Union General McClellan during the Virginia Peninsula campaign, and played major roles in the battles of Antietam, Fredericksburg, Gettysburg, and in the many battles near Richmond in 1864.

And there was Colonel John Singleton Mosby from Virginia. Mosby started the war as a private and was soon commissioned an officer. He eventually commanded a cavalry battalion called Mosby's Raiders, cutting supply lines, capturing couriers, and generally harassing Union forces in north-central Virginia. Mosby got the nickname "Gray Ghost" for his troops' ability to elude their pursuers and melt into the countryside.

Following this overview of Confederate commanders, we will learn about Union officers as we discuss the campaigns and battles where they commanded.

THE CIVIL WAR BEGINS

The Civil War is a long and bloody story. The Union and the Confederacy fought over a hundred battles, on land and sea, and in half the states. Virginia saw as many major battles as the rest of America combined. Thousands of books have been written on the War. What follows is not a comprehensive or military history of the Civil War. It is an attempt to explain how the War progressed from beginning to end, by describing the major battles, the turning points, and the leaders and commanders. I will use names, dates, and numbers, for I think they help understand the outcomes of each battle and the overall progress of the war. It is not important to become an expert on the Civil War, but it is important to know how the war was won, and lost.

War fever ran very high in 1861. Both sides were sure the war would be short, over in a battle or two; the South especially thought the North would relent and accept secession after a short period of violence. Southerners had long felt a separate identity from the rest of the United States. On both sides, the raging controversy over slavery just aggravated differences they felt, such as culture, climate, city vs. country life, southern accents, and rival ancestries. Although many families and friendships straddled the Mason-Dixon Line, Northerners felt the same differences and by 1861 they could no longer understand the South's attachments to its "peculiar institution." They also were ready to fight.

What neither side anticipated was the bloody, four-year struggle ahead of them, and how the new weapons of war would cause so much pain and loss. Half as many men were casualties (killed or wounded) in several Civil War battles as were lost in the entire American Revolution. Artillery used solid shot and explosive shells to destroy distant targets, and also fired canisters loaded with "grape-shot," small balls that killed many men at short range. The average infantryman's rifle fired a "Minie" ball (named for its developer, Claude-Etienne Minie) that shattered bones on impact, and rifling gun barrels had improved accuracy over the muskets used 80 years earlier. Midway through the war, both sides introduced repeating rifles and a few Union units used Gatling guns, the precursor to the machine gun.

Because nineteenth century wars were fought mostly by volunteers or conscripts inducted by the individual states, their units were identified by their own state. For example, at the Battle of Antietam, the 12th Massachusetts Infantry and the Louisiana "Tiger" Brigade both suffered high losses in a section of the battle called the Cornfield. Both sides used traditional army terms to designate units in the military hierarchy. Four to six companies of infantry, about 100 men each, made up a regiment; four or five regiments made up a brigade of about 2,000 men; two to four brigades made up a division which varied from 5,000 to as much as 10,000 men, and three or four divisions made up a corps. And an army was as many corps as a commander could assemble, and they got especially large on the Union side, sometimes over 120,000 men. At every one of these levels there was a commanding officer, who was usually a colonel at the regimental level and a general at the brigade level and higher.

The scale of Civil War fighting eclipsed anything Americans had seen, with most of the large battles fought by over 100,000 men in the field. Yet military tactics too often relied on the frontal assault against a defensive line, causing massive casualties that climbed higher every year. By the end of the war, there was hardly a family in either the Union or the Confederacy that was not affected by the death or wounding of a son, brother, or father.

FIRST BATTLE OF MANASSAS

On July 21, 1861, the Union and Confederate armies met for the time in the First Battle of Manassas (also called the First Battle of Bull Run). General Ervin McDowell and 35,000 Union troops confronted about 22,000 Confederates commanded by General P.G.T. Beauregard at Bull Run Creek, near the city of Manassas, Virginia. Manassas is 30 miles west of Washington and it was strategically important as the junction for two railroad lines. Naively expecting a half-hearted fight from "the Rebels," citizens from the District of Columbia rode in their carriages to watch. Only about 18,000 Union troops got into the fight, and they made gains early that day and were near victory. But mid-day, General McDowell paused and failed to press his advantage, while Confederate reinforcements from Shenandoah Valley under General J.E. Johnston arrived by train in Manassas, bringing their total number to 34,000. The Northern army was sent running when the Confederates regrouped and counterattacked. The civilians' scurrying carriages clogged the roads heading east, interfering with the Northern retreat.

THE PENINSULA CAMPAIGN

President Lincoln replaced McDowell with General George B. McClellan, whom everyone considered an innovative and strategic leader. McClellan had overseen construction of defensive forts ringing Washington, and people admired how quickly he trained and equipped the new Army of the Potomac. In March 1862 Lincoln sent McClellan and the Army on a great expedition down the Potomac and Chesapeake Bay toward Norfolk, on the Virginia coast. Their goal was to attack Richmond from the east, moving along the Virginia peninsula between the York and James Rivers.

The campaign had to wait until after the Battle of Hampton Roads, in which the Confederacy nearly broke the Union Navy's blockade of Norfolk harbor. General McClellan sailed from Alexandria, Virginia on March 17, with a massive force of 121,000 men, 1,150 wagons and 15,000 horses, and 44 artillery batteries (a battery usually consisted of 4 to 6 cannons). The Peninsula Campaign was a grand design, but it was hampered by two major problems. First were the swamps along the 70-mile approach to Richmond, which required constant bridgework and other engineering feats to transport troops, cannons and supplies.

The other problem was McClellan himself. Self-important and highly analytical, he was reluctant to accept major risks to his plans. He believed his own worst case scenarios, and he often exaggerated his needs for resources to protect himself. Throughout the campaign, McClellan demanded more supplies and reinforcements. When he finally reached the outskirts of Richmond after five inconclusive battles, he dug in and asked for even more reinforcements. He fell for a Confederate charade where they marched troop formations in circles to appear to have more soldiers than they actually did.

General J.E. Johnson was wounded and left the battle and Robert E. Lee took command of the defending Confederate army. With the Army of the Potomac stuck short of Richmond, General Lee went on the offensive against McClellan. The Peninsula Campaign culminated with the so-called Seven Days Battle, a series of six battles from June 25 to July 1 1862, in which Lee pushed McClellan back towards the James River. McClellan's army won the last battle at Malvern Hill, but he had hopelessly lost the initiative. The South's losses over the Seven Days, about 20,000 casualties were about twice the North's losses, but McClellan still believed he faced superior opposition. Lincoln ordered him to abandon the campaign and return to Washington.

The Peninsula Campaign was a failure and a waste of men, resources, and time, and the blame clearly lay with the commander of the Army. But President Lincoln thought there was no leader strong enough to replace him. Disgraced as he should have been, General McClellan held onto his job.

ADVANTAGES: INDUSTRY AND POPULATION VS. RAW SPIRIT

Seeing that the Confederacy had such strong military leadership, you can understand how the Southern fighting man was a highly motivated soldier. Most "Rebs" had no slaves and no vested interest in preserving slavery, but they resented Northern interference and were committed to their homeland. Even when the war went against them and Union troops had invaded and divided the South, Southern troops maintained the same spirit of defiance as at the beginning. They believed their cause was just, and they would ultimately prevail. For much of the War the South had the dual advantage of fighting on their home ground, and fighting in defensive positions against Union invaders.

But economic forces can trump the fighting spirit, and sheer resources can determine a war's winners and losers. At the outset of the Civil War, Southern leaders assumed their independence was guaranteed since all of Europe craved their cotton. "King Cotton" was not just an industry but a conviction that Britain, France, and other cotton importers would never let the South go down, and intervene to help them. However, while European cotton weavers did suffer when the Union blockaded southern ports, putting 330,000 British textile workers out of work in 1862, they made up the shortfall with cotton from Egypt and India, and even the northern states. Britain had ended its own slave trade forty years earlier. Britain and France never did intervene in the American Civil War, and neither their leaders nor their people had much sympathy for the cause of Southern slavery.

The North held huge advantages in terms of people, manufacturing capacity, and financial resources. Just as America overwhelmed the smaller nation of Japan in World War II, the North led the South in almost every area of production. The best way to understand this is to look at the following chart.

Population Counts	**North**	**South**
1860 Census	18,936,579*	5,449,467 whites, 3,521,111 slaves
Men in arms at war's peak	959,460	481,180
Economic Capacity, in Ratios – North: South		
Wealth	3 : 1	
Free males aged 18 to 60	4.4 : 1	
Iron production	15 : 1	
Coal production	38 : 1	
Firearms production	32 : 1	
Wheat production	412 :1	
Textile production	14 : 1	
Merchant ship tonnage	25 : 1	
Railroad mileage	2.4 : 1	
Cotton production	1 : 24	

*Representing 19 Union states, not including approximately 3 million people in the four Border States that contributed to the Union war effort.

It is obvious that the ONLY economic resource favoring the South was its cotton production. Southern heavy industry existed in just a few cities, such as Richmond, Nashville, Charleston, Atlanta, and New Orleans. The South soon suffered from a scarcity of raw materials, some as soon as war broke out. For example, look at the Tredegar Iron Works near Richmond. Tredegar was America's third largest iron manufacturer and employed 800 people making cannons, railroad track, and metal for ships. But as the war approached it was going bankrupt due to high raw material costs and the wages it paid workers from the North, who hated working next to slaves. The Civil War only made matters worse for Tredegar, when iron was in short supply.

FINANCING THE WAR—AMERICA'S FIRST PAPER MONEY

Given these strategic disadvantages, it's no surprise that the Confederacy's financial problems began early in the war. They used their first $15 million loan from a French bank to buy arms abroad, and had trouble getting loans from there on. The Confederate Treasury resorted to printing new money. Its currency in circulation grew from $30 million at the end of 1861 to $100 million in March 1862, $200 million in August, and $450 million in December. It doubled again in 1863 to $900 million, and kept growing. The premium people paid in currency for the same amount in gold increased with the amount of paper money in circulation. At the end of 1862 the conversion rate was three Confederate dollars for a gold dollar, which went to twenty dollars for a dollar of gold at the end of 1863. Runaway inflation in the South doomed the Confederacy as much as any victory won by Union armies.

But what about the Union's ability to pay for the war? The US had an excise tax and imposed the first national income tax during the war, but taxes only covered a quarter of the cost. (The income tax ended in 1872.) Lincoln's administration asked for loans from major banks in New York, but were charged interest rates of 24 to 36 percent. Lincoln of course balked. Starting in August 1861, Congress authorized $50 million in greenback Demand Notes to pay the government's bills. But the amount of Demand Notes issued was woefully insufficient to meet the war expenses of the government.

The solution came from Colonel "Dick" Taylor, an Illinois businessman serving as a volunteer officer. Taylor met with Lincoln in January 1862 and suggested issuing unbacked paper money. Taylor said, "Just get Congress to pass a bill authorizing the printing of full legal tender treasury notes... and pay your soldiers with them and go ahead and win your war with them also. If you make them full legal tender... they will have the full sanction of the government and be just as good as any money; as Congress is given the express right by the Constitution." Congress passed the Legal Tender Act in February, and the result was $150 million in greenback United States Notes, and the birth of paper money in America.

As the government issued hundreds of millions in greenbacks, the value of the greenback against gold declined, though nothing like the Confederate dollar. In the spring of 1863 the conversion rate was $1.52 for a gold dollar. It recovered after Gettysburg, but fell again to $2.58 in July 1864. When the Union won the war in April 1865, it recovered to $1.50. The highest level of United States Notes outstanding at any one time was $447,300,203. Through the National Banking Acts of 1863 and 1864, Treasury Secretary Chase established a national banking system that solved the problem of notes from different banks circulating all at once.

SECOND MANASSAS, THE FIRST SOUTHERN INVASION, AND ANTIETAM

After his victory over McClellan in the Peninsula Campaign, CSA President Jefferson Davis made General Lee Commander of the Army of Northern Virginia, with the mission of keeping Union armies away from Richmond. President Lincoln formed a second large command called the Army of Virginia, and placed it under General John Pope. In the summer of 1862, the Union was firmly in control of northern Virginia (across the Potomac River from Washington), and General Pope's first objective was to extend Union control deeper into Virginia and into the Shenandoah Valley.[33]

For his part, General Lee saw Pope's new Army as an opportunity to divide and conquer Union forces. Lee needed to destroy the Army of Virginia before McClellan could return from Norfolk with the Army of the Potomac. He sent General

Jackson's Corps to attack Pope at Cedar Mountain in central Virginia on August 9 1862. Pope withdrew to the north, but then Jackson marched around Pope to capture the supply depot in Manassas Junction, which at this time was held by the Union.

All the armies in Virginia clashed in the Second Battle of Manassas on August 28-30 1862. The Second Battle of Manassas was bigger and deadlier than the first, with 55,000 Confederates facing 62,000 Union troops. The battle began with General Pope chasing Jackson's corps, which had moved north of town after taking the Union depot. On August 29, Pope's and Jackson's men fought across an unfinished railroad bed, suffering heavy casualties on both sides. The two-mile long, six-foot tall embankment provided excellent cover for Jackson's men who, though outnumbered, fought off Union charges the entire afternoon.

But General Pope was unaware until too late that General Lee and General Longstreet's corps had broken through a small mountain pass about 15 miles west, and were moving on his left flank. On August 30, after massed Confederate artillery stopped an advancing Union Corps, Longstreet's 28,000 men made a giant surprise attack out of the protective woods. Pope managed to regroup and retreated his army 10 miles east to the safety of Centreville. A single Union brigade covered the Union retreat from Henry Hill, the scene of the First Battle of Manassas, protecting Pope's army from total annihilation. Union casualties at Second Manassas came to 13,000 killed or wounded and the Confederates lost 8,300. Just as bad was the blow to Northern morale, with this terrible defeat coming so soon after the disaster of the Peninsula Campaign.

General Lee decided the time was right for a counter-attack into the North. He organized a campaign to march north from Manassas, cross the Potomac River into Maryland upstream from Washington, and circle eastward and capture the city. Lee brought both Jackson's and Longstreet's corps, nine divisions in all with over 40,000 men. He was determined to move fast and maintain the element of surprise, and his soldiers, though tired and dirty and many lacking regular uniforms, were eager to follow and end the war. It was said in Leesburg, the last town in Virginia before the river, that you could smell the Confederate army approaching before they marched through. About a week after leaving Manassas, much of Lee's army crossed the Potomac at a shallow point called White's Ford.

Near Frederick, Maryland, the Confederates learned that McClellan was bringing up the Army of the Potomac, with six different Corps commanders leading 18 divisions totaling 75,000 men, and was moving westward to find Lee. General Lee was forced to retreat in the same direction, moving over a short mountain ridge that forms the northern end of the Blue Ridge Mountains.

In the Union camp east of the mountains, in the same pasture the Confederates had just abandoned, a soldier happened to find a copy of General Lee's battle plans, used to wrap cigars and dropped near a fence. The plans were presented to General McClellan. They revealed how Lee had divided his forces, sending Jackson with four divisions to seize the federal arsenal at Harpers Ferry, and Longstreet with a small force northwest to Hagerstown. If McClellan had exploited this intelligence windfall and moved quickly with overwhelming force to destroy Lee's isolated force of 30,000, he could have ended the war. But McClellan remained cautious by nature, and waited 18 hours to attack, a delay which some said later, bordered on treason.

General McClellan continued west across the mountains to face Lee's army head on at Sharpsburg, just across Antietam Creek. On September 14 the Confederates stalled McClellan trying to cross the ridge in the Battle of South Mountain. This gave Lee time to regroup all his forces but one division, still in Harpers Ferry.

What followed on September 17, 1862 in the Battle of Antietam was and remains the bloodiest single day in American history. With three separate Union assaults against a strongly defended, three-mile-long Confederate line, and outnumbered nearly two to one, General Lee barely held on by shifting his forces against McClellan's poorly coordinated attacks. In the morning, Southern troops drove back Union charges in savage fighting across a cornfield.[34] At mid-day, McClellan sent a frontal assault against Confederates protected by a sunken road, called "Bloody Lane", that left the fields and the road littered with bodies. It was only in the southern side of the battlefield where General Ambrose Burnside was able to overcome Confederate sharpshooters at a stone bridge over Antietam Creek, and get substantial numbers of Union troops into the fight on Lee's right.

"Bloody Lane", Battle of Antietam

Late in the day General Lee saw he was losing a third of his men. He would have lost the battle if not for being reinforced by General A.P. Hill's division, which rushed north from Harpers Ferry, covering the 20 miles in just four hours. The battle's losses were terrible and almost evenly divided between North and South; combined casualties were 3,654 men dead and over 22,700 wounded or missing. Three generals were killed on each side. After the battle, witnesses said you could walk across parts of the battlefield stepping on bodies, and not touch the ground.

At nightfall both sides were exhausted. On September 18,

General Lee prepared for another attack, which never came. That evening, Lee and his Army of Virginia retreated west across the Potomac at Shepherdstown, Virginia, and were gone the next morning. General McClellan chose not to attack nor to pursue Lee when he still held the advantage – and for President Lincoln, this was the final straw. As historian Steven Sears wrote of McClellan in *Landscape Turned Red*, "In making his battle against great odds to save the Republic, General McClellan had committed barely 50,000 infantry and artillerymen to the contest. A third of his army did not fire a shot. Even at that, his men repeatedly drove the Army of Northern Virginia to the brink of disaster, feats of valor entirely lost on a commander thinking of little beyond staving off his own defeat." McClellan lost his command and was replaced by General Ambrose Burnside.[35]

During the battle, a woman named Clara Barton brought supply wagons with bandages dangerously close to the fighting to help surgeons care for the wounded. Clara Barton had been working as a patent recorder in Washington when after the First Battle of Manassas, she realized how the high casualty numbers were overwhelming the Army's capability to save lives. She got a quartermaster's pass to visit the battle lines, so close a bullet went through her clothes. Barton cared for Union and Confederate soldiers alike at Antietam and later, at Fredericksburg. After the Civil War, she founded the American Red Cross, modeled on the Red Cross movement she saw on a visit to Europe where she witnessed the Franco-Prussian War.[36]

THE EMANCIPATION PROCLAMATION, FREDERICKSBURG, AND CHANCELLORSVILLE

Just before the Battle of Antietam, President Lincoln had decided the time was right to declare that in saving the Union, the war was also being fought to end slavery. The issue that started the war, limiting the spread of slavery into newly admitted states, no longer mattered. Lincoln realized emancipation must be linked to the war, but in a political calculation, he knew he needed a military victory to bring the people to his cause. Many Northerners still considered the black man, even a freedman, to be inferior to white men. Lincoln had to forestall a backlash against his new policy, and the defeat of Lee's army at Antietam was just what he needed.

Lincoln meets McClellan after the Battle of Antietam

On September 22, 1862, Lincoln announced the Emancipation Proclamation, which would take effect on January 1, 1863. The Union would liberate all slaves in territory and states captured by the North. Frederick Douglass' opinion of Lincoln was "From the genuine abolition view, Mr. Lincoln seemed tardy, cold, dull and indifferent, but measuring him by the sentiment of his country…he was swift, zealous, radical, and determined."[37] The Proclamation was highly acclaimed in the North, and made him a hated man in the South. Slaveholders worried for good reason their slaves would try to run off. The Proclamation also reversed Union policy denying blacks the chance to fight in the Army. By the War's end over 200,000 blacks from the North or the Caribbean, and escaped slaves from the South, joined the Union army in their own regiments, and many fought bravely for the new, official cause of freedom.

But the South continued winning battles. In a four-day campaign in December 1862, new Commander General

Ambrose Burnside and the 100,000 man Army of the Potomac tried to seize the initiative with a new drive south from Washington. The Union had occupied Fredericksburg Virginia, a small city of 5,000 halfway between Washington and Richmond, for four months early in the year, a time when many slaves fled North for freedom, but it was now back under Southern control. Burnside planned to retake Fredericksburg by building pontoon-boat bridges across the Rappahannock River on the north edge of town.

General Burnside had to wait two weeks for the pontoons, which allowed General Lee and his corps commanders General Jackson and General Longstreet, and 70,000 Confederates ample time to organize a defense. Longstreet's corps placed artillery on a ridge at Marye's Heights, nearly two miles south of the city. Just below the artillery, Confederate infantry lined up behind a four-foot stone wall. It was a near perfect defensive arrangement. General Jackson's corps dug miles of trenches running to the southeast toward an area called Prospect Hill, and installed some of the heaviest artillery used in the War. Most of Fredericksburg evacuated, and snipers occupied houses next to the river, shooting at Union engineers trying to connect the pontoons together, and repeatedly driving them back for cover. Out of frustration, Burnside ordered artillery fire on the houses – the first attack on civilian property during the War.

Once he had the town secure, Burnside's next target was Lee's forces, strung out in a five-mile line south of town. On December 13, he sent 60,000 men in six divisions south of the city to attack Prospect Hill. Burnside's plan was to take Prospect Hill, but use the other 40,000 men in a diversionary assault on Marye's Heights. However, only one division, under General George Meade (the Union commander at Gettysburg in 1863) managed to break through near Prospect Hill, and was soon forced back. Only one other division supported Meade; owing to misdirections, the other four divisions stayed idle throughout the day's fighting.

At that same time, Burnside's diversion at Marye's Heights was turning into a bloodbath. In the morning, five waves of Union troops marched south one after another, crossing a canal, muddy fields, and over 600 yards of open ground, and all meeting the same fate. Solid cannon shot and exploding shells killed hundreds and broke their ranks, while they were still hundreds of yards away. As they got closer, canister rounds mowed more men down, and then they were hit by volleys of rifle fire from Confederates concealed by the stone wall. Burnside worried about a counter-attack and he doubled down on this tactic. Seven Union divisions were sent in, generally one brigade at a time, for a total of fourteen individual charges. All of them failed, costing the Union nearly 8,000 casualties.

Many units attacking Marye's Heights had casualty rates nearly 50 percent. In one of the South's most lop-sided victories, the Union suffered a total of 9,600 casualties, with 1,770 captured or missing and 1,284 dead, while General Lee's casualties were less than half. General Burnside retreated to Washington on December 15. Watching the carnage at Fredericksburg, Lee is known to have said, "It is well that war is so terrible. We should grow too fond of it."

President Lincoln soon replaced Burnside with General Joseph Hooker. Hooker made improvements in Army organization, sanitary changes and hospital reforms, and he raised up their sinking morale. He was considered tough, a fighting man's general, but under Hooker the North suffered another bloody loss to Lee and Jackson at Chancellorsville, Virginia in May 1863.

General Hooker had overwhelming numbers of men, 133,000 troops in seven full Corps and 21 divisions. But General Lee daringly divided his forces, sending Jackson through forest roads on a wide flanking maneuver that sent the Union IX Corps troops into headlong retreat. Hooker fell back into a defensive posture, and Lee was able to launch repeated, mostly successful attacks over the course of May 2-3. One of Hooker's field commanders carelessly abandoned a key hill and gave the Confederates an ideal spot to rain artillery shells down on Union positions. Owing to a combination of weak leadership, poor coordination, unfamiliarity with the terrain, and General Hooker being knocked unconscious for hours, the Union lost decisively and retreated north again.

DAVID PAINE

Chancellorsville was a bloodbath to match Antietam. Including the number of men killed, the Union lost 17,200 men, and the Confederacy 13,300 casualties. About 5,000 of the Union's losses were prisoners captured by Jackson's surprise attack on the IX Corp. Lee's skill and his men's determination had saved Richmond for the third time.

General Thomas "Stonewall" Jackson

But relative to the overall number of troops and men available to join the War, the South suffered higher losses than the North, and this pattern became more troublesome as war dragged on. Worst of all for the South at Chancellorsville, Confederate General Stonewall Jackson was killed at night by friendly fire, by men who had mistaken him for a Union patrol. The South won the battle, but lost one of its most valued commanders.

Until the Emancipation Proclamation, black Americans had only served in the Army in support jobs or as cooks. Now they

102

were fighting in their own units, with white officers. The most famous of these units was the 54th Massachusetts Infantry Regiment. The 54th first fought in Georgia and in July 1863 stormed Confederate Fort Wagner, near Charleston, South Carolina. They were badly outnumbered and the attack was a failure. Nearly 300 of the 54th were killed and the bodies of both soldiers and officers thrown into a mass grave.[38]

THE WAR AT SEA AND THE RIVERS

Here we come to another of the South's disadvantages – when war broke out, it had no navy and had to build its fleet almost from scratch. What the South accomplished with its fleet was as amazing as its resilience on the battlefield, for the Confederate Navy was able to match Northern fighting strength in several engagements.

Wikipedia lists fifty separate naval battles during the Civil War. Most battles were fought along the southern coastlines of the Atlantic and the Gulf of Mexico, including the harbors of Port Royal, Charleston, Galveston, and Corpus Christi. A key turning point in the naval war was the Union capture of New Orleans by Admiral David Farragut after the Battle of Forts Jackson and St. Philip on the Gulf of Mexico, in April 1862. The greatest Union Navy victory of the war was the Battle of Mobile in August 1864, which sealed off the last major Southern port. Important battles were also fought by steam-powered paddleboats and gunboats along the Mississippi River. In May 1862, the Confederate River Defense Fleet fought off Union Ironclads at Fort Pillow, Tennessee. But soon afterward, the Confederates fought and lost their last defense of the river in the Battle of Memphis.

The Average Joe probably knows that the world's first battle between armored ships happened in the Civil War. In March 1862, the Union *Monitor* and the Confederate *Virginia* fought something of a duel in the Battle of Hampton Roads, just before McClellan's Peninsula Campaign. The *Virginia* was an Ironclad, essentially an overhauled brig with slanted iron plates to deflect cannon fire, and several gun portals on each side. The *Monitor* had an innovative design, a flat top with a single revolving cannon turret. The battle ended in a draw, with both ships damaged, and withdrawing from the fight.

The Union and the Confederacy both fought with Ironclads, which were especially useful in shoreline and river fighting. The Union built several *Monitor*-class ships, however they proved to be slow and of limited use in later naval battles. For example, in the First Battle of Charleston Harbor in April, 1863, nine Monitors were unable to get in position to penetrate the harbor defenses. Still, the Ironclads and the Monitors caught the imagination of shipbuilders and changed the shipbuilding industry forever.

Confederate Ironclad CSS Chicora

The North's industrial advantage meant the Confederate Navy was doomed. By early 1864, with the Union in control of the Mississippi River and full blockades of Southern ports, the Confederacy was an imprisoned country with no hope of breaking out.

THE WESTERN THEATER OF THE CIVIL WAR

Most Civil War battles, small and large, were in Virginia and other mid-Atlantic states. Yet major battles did take place in the "western theater", across the Appalachian Mountains and in the Mississippi River valley, and even in the far West.

Texas maintained control of its western borders, allowing

the Confederacy to seize and claim the lower portions of New Mexico and Arizona, calling it the Arizona Territory. In early 1862, the Confederacy launched the New Mexico campaign into the northern part of the Territory. The South's goals were to intercept shipments of gold from California to the North, and to draw Union forces away from other theaters of battle. After the South won a battle at Valverde they drove north toward Fort Union. They were winning at Glorietta Pass, when Northern troops destroyed their supplies and wagon train. The Confederates were forced to pull back to Texas, and the New Mexico campaign failed.

In late 1861, once Kentucky was secure and the Ohio River under Northern control, the next Union objective was to control the Mississippi River and cut the Confederacy in half. The Union had already taken New Orleans after Admiral Farragut's campaign in the Gulf of Mexico, but Southern shipping and armaments still flowed along the Mississippi from Tennessee down to Louisiana.

The campaign in Tennessee is where Union General Ulysses S. Grant first made his mark. In February, 1862 Grant's army took Confederate Fort Henry on the Cumberland River in northwest Tennessee, then immediately launched a successful attack on the more heavily defended Fort Donelson, where Grant took prisoner over 12,000 Confederate soldiers. These victories opened the Cumberland River to Union movement and threatened the South's industrial and weapons centers in Nashville.

On April 6-7, General Grant fought a large Southern army under General Albert Sidney Johnston (not to be confused with J.E. Johnston) in the battle of Shiloh, on the Tennessee River near the state border of Mississippi. Grant and six divisions of his Army of the Tennessee had moved south through Tennessee, dividing the state and separating Confederate forces.[39] Early in the morning of the first day, the South attacked and surprised Grant's troops in their camps, hoping to push them into a nearby swamp. Union troops were barely able to escape under the protection of hastily assembled artillery. Later that day, General Johnston died from a leg-wound, and was succeeded by his second-in-command, General P.G.T.

Beauregard.

General Beauregard became overly confident and in fact telegrammed CSA President Jefferson Davis, claiming victory was at hand. But on the second day Grant, who was now reinforced by four divisions under General Don Carlos Buell, rallied with a dawn counter-attack. General Beauregard's army was weakened and low on ammunition, and retreated south into Mississippi. The Battle of Shiloh came prior to Antietam, and was the first major blood-letting of the war, with over 1,700 dead on each side, and 11,200 Union and 9,000 Confederate casualties.

The Northern public and newspaper condemned Grant for his high casualties and accused him of being drunk and unprepared for the initial attack at Shiloh. Union General William Sherman was praised for rallying the frightened, retreating troops, and then for pursuing Beauregard's army the day after the battle. But President Lincoln replied with one of his famous quotes about Grant: "I can't spare this man; he fights."

Still, Grant was demoted and placed under General Henry Halleck. Halleck successfully coordinated a gunboat campaign on the Mississippi River, which took control of Memphis in May 1862. He was then promoted to General in Chief of all Union armies, and went to Washington. Ulysses Grant got his old job back as commander of the western armies.

VICKSBURG AND CHICKAMAUGA

Having now taken control of the great river down to Memphis, General Grant laid siege to Vicksburg, Mississippi. Vicksburg was vitally important as a Confederate hilltop fortress and a strongpoint blocking Union traffic on the river; Jefferson Davis said "Vicksburg is the nail head that holds the South's two halves together." Its natural defenses helped it resist Union assault in May and again in June by Admiral Farragut, who had sailed up the river from New Orleans.

The Vicksburg Campaign was six months long and a frustrating experience for Generals Grant and Sherman, his chief field commander. At the end of December 1862,

Sherman's forces came down the river and disembarked just north of the city, but were repulsed in a two-day long attack. Grant attempted to move inland from the east toward Vicksburg, but Confederate cavalry disrupted and destroyed his supplies. Grant also tried two times to build a canal west of the Mississippi so as to bypass Vicksburg, and each of the canal projects failed.

General Grant was known for his determination. In his final plan, Grant's army marched south through Louisiana, crossed the Mississippi River to the east, supported by Union Admiral David Porter and a naval bombardment at Grand Gulf, Mississippi. After winning five battles in 17 days, Grant captured the state capital of Jackson. He then laid siege to Vicksburg with five army corps and 75,000 men, and Vicksburg surrendered on July 4, 1863. Vicksburg was one of the most important turning points of the war, not least since it came a day after the Union victory at Gettysburg, Pennsylvania.

The Union was winning the war west of the Appalachians. But they suffered one more bloody defeat at Chickamauga Creek in northern Georgia. General William Rosecrans and the Army of the Cumberland had seized Chattanooga, Tennessee, but Confederate General Braxton Bragg, with a slightly larger force, was determined to reoccupy the city. On September 19, 1863 Bragg attacked Rosecrans' lines but could not break through. The following day, owing to a miscommunication, Rosecrans opened a gap in his own lines, which Bragg immediately exploited. A third of Rosecrans' army retreated in disarray, and the remaining forces retreated to Chattanooga, where they would fight again in two months' time. Chickamauga was one of the war's highest casualty counts, over 16,000 Union and 18,000 Confederate troops, including nearly 4,000 dead.

GETTYSBURG AND THE SECOND SOUTHERN INVASION

In early 1863, Robert E. Lee was named Commander of all Confederate armies. Lee was now feeling the strain of the long war, and watching the South unravel with dwindling resources, financial crises, and weak leadership in Richmond. Lee determined once again to end the war with an attack on Washington, and again with the encircling maneuver through the North.

In June 1863, General Lee and an army of 75,000 crossed into Maryland, and this time went straight through into Pennsylvania. He sent J.E.B. Stuart's cavalry to scout ahead. Stuart collided with cavalry detached from a Union army of 90,000 under General George Meade. General Meade was the new commander of the Army of the Potomac, and until this time he had little idea where to find Lee's army.

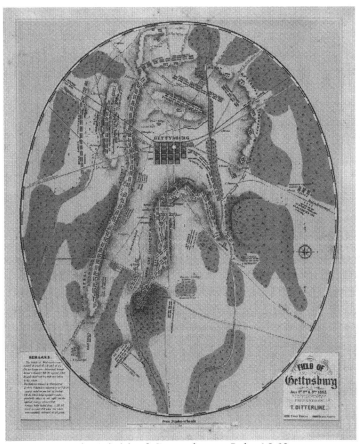

The Field of Gettysburg, July 1863

With the armies now alerted to the other, Union forces quickly moved into Gettysburg, the nearest crossroads in the Confederate's path. What followed was a three-day battle with the highest casualties of the Civil War, and which marked the beginning of the end for the Confederacy. On July 1, Union forces fell back in fighting northwest of Gettysburg. General Meade deployed his men along a north-south line called Cemetery Ridge, stretching south from the town and across a broad field from the Confederate line. On July 2, Union and Confederate troops charged each other back and forth across the "Peach Orchard". At "Devil's Den" on the southern end, there was desperate combat over rocky outcroppings held by the North, and in a wooded area on the left Union flank called Little Roundtop.

Thousands were killed on each side, and in each section of the battle. The Confederates under General John Hood tried a flanking maneuver on the extreme Union left at Little Roundtop. Union troops there were outnumbered and out of ammunition, and in desperation Colonel Joshua Chamberlain ordered a bayonet charge down the hill. Military historians call the Union's successful defense of this spot the single most crucial action in saving the battle.

The Confederates also sent a large flanking attack on the Union right at Culp's Hill. They could not overcome the strong Union defenses with its fortified breastworks, and were beaten back after fighting that carried on into the night, suffering heavy losses. General Lee instructed his commander General Ewell to try again the next morning, but Union artillery delayed the attack. The Confederates charged three more times before giving up at noon.

July 3, 1863 was the decisive day of the battle. That afternoon, believing the Union center at Cemetery Ridge was thin, General Lee ordered a frontal assault across a mile-wide field. He gave the job to three divisions, 12,500 men in total. General George Pickett was just one of the three division commanders, but history has permanently attached his name to the disaster that day. The Confederate artillery barrage before the attack was ineffectual. Pickett's division and the two others had to march east across the open field, completely exposed to

Union artillery. Union soldiers shouted "Fredericksburg! Fredericksburg!" as they concentrated rifle fire on their enemy. Thousands of Confederates were slaughtered before they reached Cemetery Ridge, where they were pushed back. "Pickett's charge" had 50 percent casualties; it was the Confederate's greatest debacle, and it closed the battle. As he did at Antietam, General Lee escaped to the South the following day, thus ending forever his goal of taking the Northern capitol, and ending Southern hopes of negotiating peace with the North.

The Battle of Gettysburg had the highest casualties of the Civil War, with combined losses of nearly 8,000 dead. Total casualties including dead and wounded were 51,000, 23,000 from the North and 28,000 from the South. Gettysburg also made clear that the Civil War was a matter of attrition; as many men as might die, the winner would be the side able to fight the longest. After Gettysburg, military tactics shifted to rely less on the costly frontal assault and more on attacks from protective trenches and earthworks.

On November 19, 1863, President Lincoln visited the battlefield at Gettysburg to commemorate the new cemetery established there. The field was still strewn with the debris of war and the carcasses of horses. Lincoln's short speech, the Gettysburg Address, has come to be known as the most complete and heart-felt expression of gratitude for sacrifice in the name of freedom. Lincoln declared their purpose that day was "that we here highly resolve that these dead shall not have died in vain—that this nation, under God, shall have a new birth of freedom—and that government of the people, by the people, and for the people shall not perish from the Earth."[40]

ULYSSES GRANT TAKES COMMAND

New York City was a Northern town, but its economy relied on exports, nearly half of which was Southern cotton. Mayor Fernando Wood once called for the city to declare its independence from the state, and from Washington. Many workers in New York, and many of them Irish immigrants, sympathized with the South, and especially resented that a man with money could buy his way out of the Army draft by paying $300 to hire a substitute. On July 13, 1863, ten days after Gettysburg, New York erupted in rioting over the draft, which turned into a race riot. The rioters attacked police offices where draft numbers were pulled; set offices, churches, and public buildings on fire; smashed streetcars, and set about lynching blacks. The New York City draft riots were and still are the worst civil disturbance in America. At least 120 people were killed and 2,000 injured. The riot was brought under control after three days when soldiers arrived from the Army, the Marines, and the New York Militia. The draft resumed on August 10, without incident.

General Meade may have fought off General Lee's invasion, but he made the same mistake as McClellan at Antietam: he refused to pursue and destroy the Southern army. Meade even revealed his thinking after the battle when he declared the battle had been fought to drive off an invader.

President Lincoln saw a winner in General Grant, who never gave up in his western campaigns. Ironically, Grant had been a loser much of his life. After graduating as a lieutenant from West Point, he fought in, and hated, the Mexican-American war. He left the army for civilian life, and proceeded to fail as a merchant, a farmer, and a salesman. He took to heavy drinking, and today he might be considered an alcoholic. But the Army was Grant's true calling. He entered the war starting as a colonel and quickly rose to general rank. After Vicksburg, Lincoln recalled Grant to Washington and gave him overall command of the Army. Congress reinstated the three-star rank of Lieutenant General just for Grant, which no man had held since the Revolution.

Ulysses S. Grant (1822-1885) was one of the most remarkable military men of his time. He was relatively short, very quiet, reserved in his comments, meticulous, and an expert in logistics; he was a superb horseman, an asset quite valuable to an officer in an army on the move. Most importantly, where General McClellan was cautious, Grant was bold and confident of his assessments, and ready to move when he had battlefield superiority.

A new Union war strategy took shape in 1864. Lincoln and

Grant decided on a two-pronged approach, where Grant would move again on Richmond, and General William Sherman would move from the west on Atlanta and on to the Atlantic coast, cutting the Confederacy once again, into three parts.

SHERMAN'S MARCH, AND GRANT'S OVERLAND CAMPAIGN

About this time, Lincoln was being opposed for reelection by none other than George McClellan, who was nominated by the "Copperheads," the Democrats who wanted to negotiate for peace and let the South secede. As with the Emancipation Proclamation, Lincoln had to tread lightly to keep the people on his side for reelection. He got the victory he needed in September 1864, when General Sherman defeated General J.E. Johnston and conquered, and burned, Atlanta. Sherman had assembled three Union armies, the Army of the Tennessee, the Cumberland, and the Ohio. With these 98,000 men Sherman proceeded to fight, burn and pillage a 60-mile wide path the remaining distance to the ocean, taking Savannah on December 21, 1864. By Christmas much of the South was short of all types of food and supplies, and millions were starving.

General William Sherman (1820-1891) was to Grant in some ways what Stonewall Jackson was to Robert E. Lee. Sherman was also a West Pointer and had served in California during the Mexican American War. He then became a banker, and in 1859 the superintendent of a military academy in Louisiana. Sherman was somewhat sympathetic to the South, but more dedicated to the Union, and opposed to secession. When war broke out he resigned his position and returned north.[41] Sherman reluctantly joined the army again, and like Grant he rose through the ranks and proved to be a tenacious fighter. He is perhaps best known for his quote from late in the war, "You cannot qualify war in harsher terms than I will. War is cruelty, and you cannot refine it; and those who brought war into our country deserve all the curses and maledictions a people can pour out. I know I had no hand in making this war, and I know I will make more sacrifices to-day than any of you to secure peace." Sherman was fighting total war, and he fought it in Georgia in 1864 and South Carolina in 1865.

Meanwhile, General Grant was having a much tougher time. In early May 1864, Lee fought Grant to a standstill in the Battle of the Wilderness, so-named for a village in the forests of central Virginia. Grant's forces included four large corps and a cavalry corps under General Philip Sheridan, 118,000 men in all. He far outnumbered General Lee, who had 64,000 men in three smaller corps, plus J.E.B Stuart's cavalry. The South held a strong defensive advantage, but Grant's strategy this time was not to allow any army much time to recover between battles, and to keep pressing Lee and move south toward Richmond.

Grant and Lee fought again at the Battle of Spotsylvania Court House from May 8 to May 21. After Wilderness, Grant sent two corps to the crossroads at the Court House to bring Lee onto more favorable terrain, but Lee sent General Anderson with troops along a parallel route that got there ahead of the Union forces. On May 8 Anderson stopped the Union advance at Laurel Hill.

This bought General Lee time to prepare a defense. As they did at Fredericksburg, Confederate troops dug four miles of trenches, stacking earth four feet high and standing in the holes dug for the wall. On May 9, Grant's commanders built their own fortifications; VI Corps commander John Sedgwick was killed by a Confederate sniper while inspecting his lines, after having just said, "They could not hit an elephant at this distance." General Sheridan's cavalry departed to look for J.E.B. Stuart's cavalry, which they defeated two days later in the Battle of Yellow Tavern, killing Stuart in the process. But without Sheridan, Grant lacked his best means to gather intelligence, and this was to cost him dearly.

Fighting resumed on May 10; General Winfield Hancock's II Corps nearly made a breakthrough but was stymied by Lee's uncanny ability to send Confederate reinforcements just where they were needed. On May 12 Grant launched his grand attack on a section of the Confederate line called the "Mule Shoe salient", since it stuck out from the line like a horseshoe. Starting at 4:30 in the morning with a 15,000 man charge under General Hancock, fighting at the Mule Shoe turned into 24-

hours of intense hand-to-hand combat. Horse-drawn artillery joined the battle and cut men down at close range. Some of the War's most concentrated fighting was at a section dubbed the Bloody Angle, where the landscape was flattened and all trees and foliage destroyed. Bodies piled up three and four deep at the trenches.

The battle was interrupted by five days of continuous rain. On May 18, mistakenly thinking that Lee had ordered most of his army to the east, Grant attacked again near the salient, and was driven back by Confederate General Richard Ewell's Second Corps. Grant then abandoned and moved around Spotsylvania and pushed on with his strategy to keep General Lee on the run. Estimates vary, and most historians say the battle cost 18,000 Union casualties with 2,725 dead, and 12,000 Confederate casualties including 1,500 dead and nearly 6,000 captured or missing.

Grant met Lee again just a week later in a smaller battle at the Anna River, 25 miles to the south. He suffered his bloodiest loss at Cold Harbor (which was not a harbor but named for Cold Harbor Tavern), near Mechanicsville and northeast of Richmond. On May 31, 1864, Union cavalry seized the Cold Harbor crossroads, and on June 1 and June 3 Grant attacked elaborate Confederate defenses to the west. For the next week the armies opposed each other in a stalemate, until Grant again moved south to prepare an attack on Richmond from the east.

On June 11, 9,286 Union cavalry under General Philip Sheridan, and 6,762 Confederate cavalry under Generals Wade Hampton and Fitzhugh Lee fought the largest, all-cavalry battle of the war at Trevilian Station, east of Charlottesville, Virginia. General Sheridan was defeated with losses of over 1,500 men (150 dead), and retreated east to rejoin Grant.

Altogether Grant's forces had about 50,000 casualties, but Lee's losses of 20,000 were more damaging, for the South had run out of fighting men. While Grant did not yet succeed in taking Richmond, what became known as the Overland Campaign—at Wilderness, Spotsylvania, Anna River, and Cold Harbor—was a turning point for putting the South on permanent defensive. Except on one significant occasion.

THE LAST SOUTHERN INVASION

General Lee had failed to capture Washington in both his campaigns, but in June 1864 he sent a small army under General Jubal Early into Maryland one more time, to threaten the city, and relieve some of the pressure Grant was putting on him in Virginia. General Early and 16,000 men went north through the Shenandoah Valley, after defeating a Union army under General David Hunter in Lynchburg. In Maryland on July 9, Early came up against less than 6,000 Union defenders under General Lew Wallace (who would later be known as author of the novel *Ben Hur*) in the Battle of Monocacy, near Frederick. General Early launched five infantry and cavalry attacks on the Union line until it crumbled and sent Wallace's army in retreat toward Baltimore.

The Confederates clearly won Monocacy, but they lost a crucial day in their advance on Washington. Two brigades from VI Corps of Army of the Potomac arrived on July 11, just as General Early, whose infantry was now reduced to 8,000 men, came near the city. Confederate artillery exchanged fire with the Union at Fort Stevens, just six miles north of the Capitol Building, and the next day General Early was forced to abandon the attack and return south. President Lincoln and many others came to watch Washington being saved right in front of them.

THE SIEGE OF PETERSBURG AND RICHMOND

In July 1864, General Grant was able to close on Richmond and the nearby city of Petersburg, and began a siege that lasted through March 1865. The Armies of the James and the Potomac combined for a force numbering over 100,000 men, against 50,000 men under General Lee. The Siege of Petersburg and Richmond was partly open battle and partly trench warfare. The Union hoped to cut off Richmond's railroads and supplies, and dug trenches 30 miles from east of Richmond to southeast of Petersburg. Late in July Grant attempted to hurry the siege by digging a tunnel under Confederate lines, and blowing a giant hole for Union troops to emerge and attack. The Battle of the Crater backfired badly when they were trapped in the hole and picked off by Confederate snipers. Union losses at the Crater were nearly triple the Confederates' losses; overall casualties during the siege were about 42,000 Union and 28,000 Confederate troops.

In January 1865 General Sherman's huge force continued its march north from Savannah into South Carolina, dishing out extra punishment to the state they called "the cockpit of secession," and then into North Carolina. By the spring of 1865 most Southern cities and countryside were under Union control. The fall of Atlanta was a critical loss. Atlanta was a major railroad hub, so transportation across the Deep South came to a complete stop. Its economy was collapsing, and with few overseers to stop them, slaves were deserting across the South.

"The Dictator"

In March 1865, seeing that he would be overpowered by new Union forces, General Lee attempted to breakout at Fort Stedman, near Petersburg. A surprise Confederate attack opened a 1,000 foot gap in the Union line, until Union artillery and troops counter-attacked. On April 1, 1865, after eight months of siege, Lee's Army evacuated to the west, and Richmond and Petersburg finally surrendered. Union artillery had used a huge, 13-inch mortar cannon called "The Dictator" to level the cities. Jefferson Davis and his remaining government fled to Danville, Virginia, hoping to keep up the fight, but in denial of the inevitable.

Northwest of Richmond, Lee fought rear-guard actions as Grant advanced. On April 9, Lee's army of under 30,000 men was surrounded by superior Union forces. Lee met Grant and surrendered at Appomattox Court House, Virginia, about fifty miles west of Richmond. Grant's terms to Lee were generous. He allowed Confederate officers to keep their guns, and all soldiers their own horses, on the promise to return home and not fight any longer. Jefferson Davis soon fled to Greensboro, North Carolina, hoping to rendezvous with General J.E. Johnston, but Johnston surrendered his army to General Sherman on April 26.

The Civil War was over. About 620,000 men were dead. Less than half these men died on the battlefield; many more died from their wounds, or from cholera, dysentery, and other diseases suffered on the campaign. About 56,000 men died from starvation and disease in prison camps, where camp commanders did not have enough food or medicine for the huge numbers of prisoners.[42] Tens of thousands were mutilated by amputation, some of which were necessary to save their lives, and some, performed by panicked battlefield surgeons, probably unnecessary.

President Lincoln had tragically few days to savor the Union victory. The Average Joe probably knows the story of Lincoln's assassination on April 14, so we will not detail those events here. General Grant later related how Lincoln had described his dreams, where "he seemed to be in some singular, indescribable vessel and…he was moving with great rapidity to an indefinite shore." Did Lincoln have a premonition of his death? Others described him as more cheerful than they had ever known him. When Lincoln died on April 15, surrounded by the men in his Cabinet, Secretary of War Edwin Stanton broke a long silence by saying, "Now he belongs to the ages."

The assassin, actor John Wilkes Booth, died trying to escape a barn where he was hiding, after it was set on fire by Union troops. Eight other members of his conspiracy were convicted, and four of them hanged. The same evening that

Lincoln was assassinated, Secretary of State Seward was attacked in his home by another conspirator and stabbed in the face and neck. He survived, and served in the same position in Andrew Johnson's Cabinet.[43]

Jefferson Davis was suspected of aiding the conspiracy, though he was surely innocent. After his capture he spent nearly two years in solitary confinement in Norfolk and upon release he left for Quebec, and stayed until receiving amnesty in 1868. He returned to live in Tennessee and Mississippi until his death in 1889. His funeral was attended by over 100,000 people.

Robert E. Lee was broken in spirit by the war. He served as president of small Washington College, and died in 1870. People were astonished to learn he was only sixty-three years old.

CHAPTER SIX—1865-1875, THE RECONSTRUCTION ERA

The fighting stopped in April 1865, but issues dividing the nation were by no means solved. The South was in ruins. Tensions between North and South did not disappear. Most of the South went under a military occupation that lasted for years. It would be more than ten years before all the seceding states were fully "reconstructed" as members of the Union, and even that outcome was far from meeting the war's original objectives.

The South was devastated by the war. Three million slaves were now free but largely unprepared to fend for themselves. The Southern plantation economy was dying, the infrastructure (roads, railroads, bridges and communications) was wrecked or in disarray, half of its cities were piles of rubble, the banks were closed, and there was no capital available for business. Black and white people were starving all over the South. After losing a quarter of a million men, there were few Southern leaders to bring life back to order. Civil governments had completely broken down in the Deep South states most recently conquered during the war; crime and chaos was spreading across the region. In the North, war debt and the losses of both state and federal governments meant very little could be spared to help the South.

There was also the political dimension of the Reconstruction period. History has shown that, much like our current time, political animosity overwhelmed the process of solving easily-identified problems. President Lincoln had plans for a relatively generous and conciliatory reconstruction; but after his assassination, Republican leaders in Washington were in no mood for reconciliation with their erstwhile enemies. Thus began a bitter dispute between Andrew Johnson, the new president who succeeded Lincoln, and the "Radical" Republicans who genuinely wanted to help the newly freed slaves, but in a few cases were intent on punishing the South.

Reconstruction is the name given to the period 1865-1877 and also to new legislation in Washington, recognizing that nearly a century's worth of division and four years of murderous battle had severely fractured the nation. Abraham Lincoln may actually have been naïve to think Reconstruction would go smoothly. There was still more upheaval, argument and violence to come, with even more devastating consequences to whites and blacks in the South and race relations for years to come.

FIRST RECONSTRUCTION, AND THE 13TH & 14TH AMENDMENTS

Andrew Johnson (1808-1875), 17th President of the United States, was President Lincoln's nominee for Vice President in the 1864 election. Choosing Andrew Johnson for VP was a calculated political act by Lincoln. As a former Democrat, governor and senator from Tennessee, Johnson's name on the ballot helped Lincoln reach out to Democrats who might have voted for George McClellan. But Johnson lacked Lincoln's calm demeanor and political skills. When he became president after Lincoln's assassination, he failed to comprehend his tough, new challenge to heal the nation. Though Johnson fought hard to implement the dead man's plan for reconstruction, he never came to terms with the Radicals for any sort of compromise.

Before he died, Abraham Lincoln had planned a set of requirements for the secessionist states. Each state could apply for readmission once its legislature had officially abolished slavery; citizens were asked to swear allegiance to the Union, (except for high-ranking Confederate officers or officials, who would be considered case-by-case); and after ten percent of the citizens had sworn the oath, the state was eligible for readmission. Immediately after the war the federal government confiscated property of the Confederacy, and the lands and abandoned property of many Southern leaders, though much of this was repatriated to its original owners, by President Johnson. The 13th Amendment to the Constitution, which outlawed slavery, was passed by Congress and ratified by all the states in December 1865, including the Southern states which had by now organized new governments and elected new representatives and senators for Congress.

Northern philanthropists like George Peabody contributed millions to help the South rebuild and open schools for former slaves. In mid-1865 the federal government took a major step to help the South get back on its feet. It established the Freedmen's Bureau under the War Department, which was essentially a network of welfare stations to provide food, clothing, education, and emergency supplies to those in need. By all accounts the Freedmen's Bureau successfully fulfilled its mission. It saved thousands of people from starvation, both black and white, helped over 100,000 former slaves learn to read, and settled thousands of black families on 400,000 acres of farmland that was confiscated by federal troops. There was an unfortunate false rumor the Freedmen's Bureau would give every former slave "40 acres and a mule" from confiscated lands, perhaps because in many cases, that did happen.

Two new phenomena became well known in the South during the Reconstruction era: Carpetbaggers and Scalawags. Carpetbaggers, who got their name since many arrived with suitcases made from carpet remnants, were northerners who travelled South to exploit new opportunities by running Freedmen's Bureaus or to start a business. Many also went into politics to enforce Radical Republican policies in the Second Reconstruction. Scalawags were southerners who joined forces with the new, federally imposed state governments after the war. Carpetbaggers and Scalawags did much good reconstructing the South; however, the rotten apples among them gave them all a bad name. They learned how to milk the new, poorly-controlled state and country treasuries for their own enrichment. For example, carpetbagger governor Henry

Clay Warmoth of Louisiana, accumulated a fortune of $4 million on a salary of $8,000 a year.[44] Southerners learned to hate their new governments with a discontent that smoldered during Reconstruction.

Worse were the "Black Codes" being instituted across the South. While they varied from state to state, legislatures established laws to control former slaves by prohibiting them from owning guns, barring them from all but farm labor, traveling or leaving jobs without permission, preaching without a license and denying them the right to vote. Disarming black Americans left them defenseless against a vicious Southern backlash. Radical Republicans understood that the Black Codes were a new form of slavery, and acts of defiance against Northern victory in the war.

Military occupation and the Freedman's Bureau helped protect Southern blacks from the worst effects of the Black Codes, but they could not last forever. The Republican Congress passed a bill strengthening the Bureau; but President Johnson vetoed it, out of conviction that it violated states' rights. Then he made matters worse by denouncing the Radicals in public, calling them enemies of the union equal to the Confederates. This cost Johnson valuable support in 1866, when Congress passed a new Civil Rights bill, declaring the Negro (to use the old term) a citizen with all the rights belonging to him. This time Johnson's veto was overridden and Congress followed up with a new bill for the Freedmen's Bureau, which also survived his veto.

Congress' next move was to pass the Fourteenth Amendment to the Constitution. It has four sections, the most pertinent being sections 1 and 2. Section 1 stated that all citizens born or naturalized in the United States are thereby citizens, and not to be deprived of their rights without due process. Section 2 dealt only indirectly with voting rights for Southern blacks, saying that states denying this right would suffer proportional loss of representation in Congress. The Amendment was submitted to all the states for ratification, with the implication that seceding states must ratify or face the consequences of extended occupation and reconstruction. Tennessee, with a Republican governor, was the first state to ratify and be readmitted to the Union in 1866.

The Freedmen's Bureau lasted until 1868 and was the hallmark of what is known as the First Reconstruction. The Second Reconstruction came about with the Radical Republicans' anger over inherent weaknesses in the first plan, and even more over signs of Southern intransigence. In spite of the loyalty oaths and the bars against former Confederate leaders, many were being elected and returned to Congress, most notably former CSA Vice President Alexander Stephens.

THE RADICALS STRIKE BACK—SECOND RECONSTRUCTION

Andrew Johnson

President Johnson continued making intemperate attacks on his enemies while campaigning in the mid-term elections of 1866—not for the Republicans but the Democrats! This tactic of course backfired, and an even larger Radical majority was elected to serve in 1867. Leadership of the Reconstruction now firmly passed from the president and the moderates to Congress and the Radicals. They promptly passed new Reconstruction Acts along lines meant to bring the South back under control. One Act divided the South into five military districts of two states each, with a general officer in charge of each district. Among other requirements, Southern states now had to modify their constitutions and give ex-slaves the right to vote.

The chief impact of Congress' new Reconstruction Acts was to render the new Southern state governments illegal until they complied with the new laws. The new military governors strengthened controls that had been relaxed the previous year. The Republicans not only controlled Congress, they had strong backing from business and financial leaders in the northeast, who in return got high tariffs, sound currency with hard money policies, and subsidies for railroad building in the West. The First Reconstruction was now officially dead, and President Johnson's relations with Congress were virtually poisoned with hate.

There were big changes with the new "thorough" Reconstruction. With wider voting rights, the Republicans including Radicals, carpetbaggers, and black Americans took control of every Southern legislature. Congress saw its first black representatives and senators. The first black American elected to a full term in the U.S. Senate was Blanche Kelso Bruce of Mississippi, who investigated banking scandals and later served as President Hayes' Secretary of the Treasury. These new Republican leaders pushed through plans for educating blacks and provided more assistance for the rural poor. With federal help they continued rebuilding Southern roads, bridges, and public buildings demolished during the war. Across the South, Union League chapters were formed as all-black auxiliaries of the Republican Party, and a mission to enroll new voters and promote civic projects.

This could have been the golden era of the South, if not for the corruption that accompanied it. As noted before, carpetbaggers and scalawags were virtually unaccountable and took the opportunity to loot the state treasuries. Some of the new black legislators had trouble conforming to norms of behavior expected in their office and came under ridicule. The states piled up huge deficits, and levied taxes so burdensome they depressed property values. The worst crimes were committed by officials who learned to manipulate the system and their black comrades, betraying everyone's ideals and the public trust.

Meanwhile, Southern blacks faced a new threat from white vigilante groups. The Ku Klux Klan was formed under the leadership of Confederate General Nathan Bedford Forrest, who had ordered the massacre of nearly 200 black Union soldiers at the Battle of Fort Pillow in 1864. The KKK operated in secret, riding in bands at night, wearing white robes and hoods to disguise themselves. At times the dispensed justice to lawbreakers, but their main targets were ex-slaves and scalawags. Over 3,000 black men and 1,000 whites died in a reign of terror lasting nearly ten years with attacks on black militiamen, new black voters, and meetings of the Union League. The KKK were well organized but not as violent as the ruffian groups they inspired, who tortured and murdered blacks and their white allies. They considered disbanding in 1869 and they faded away in the 1870's (to be reborn in 1915), however they had unleashed forces they were powerless to stop. Between the Black Codes and the Klan, a new regime of racial hatred was born across the South that had not existed before.

IMPEACHING PRESIDENT JOHNSON

Radical leaders of the Republican Party asserted high ideals trying to stop the new regime. However, their conflict with President Johnson turned into a serious political battle that nearly threatened the Constitution and its system of checks and balances. The two most important men leading this fight were Thaddeus Stevens of Pennsylvania, Speaker of the House of Representatives, and Senator Charles Sumner of Massachusetts. Senator Sumner had a political and a personal reason for his crusade: In May 1856, during the debate on the Kansas-Nebraska Act, Representative Preston Brooks of South Carolina had severely beaten Sumner with his cane on the floor of the Senate as punishment for an innuendo-laden speech he had just given. Sumner received a concussion and spinal cord damage, and could not return to the Senate until 1859.

President Johnson continued feuding with Congress. Where once he had wanted a Reconstruction that freed the slaves and amicably brought Southern states back to the Union, now he was a full-blooded defender of the South and took every Congressional law as infringement on his rights as president. By 1867 the situation in Washington had deteriorated to the point that the Radicals decided to get rid of Andrew Johnson.

With its new veto-proof majority, Congress's power looked invincible. In March 1867, Congress passed the Tenure of Office Act, which stripped the president of his right to fire any official whose appointment had been approved by Congress. As it was, President Johnson was already battling with his Secretary of War, Edwin Stanton, who was most influenced by the new Republican politics. Johnson also believed—with good reason—that the Tenure Act was unconstitutional, so he tested Congress' determination by firing Stanton and turning his authority over to General Grant.

The Radicals exploded. President Johnson was falling into their trap, and they began impeachment proceedings. In February 1868, Johnson was impeached by the House of Representatives. According to the Constitution, impeachment in the House must be followed by trial in the Senate and approved there by a two-thirds majority, or 36 of the 54 Senators of the time. Johnson's Senate trial dragged into a three-month long process. In his defense, Johnson explored legal precedents going back years to exonerate himself of the charge of breaking the law. It became high drama across the city of Washington, with tickets being sold for seats in the Senate gallery.

The impeachment verdict, which once looked so certain, was a surprise to the nation. Seven Republican Senators refused to vote with the Radicals, leaving the vote at 35 to 19, just one count short of the two-thirds majority. Johnson was acquitted, and allowed to serve the remainder of his term as president.

How did this happen? The story of Johnson's impeachment holds several different lessons for us, some of them contradictory. Was Andrew Johnson unfairly persecuted by a power-hungry Congress, and escaped impeachment when just one more Republican senator felt the weight of history on his conscience? According to this view, if the Radical Republicans in Congress had prevailed, it could have set a precedent severely limiting presidential prerogative and power. Johnson may have been unpopular and only put in office due to Lincoln's assassination, but the office of the presidency could have been permanently damaged, and with it the system of checks and balances so deliberately and carefully built into the Constitution by America's Founders.

Or, as Professor Jeffrey K. Tulis of the University of Texas suggests, did Johnson truly abuse his power and then use a hyper-legal defense to frame his impeachment as a narrow trial over very specific crimes? Johnson not only fought an ugly and public fight with the Republicans, he went overboard appeasing the South, and fired a government official (Stanton) in violation of an act of Congress. He, not Congress, was upsetting the careful system of checks and balances. The mere fact that the impeachment vote favored Johnson by just one vote indicates that there are no easy answers.[45]

There is a danger when impeachment occurs under such politicized circumstances. The Framers of the Constitution probably imagined that impeachment would only be necessary when a president was guilty of a traitorous act, or committed a felony or some other clear-cut crime, not just because of a political feud. They probably didn't envision the complex web of allegiances and passions following a terrible war, as happened in 1867.

The impeachment of Andrew Johnson cannot be properly understood in this book. It is up to every Average Joe to contemplate the meaning and the proper circumstances for impeachment. I urge you to give it some extra thought and research, for good government should never be taken for granted, and our freedoms are too precious to let them be trampled by abuse of presidential authority.

It's worth noting at this point that Johnson's Secretary of State, William Seward, who held his position since Lincoln's cabinet, is credited with purchasing the Alaska Territory from

Russia in 1867. Seward first offered $5 million, and the final price was $7.2 million. Given that most Americans thought of Alaska as a frozen wasteland, the purchase came to be called "Seward's Folly."

PRESIDENT ULYSSES S. GRANT

The Republicans failed to impeach Johnson, but their favorite man won the presidency in the election of 1868. President Ulysses S. Grant (1822-1885) of Point Pleasant, Ohio, was the hero of the Civil War and won a landslide victory in the Electoral College against Democrat Horatio Seymour of New York. However, the popular vote showed narrow Republican majorities in the North, and in fact, Grant might have lost without the votes of new freedmen in the South.

The Fourteenth Amendment had been designed for the Southern vote, and it was blatantly hypocritical, since many Northern states did not give blacks the right to vote. In 1869 Congress corrected this with the Fifteenth Amendment, guaranteeing the right to all male citizens regardless of "race, color, or previous condition of servitude." Black Americans across the nation were now enfranchised, and sure to vote Republican.

President Grant was a military man, and needed time to adjust to the political demands of his job. He was usually content to work with the Republican leaders in Congress. His early appointments were often misguided, with men in cabinet positions and other offices who couldn't do their jobs. The greatest exception to this was Grant's Secretary of State, Hamilton Fish, a former governor of New York who served during Grant's second term. Secretary Fish settled claims against Great Britain over their support of the Confederate Navy during the Civil War by receiving a $15 million settlement, and he implemented civil service reforms inside the State Department.[46]

But Grant almost got into serious trouble in his first year, with the famous "gold corner conspiracy" of 1869. Speculators Jay Gould and James Fisk of New York were using their influence with Grant's friends and relatives to induce the president to stop sales of gold by the US Treasury. On a normal basis, the Treasury sold its gold to manage international trade and it accrued gold the same way. Both Gould and Fisk courted the president on his visits to New York, but Gould worked on Grant primarily through his brother in-law Abel Corbin. Corbin advised Grant that holding gold would drive up its value and bring the dollar lower, and cause mid-western grain crops and other exports to move rapidly for sale in Europe. With this advice, Grant ordered the Treasury to suspend all sales of gold, unless directly ordered by the president.

Gould and Fisk had been accumulating millions of dollars in gold coins and brought others, including Corbin, into the scheme by convincing them the president was in on it. Their plan was, after using the government to help corner most of the gold supply and drive up its price, to suddenly dump it and reap the profits. Gould held $40 million in gold, twice the amount normally in circulation. On September 24, gold opened at $142 and went up to $162. This was not yet at Gould's target of $180, but Grant was alerted to what was happening on Wall Street, and he gave immediate orders to the Treasury to sell gold. This quickly sent the price back down. The speculators dumped all they could by Monday, and it is not clear how much money they made. However, the attempt to corner gold did cause a temporary panic in the markets and left a black mark on Grant's administration.[47]

President Grant was a hard money man and opposed to the greenbacks that were still in circulation after the Civil War. In January 1875, Grant succeeded in getting Congress to pass the Resumption Act, which withdrew all greenbacks from circulation by 1879, and returned the nation to the gold standard.

THE END OF RECONSTRUCTION

In time, the rigors of military occupation wore on both the North and the South. Friction between Republican-controlled governments and resentful whites in the South got worse. Eight states had been readmitted to the Union by 1868, including Tennessee, North Carolina, South Carolina, Arkansas,

Alabama, Georgia, Louisiana, and Florida. (Mississippi, Virginia, and Texas were as yet "unreconstructed".) As member states once more, they participated in national elections. A federal commission investigated the Klan and its spinoff gangs, resulting in the Enforcement Acts in 1870 and 1871. President Grant used powers these Acts gave him to crack down on the perpetrators with additional federal troops. The state of Georgia was in such turmoil that in 1869 it was reoccupied and put under a third Reconstruction, and readmitted again to the Union in 1870.

Hard feelings in the North started softening as word got out about corruption and embezzlement in the South, and the plight of poor Southern farmers. Gradually a reform movement was born on both sides of the Mason-Dixon Line. Southern reformers were business minded and wanted to move beyond the old antagonisms; in the North, a new reform-minded wing of Republicans calling themselves the "liberals" worked to help fund Southern businesses.

President Grant easily won re-election in 1872. On the surface, Reconstruction was plodding along but the Democrats were steadily returning to power in the South. They retook the Tennessee state government in 1869. Virginia, West Virginia, Missouri, and North Carolina followed in 1870, then Georgia in 1871, Alabama, Arkansas, and Texas in 1874, and Mississippi in 1875. Florida, Louisiana, and South Carolina remained under occupation until 1877 and went Democrat as soon as the troops left.

Whites across the South eventually reconsolidated their power, this time not by directly violating federal law, but through Jim Crowe laws that kept most blacks as second-class citizens. Voting was restricted by literacy tests, poll taxes, and outright intimidation. Since schools for blacks were segregated and inferior to white schools, literacy was a persistent obstacle for Southern black for decades to come. Through the end of the nineteenth century and beyond, few blacks were able to vote in the Deep South.

Capital for development continued to be scarce for many years. Southern states often got the losing end of the deal when Washington apportioned funds for roads, public construction, and railroads. With most cities in need of rebuilding and its transportation largely in ruins, the South lagged far behind the rest of the nation for the rest of the century. Racial segregation in the South went hand in hand with under-development and regional backwardness, each holding the other back.

GRANT'S LEGACY

President Grant believed firmly in republican government and the Union cause. Referring to the Fugitive Slave Law and to Lincoln's statement that no state could remain half free and half slave, he wrote:

Slavery was an institution that required unusual guarantees for its security wherever it existed, and in a country like ours where the larger portion of it was free territory inhabited by an intelligent and well-to-do population, the people would naturally have but little sympathy with demands upon them for its protection.[48]

During the Civil War, France had taken advantage of America's trouble to establish a monarchy in Mexico. In 1862 Emperor Napoleon III sent French troops to Mexico and installed Austrian Archduke Ferdinand Maximilian as Emperor Maximilian I of Mexico. President Benito Juarez established a Mexican government-in-exile in northern Mexico. When the US Civil War ended in 1865, General Grant sent General Sheridan with 50,000 troops to the Rio Grande River, ready to assist Juarez and drive France out of Mexico. Fortunately war was unnecessary; the French backed down and withdrew their troops. Juarez returned to the Mexican presidency, and Maximilian was executed in 1867.

Ulysses Grant retired in 1877 after his eight years in office. Grant and his family and went on a world tour, and were greeted by large crowds in England and met Queen Victoria in London. Next he met Pope Leo XIII, Chancellor Otto von Bismarck, and travelled on to the Holy Land, India, Southeast Asia, and China, where he helped settle a dispute between China and Japan over the Ryukyu Islands (Okinawa). Back in

America, Grant needed money, and in 1883 he made very risky investments in his son's brokerage firm in New York. The firm went bankrupt and left Grant destitute.

Grant had avoided writing about the Civil War but now this was the only way he could earn any money. At the urging of his friends including Mark Twain, Grant wrote his lengthy *Personal Memoirs*, which was a huge success. It was not only popular with war veterans but critics called it one of the greatest memoirs written, and it remains the best written by an American leader. But Grant was also suffering with throat cancer; he finished the book just two days before dying on July 23, 1885. His funeral train from upstate New York was visited by a quarter of a million people, and tens of thousands attended his funeral in New York City, where his pallbearers included both former Union and Confederate generals. In 1897 he was laid to rest at the General Grant National Memorial, better known as Grant's Tomb, the largest mausoleum in America.

Ulysses S. Grant, Official Portrait

CHAPTER SEVEN—SETTLING THE WEST

After the Civil War, Americans and the United States government renewed their focus on settling the West. The great expanses west of Texas, Missouri, and the upper Mississippi River were mostly wild, populated by American Indians, and uninhabited. Millions of citizens and immigrants dreamed of settling the land, and the policy of Washington, DC was to bring all the Territories in as member states of the Union.

In 1870, the United States included 37 states and 10 territories, plus the Department of Alaska. The Nevada and Nebraska territories became states during the 1860s and Colorado in 1876, which is the reason it is called the Centennial State. The territories between the eastern half of America and the Pacific area were still being settled. There would not be another new state until 1889.

LIFE ON THE FRONTIER

After the Civil War, the US Army devoted more resources toward fortifying the "Wild West." Forts were built in every territory as barracks for troops and as protection from American Indians. New towns sprang up across the thousands of miles of unsettled territory, from New Mexico and Arizona on the Mexican border to the Dakotas and Montana on the border with Canada.

The Homestead Act of 1862 was an important Republican initiative to populate the West with independent farmers. It gave a new settler title to 160 acres of land in the western territories, provided the settler stayed there and farmed the land at least five years. This was followed by the Timber Culture Act in 1872, which granted an existing homesteader who would plant 40 acres of trees title to an additional 160 acres. The Timber and Stone Act of 1878 sold land that was unfit for farming to those willing to log or mine the land for $2.50 per acre. While the first two acts successfully met their goals of bringing farmers to the territories, the Timber and Stone Act backfired. Land speculators hired individuals to purchase the lots and sell them to the company, after nominal compliance with the law. Together, however, these acts in the late 1800s must be considered among the most generous actions ever taken by a government to help the ordinary man become a landowner.[49]

Farming the arid Great Plains region of Kansas, Iowa, Nebraska, Minnesota, the Dakotas, and eastern Colorado was a harsh life. Rainfall was low, barely enough for most crops, and whatever trees existed were soon chopped down for homes and firewood. Cold winds blew half the year. Settlers had to endure blizzards, tornadoes, and plagues of locusts every 8 or 10 years. In areas with few trees, settlers had to build their homes with sod siding and roofs. These people probably decided the Homestead Act was the government betting 160 acres you couldn't live ten years on the frontier.

But the settlers kept coming—farmers from the East wanting a new start, and a new wave of immigrants, especially eastern Europeans and Scandinavians. For these people frontier life was worth the risk; it was their chance at prosperity and abundance, and if not for them, then for their children. And within a generation, a newly settled area usually went from wilderness to towns and civilization.

The word frontier has several meanings. In the 1800s the Frontier was the broad line, slowly moving West, that separated towns and cities where the law prevailed and people could safely prosper, from lands where businesses were few and settlers were on their own. The Frontier was also a state of mind, defining the quality of life in a certain area, which would have different definitions depending on the person. In 1893, historian Frederick Jackson Turner wrote that the Frontier mentality was characterized by "that coarseness and strength combined with acuteness and inquisitiveness: that practical inventive turn of mind…that masterful grasp of material things lacking in the artistic but powerful to affect great ends; that restless, nervous energy; that dominant individualism, working for good and evil…with exuberance that comes from freedom."[50]

But most importantly, the Frontier was a legal definition. The federal government defined the Frontier as a region where population density was between two and six persons per square mile, on average. As more settlers streamed in, the Frontier line kept moving west, toward the Sierra Nevada Mountains of California, further and further, with smaller pockets of unsettled land remaining until there was no Frontier left, from a legal standpoint. That event occurred with the census of 1890.

From television and movies we all recognize the Conestogas, or covered wagons that brought most settlers West, banded together to form wagon trains. Their destinations varied, depending on the times and which new areas were being homesteaded. Long distance travel for those who could afford it was by stagecoach, at least until the railroad reached town. By 1875 stagecoaches were reaching every city and town in the West. Although very uncomfortable and not safe from attack by thieves or Indians, the stagecoach was fast. Passage from St. Louis to the Pacific cost about $200, with lower fares for shorter distances. Another important supply line before the railroad was oxen-pulled freight. Freight-wagon trains were a multimillion-dollar business, invaluable for bringing goods to settlers in the plains and around the Rockies. A typical freight wagon train was hundreds of wagons stretching over a mile in length.

MINING AND CATTLE RANCHING

The mining industry was a key enticement that brought people West. Gold was the first big draw, starting with the gold rushes in California in 1849, at Pikes Peak in Colorado and in Nevada in 1859, and Idaho in 1860.[51] Most miners failed to strike it rich, but some became fabulously wealthy and retired to San

Francisco for a life of leisure. A typical mining town was a rough, ramshackle place with few homes, but always a saloon where miners blew off steam and found the few available women willing to live, and make her living, there. Most of these towns crumbled away when the miners left, leaving ruins and ghost-towns we can still visit if we're willing to get off the highway. The last gold rush in the continental states happened in the Black Hills of Dakota, in 1876.

Gold fever subsided as large mining companies bought the miners' claims, and when it was discovered bigger money could be made mining for copper and more mundane metals. This was especially true in Montana, which attracted gold miners first, and where the discovery of copper resulted in the world's largest copper smelter being located in Anaconda. Silver was also abundant and mined around the Rocky Mountains.

The most important industry in the West was cattle herding and ranching. Cattle breeding was born in Mexico in the days of the Spanish colonies, from where it spread to Texas. More than 200 years of breeding resulted in a hardy stock of cow; it was fast, strong and featured a huge set of horns. In the early years 1830 to 1870, cattle were herded from grazing grounds in the Southwest and driven north toward the cattle towns for fattening and slaughter. A typical cattle drive was over a thousand head of cattle, herded by twenty men on horseback with a few wagons for provisions. It would usually cover about 500 miles, or more than a thousand miles depending where the herd started; most herds originated in south Texas, with destinations at railheads in Abilene, Wichita, and other points in Kansas. The most common route was the Chisholm Trail, named for an Indian trader, Jesse Chisholm.

The cattle industry went through some changes in the mid-1870s. Cattle were able to survive the cold winters in the high plains, and they could roam free until time for the annual round-up. A new technique for inexpensive production of barbed wire drove the cost down from $20 per 100 pounds of wire in 1874 to $1.90 in 1896. Now it was cheaper to fence the herds into large ranches, and cattle ranchers kept their herds nearby instead of driving them cross-country. The industry shifted toward local ranching and the ranchers acquired the power to control entire towns and counties where they ranched.

Cattle ranchers in Kansas, Nebraska and Wyoming—who preferred to be called cattlemen—were the most powerful men around. Raising cattle on their own lands, with no payments owed to the government for grazing rights, herding the animals onto the nearest train, and managing their entire business up to the point of sale, they grew rich and attracted capital for expansion from banks and investors around the world. The Wyoming Stock and Growers Association developed laws that virtually covered the territory, controlling cattle branding and round-ups, and discouraging over stocking. However, two severe winters in 1886 and 1887 killed most profits from cattle ranching. The cattlemen were forced to diversify their business, with more farming and smaller herds.

COWBOYS, LAWMEN, AND OUTLAWS

A Cowboy at Work

With cows you also got cowboys. The cowboy's fame spread far and wide, and by 1860 the Western legend of the cowboy was born. He could ride his horse for hours, lasso a steer on the run, sleep in the wilderness, and cross miles of desert when he had to. Hollywood has exaggerated the cowboy's violent side, but he was sure to carry a revolver and be ready to defend himself. Stories of cowboy adventures filled the dime-store novels printed for people back East who hungered for a taste of the West themselves.

The greatest Western stories were about the county sheriff or the federal marshal. The Sheriff was as likely to be a former policeman from the East as a cowboy who wanted a new life that put his skills with the six-shooter to work. The Marshal's job was to serve in the Territories, often working with the local sheriff. He would also range far and wide in search of fugitives and to collect a bounty. Most famous of all the lawmen was Wyatt Earp (1848-1929), the eagle-eyed shot who first became famous as a lawman in Dodge City during the 1870s. But Earp had a very rough start. He spent his childhood in Iowa, and in 1864 went with his father on a wagon train to San Bernardino, California where he found work as a teamster, and then was hired by the Northern Pacific Railroad, and learned gambling and boxing. He bounced around Missouri and Illinois, getting in trouble for a charge of horse-stealing and living in a brothel. He settled down a bit in Wichita, Kansas, serving as a deputy marshal, and in 1876 was appointed assistant marshal in Dodge City, where he made friends with Doc Holliday.

Wyatt Earp in 1869

In 1879 Wyatt Earp and his brothers moved to Tombstone, in the southeast corner of Arizona, seeking new opportunities, until they started clashing with the Clanton Gang. On October 26, 1881, Wyatt Earp, his brothers Virgil and Morgan, and Doc Holliday met two Clantons and three others in an alley near the OK Corral, killing three of them. The shootout became the stuff of legend, and it also started a year-long feud with the Clanton Gang that ended with the deaths of Morgan Earp and eighteen of the Gang members. In later years Earp and his wife Josephine turned to gold-mining in Alaska and Nevada, and in 1910 they moved for the last time to Los Angeles, where after a few more scrapes with the law, he ran a mine in the desert town of Vidal.

Perhaps second in fame to Wyatt Earp was his Dodge City associate, Bat Masterson (1853-1921). Born in Quebec, Masterson came to the West to hunt buffalo and survived an attack by nearly 700 Comanche and Cheyenne warriors in a four-day siege known as the Battle of Adobe Walls. He was elected Sheriff in Dodge City in 1877 where he rounded up the train-robber Dave Rudabaugh and his gang. Masterson was a lawman and occasional troublemaker in many places before going to New York and working as a sportswriter.

Lawman "Texas John" Slaughter (1841-1922) was a cattleman near San Antonio before moving to New Mexico and Arizona. He bought a large ranch near Tombstone, and in 1886 he was elected Sheriff of Cochise County, where he helped to capture the Jack Taylor Gang. Sheriff Slaughter carried a pearl-handled .44 and a double-barreled shotgun he called his "equalizer." The first black US Marshall in the West was an ex-slave named Bass Reeves (1838-1910). Reeves fled slavery as a boy and went to the Indian Territory (modern Oklahoma) to live among the Cherokee, where he learned to speak several Indian languages. He became a lawman about 1875 and served in the Indian Territory for 30 years, claiming to have arrested over 3,000 outlaws and fugitives. Reeves retired to Muscogee.

The best known outlaws of the time, and one of the greatest Western stories, were the James Gang. Jesse James (1847-1882) and Frank James (1843-1915) from Missouri learned the art of ambush as bushwhackers for the Confederate Army, under Bloody Bill Anderson.[52] After the war, they formed a gang with other ex-soldiers and started robbing banks across the frontier. While they justified robbing as revenge against the Union they did not care much who they killed in the process, bank staff and innocent bystanders alike. In the 1870s they turned to robbing stagecoaches and then trains, starting with a train derailment in Adair, Iowa. After settling down to farm for a couple of years, the James Gang got restless and in 1876 selected First National Bank in Newfield, Minnesota as their next target. The robbery went awry. Two gang members were killed on the scene, and the others killed or captured on the run. Only the James brothers survived. They formed a new gang operating out of Tennessee, then returned to Missouri. Jesse was killed in April 1882 by gang member Robert Ford, who in a secret agreement with Governor Thomas Crittendon, betrayed him to collect a reward. Frank James grew tired of being on the run and surrendered in October; he was acquitted of two charges against him by a sympathetic jury, and went on to lead life as a horse trainer and shoe salesman.

The most legendary outlaw was William Bonney (1859-1881), who was born Henry McCarty and is much better known as Billy the Kid. Bonney's true story is more amazing than the myths that circulated about him. Billy's life of crime began with petty theft in New Mexico territory in 1875, but he didn't become a fugitive until he escaped jail on one of those charges. He fled to the Arizona territory and made a living stealing horses. After killing a man in an argument he was put in jail, and again he escaped. Back in New Mexico in 1877, he reluctantly joined in with cattle rustlers, then left them to work for rancher John Tunstall in Lincoln County. Billy revered Tunstall and was enraged when he was gunned down by crooked sheriff William Brady and his deputies, who were working for a competing rancher.

Billy swore an affidavit against Brady and joined a posse called the Lincoln County Regulators. In 1878 they ambushed and killed Brady and several of his men. In the "Battle of Lincoln" a new sheriff came after them and seven men died, but Billy escaped. In 1879 Billy arranged a deal with territory

Governor Lew Wallace to testify on a separate crime in exchange for a pardon, but Wallace betrayed him and left Billy in jail. As you may guess, Billy escaped again. In 1880 he killed another man in self-defense in Fort Sumner, went on the run, and killed a deputy after taking a rancher hostage. Now Billy was hunted by new Lincoln County Sheriff Pat Garrett. Garrett arrested him in December 1880, and in April 1881, Billy was sentenced to hang. Waiting for punishment in Mesilla, Billy outsmarted and killed both of his captors, stole a horse, and escaped again. Sheriff Garrett tracked him down for the last time in Fort Sumner on July 14, and was lucky enough to meet Billy when he unexpectedly walked into the same room. Garrett shot Billy in the heart. Historians now say Billy only killed nine men, but in his time he was blamed for 21 deaths.

William Bonney, aka Billy the Kid

Historians have collected records on hundreds of outlaws and gangs in the Old West. Some other famous names include Butch Cassidy and the Sundance Kid, who in the 1890s had the longest string of successful bank and train robberies in history; gunfighter John Wesley Hardin from Texas, a quiet man who preached hell fire from the Old Testament, is known to have killed 27 men but claimed he killed 42; and Thomas "Black Jack" Ketchum and the Ketchum Gang, who robbed trains in New Mexico by uncoupling the mail and express cars, sending them down the track for looting. The most non-violent criminal was Charles Bowles (1829-1888), aka Black Bart. His unconventional method of robbing stagecoaches was all bluff, since his shotgun was seldom loaded. Bart lived a double life as a gentleman in San Francisco, heading east or north to Oregon to make his living. He was finally tracked down by Wells Fargo detective James Hume in 1884.

Then there was the type of man who was hard to pigeonhole, often a loner, living just inside the bounds of the law, sometimes working for the law. The most famous example was "Wild Bill" Hickock (1837–1876), born James Butler Hickok in Troy, Illinois. Wild Bill was a gunfighter, a ruffian, a crack poker player, an Indian scout and fighter for the US Army, an actor, a stagecoach driver, a city marshal (in Hays City and Abilene, Kansas), and a friend of both lawmen and outlaws across the Great Plains.[53] Harper's New Monthly Magazine interviewed Hickok in 1865, giving him the chance to build his legend by claiming he killed "hundreds" of men. In one famous incident in Nebraska, Hickok was challenged by four drunken cowboys to a gunfight; he killed three and wounded the fourth, receiving a bullet in his shoulder.

After several years as a lawman, Wild Bill married Agnes Lake early in 1876, an older woman who convinced him to give up the brothels, but he soon left her behind in Wyoming to find gold in the Black Hills. On the wagon trail there he met his kindred spirit Calamity Jane, the legendary female army scout. Hickok went to Deadwood, Dakota Territory, and apparently spent all his time with Jane or gambling. On August 2, 1876, he was killed by a young man mad with envy—shot in the head, on one of the few occasions Wild Bill couldn't sit with his back to the wall.

Speaking of Deadwood, the gold mines made it one of the richest and most cultured towns in the West. Deadwood attracted visitors from around the world who came for the beauty of the Black Hills and for the nightlife. At its peak, the Gem Theater in Deadwood performed the comic opera The Mikado for 130 consecutive nights.

These are just a few of the names that make up our Western lore and legends. But just how violent was the "Wild West?" In most of the West, there was a period of several years after a district became open for settlement and before formal protection by lawmen when an area was truly dangerous. Afterwards, the typical Western town saw very little violence. By far the most common crime, which could carry the penalty of death, was horse-stealing. It has been said that more men died in Hollywood gunfights by 1950 than were actually killed out West. Rather than glorying in the semi-fictional violence of the West, its heritage to us today should be the free spirit, and the willingness of the ordinary man or woman to take a gamble and try something new, all living in the same frontier.

Wild Bill Hickok

THE AMERICAN INDIANS

Westward expansion meant more pressure on American Indians in the West. US government policy towards Indians was never consistent, and usually dependent on the president in office at the time, or the numbers of white men on the move, or the particular tribes involved. Western settlers usually tried not to antagonize their Indian neighbors; but when there was a conflict over land, most often the Indians' interests were the last taken into consideration. There are countless books written on the American Indians, which are complex and full of betrayal and murder on both sides. This section, just like the rest of the Average Joe's Guide, is an overview of the important trends and events and not an attempt at comprehensive history. Given the American Indians' importance to our national heritage, I urge you to do your own reading.

For years prior to the Civil War, the land west of the Missouri River was considered Indian Territory. Most of the white pioneers passed through the Great Plains, bound for California, Oregon, and other points. They of course counted on the US Army to protect them. In 1851, at Fort Laramie in Wyoming, government agent David Mitchell negotiated a treaty with the surrounding tribes guaranteeing the safe passage of wagon trains. Mitchell was accompanied by an army unit of 250 men, and 10,000 Indian warriors were witnesses to the agreement. The treaty was a success, and over the next twenty years 250,000 settlers passed through the plains without incident.

As we know, this situation could not last indefinitely. During and after the War, settlers started contesting Indians for their lands. New treaties were made, sometimes paying the tribes annuities for their lands, and which always meant setting new tribal boundaries and leaving the government free to allow white settlement and railroads anywhere it wished. The Indians were usually left with inferior lands and less game for hunting.

In Colorado in 1864, the Arapaho and Cheyenne tribes were forced into a barren reservation in the southeast corner of the territory near the Sand Creek River. In anger, war parties struck out and conducted raids into the north and Nebraska, attacking settlers and wagon trains. The government offered amnesty if they returned to the reservation, but they waited too long, angering the Army commander at Fort Lyon, General Samuel Curtis. Chief Black Kettle believed the peace was secure, and the tribes returned to Sand Creek and encamped close to Fort Lyon. General Curtis ordered Colonel John Chivington to take revenge, and over 100 tribe members were brutally massacred. Though the Sand Creek Massacre was at first seen as a victory, the government investigated and made public testimony damning the attack. Col. Chivington had already resigned and was immune from military justice, although his political ambitions were ended.

Also during the Civil War was the Sioux Uprising of 1862, in Minnesota and the Dakota Territory. The Dakota Sioux had recently lost hunting grounds during negotiations in Washington and were short of food. Preoccupied with the War, the federal government was behind in payments to the Sioux for the land. The war started almost by accident in August 1862, when a Sioux hunting party in Acton Township was stealing eggs and killed five white settlers. Chief Little Crow knew war was coming and took the offensive, deciding to drive the white man out of the area. Little Crow's band killed as many as 800 men, women and children in settlements along the Minnesota River. The Army took the area back by December, captured 400 Dakota, and put them on trial. President Lincoln pardoned all but 38 of them, who were then executed in a vengeful, mass hanging. This increased tensions and led to several more years of fighting in Minnesota Territory. Little Crow was caught and killed in 1863.

Sioux Chief Red Cloud was more successful in resisting encroachment by white settlers west of Minnesota. Red Cloud wanted to defend his finest hunting grounds and fought the Army to a standstill. This victory won a treaty in 1867 giving the Sioux control of lands north and west of the Platte River. That same year the government formed the Bureau of Indian Affairs, which still exists as part of the Department of the Interior. The BIA's mission was to manage the Indian reservations, but the Army came to view BIA agents as soft and too ready to accept Indian promises.

In 1868 Chief Sitting Bull (1831-1890) of the Lakota Sioux refused to renegotiate new terms to the Mitchell Treaty. President Grant had little sympathy for American Indians, and ordered the Sioux out of their reservations, leading to years of warfare known as the Great Indian Wars of 1868 to 1876. One man who wanted to make a name for himself in the Indian War was Colonel George Custer (1839-1876), a hero of the Civil War who had held the temporary rank of General. Custer was impatient for victory against the Indians. In his first major action in 1868 at the Washita River in modern Oklahoma, he rashly slaughtered the tribe of Chief Black Kettle, who wanted peace with the white man. In 1873 Custer and his cavalry intruded into Lakota Sioux territory in the Black Hills of Dakota to protect a railroad survey (see Chapter Eight for related information). Custer announced that he found gold there, kicking off the Black Hills gold rush.

The Sioux Indian War climaxed on June 25, 1876 when Custer and 267 troops of the Seventh Cavalry Regiment were ambushed and slaughtered by Sitting Bull and Crazy Horse at Little Big Horn in southern Montana. "Custer's Last Stand" was the Army's worst defeat in the war, and ended the career of a man who had once hoped to become president. General Nelson Miles retaliated and ultimately conquered the rebellious Sioux tribes. Commander of the Army General Philip Sheridan soon ordered the Sioux people split up into six different reservations.

In 1873, Chief Joseph (1840-1904) of the Nez Perce had negotiated his peoples' right to stay on their lands in eastern Oregon. The government reversed itself in 1877 and demanded the tribe move to a reservation in Idaho. Some of the Nez Perce chiefs were for war, but Chief Joseph persuaded them to escape to Canada and join Chief Sitting Bull, who had fled there in 1876. Army General Oliver Howard fought and pursued 750 of the Nez Perce across the Idaho and Montana Territories for three months before he defeated them in the Bear Paw Mountains, just 40 miles south of the Canadian border.

The Nez Perce's tactics and skills in battle earned them widespread admiration from their adversaries and from the

American public. Chief Joseph was the only surviving leader of Bear Paw. He went to prison for eight months, while most of the Nez Perce were sent to Indian Territory in Oklahoma. Joseph was at last allowed to settle near his old homeland, at the Colville Reservation in Washington Territory. In later years he made three trips to Washington to meet Presidents Hayes and Roosevelt, and to plead for better treatment for his tribe.

GERONIMO IN ARIZONA

Indian tribes in the Southwest varied in their attitudes toward the white man. In general, the Hopi, Pueblo, and Navajo tribes were less nomadic, and more likely to farm and stay in one place. In part because the region in general was semi-desert and not hospitable, they were given large tracts of land for reservations and there was less conflict. Not so with the Apache and the Comanche, who were great horse-riders and fearless warriors. These tribes fiercely resisted the Army in the Arizona and New Mexico territories, and took decades to suppress. Their most famous leader was Geronimo, who fought bravely until his capture in 1886.

Geronimo (1829-1909) was not a chief, but a military leader. Geronimo had fought against the Mexican army going back to 1851, when they slaughtered his wife and children in their camp in Chihuahua. This experience gave Geronimo a special hatred for Mexicans, greater than any he felt for Americans. From 1850 to 1886, Geronimo and chiefs of the Chiricahua Apache lived lives of continuous raiding in Mexico and in the American Southwest, raids made either for plunder and prisoners (who were usually tortured), or in revenge for raids on the tribes. The Apache were confined to reservations but "broke out" three times, in 1878, 1881, and 1885, each time going back to raiding, plundering, and warfare. The Apaches established their base in the Sierra Madre Occidental Mountains in northwestern Mexico, and conducted raids inside Mexico and across the border in the Arizona and New Mexico territories. The Apache usually killed everyone they met in these raids, to keep the army off their trail until they were safe. In 1883 Mexico allowed the US Army to attack and capture the

Apache in their hideout, using the help of Apache Scouts trained in Fort Apache. However, Geronimo's third breakout in 1885 was still ahead.

Geronimo in 1892

On September 4, 1886, General Nelson Miles forced Geronimo's final surrender in Skeleton Canyon, in the southeastern corner of Arizona. General Miles treated Geronimo as a prisoner of war, which made him immune to murder charges the territory had ready for him. Geronimo and many of the Chiricahua Apache wound up at Fort Sill, Oklahoma in 1894, where he was given a plot of land to take up farming. In 1898 Geronimo participated in the Trans-Mississippi International Exposition in Omaha, Nebraska, and was a sensation with the crowd. After several more expositions, Geronimo rode in President Roosevelt's 1905 inaugural parade, and brought the people along the parade route to their feet. He asked Roosevelt to return to Arizona but the president refused, citing the enduring hatred for his deadly raids twenty years earlier. Geronimo died at age 80 in Fort Sill, still a prisoner of war.

The last serious incident with the Sioux, and a great tragedy, occurred in 1890. Sioux men on the Lakota Pine Ridge reservation had come to perform a style of dance that was frightened agents from the BIA. This "ghost dancing" was religious in nature and not overtly threatening, but the numbers of men involved forced them to call in the Army. Tensions rose to boiling, and many Sioux escaped to a spot in South Dakota called Wounded Knee. On December 29, the Seventh Cavalry surrounded them and demanded their weapons. According to one account, a tribesman refused to give up his valuable rifle and a shot rang out. The Cavalry quickly attacked, firing indiscriminately and killing 146 men, women and children, though other estimates are as high as 300. Thirty-five cavalrymen were also killed.

WHY THE INDIANS LOST

Historians point to two main reasons American Indians were at disadvantage in the war of conquest by the white man. Most obvious is they were seldom unified; most Indian tribes made war on each other, and they looked on both other tribes and the new white settlers as outsiders. They were almost incapable of large scale, organized resistance. Second, Indian men with a few exceptions insisted on the life of wandering, and had poorly defined boundaries to mark their territories. They had a different concept of ownership; the land provided food and game, but no one could truly claim it. They would not settle down for the life of farming the soil, as that was "woman's work." These all made their territory rights looked unreasonable to the pioneer or soldier, who didn't believe the

Indian had a serious claim to the land.

The buffalo, properly called the American Bison, was also a catalyst in the Indian Wars. The buffalo's decline meant the American Indians' decline. Until the late 1800s the plains Indians relied on buffalo for meat and hides; sometimes they killed buffalo in large numbers, but the herd population kept steady. Before the white man, there were probably 50 million buffalo across North America. But white hunters killed buffalo mercilessly, often just for their horns and little else from the carcass, also to deny them to the Indians, or clear the land for ranchers. The number of buffalo plummeted; by 1900 there was only 1,000 head of buffalo left in the United States. Losing the buffalo enraged the Indians of the plain states, and made them fight harder. But with the buffalo gone, the Indians had little choice but to make peace and live on the reservations.[54]

Without a doubt, the average frontier American's attitude was mostly contempt for the American Indian. Going back a hundred years, stories of the Indians' barbaric habits were common knowledge: how children from many tribes learned cruelty at a young age, the Indians' hideous tortures of warriors from other tribes and of white men, the massacres of families and entire villages on the frontier. Americans were not inclined to worry about fair treatment by the government. Soldiers attacking the Indians usually did so in the spirit of revenge, sinking to the same barbaric type of warfare, much as happened with a few American soldiers during the Vietnam War.

Still, too often the federal and state governments found it convenient to bend or break treaties made with the Indian tribes. Years of disease, relocation, and warfare had reduced the American Indians' numbers from about 600,000 in 1800 to less than 100,000. In 1881, Helen Hunt Jackson of Massachusetts wrote *A Century of Dishonor* to document the broken treaties and injustices brought on American Indians by the white man. Her book was influential in changing public opinion and alleviating their lives on the reservations. In 1887 Congress passed the Dawes Act, which gave an individual Indian 160 acres of land with 25 years of federal supervision before title was free and clear. The Dawes Act was manipulated by land speculators, but it was also a path to assimilation and independent living for thousands of American Indians, with its greatest successes in what became the state of Oklahoma. For the Indian who was willing to farm and settle in one place, much as the Cherokee and others had done early in the century, there was hope.

The government pressed for further assimilation with compulsory education for Indians in 1891. Visit a typical western town now, such as Phoenix, and you will see signs and roads named for the location of the territory's Indian School. Finally, in 1924, all American Indians were granted full citizenship regardless of where they lived. American Indian warriors went on to fight bravely with the white man in World War II.

THE MORMONS

Brigham Young first led the Mormons, also called the Church of Latter Day Saints, into Utah in 1847, as was described in Chapter Three. The Mormon colony was productive and energetic, and before long they turned Salt Lake City into one of the leading population centers in the West, and one of the first planned cities. They irrigated more extensively than anywhere else in the desert, and the valley surrounding the city blossomed with fruit and grain. In 1869 the Union Pacific Railroad reached the city and brought in more settlers. The size and wealth of the area attracted Gentiles (non-Mormon Christians) to settle, though the Mormons were clearly in charge. They organized the Zion's Cooperative Mercantile Association to satisfy their business needs, and none of the Gentile businesses could seriously compete with it. Salt Lake City grew to 13,000 people in 1870, and by 1890 Utah's population had soared to 210,000.

However, many of the same problems that forced the Mormons out of Illinois caused more trouble in the 1880s. Few Mormons actually practiced polygamy, but its existence and endorsement by the Mormon Church was intolerable to other Westerners. Congress passed the Edmunds Act to end bigamy and polygamy in 1882, and it was followed by the Edmunds-

Tucker Act in 1887, which included long jail terms for offenders. The Mormon Church still resisted, so the territorial governor seized Church property, ending the Mormons' tight control over the area. The Church soon outlawed polygamy and got its property back, but not all its original power. Eventually the Mormons aligned themselves with the two-party system and became better integrated with American society. Their predominance in Utah continues to this day.

CHAPTER EIGHT—1870 TO 1884: RAILROADS, PANIC, POLITICS, AND INVENTORS

It is hard to overstate the Civil War's impact on American industry and the economy in the late nineteenth century. It was a massive war that made unprecedented demands for weapons, iron, heavy machinery, food, clothing and provisions, and a transportation system to provide them. Of course America already used and shipped these things, but after the war, the manufacturing base and the infrastructure to provide them— factories, iron foundries, steel mills, oil drilling, packaging, textiles, bridges and railroads—had expanded tremendously, and was growing faster than in any European nation.

THE RAILROADS GO TRANSCONTINENTAL

The war's impact was obvious first in the nation's railroads. From the beginning, American trains were larger and used a wider track than trains in Europe. It's easy to see the railroads' growth by the miles of tracks in place. In 1870, there were 52,000 miles of railroad track, in 1880 there were 93,000 miles, and in 1890, 163,000 miles, a three-fold increase over just twenty years. As the railroads expanded the trains got stronger, bigger, faster and more comfortable.[55]

The railroad companies proliferated and competed heavily with each other. Government saw the need for railroads to supply the new territories and the growing cities of the East, and in their haste Washington and the states went overboard in subsidizing railroad operations. During the Civil War President Lincoln loaned $65 million to assist the first transcontinental railroad. This dream became a reality on May 10, 1869 when the Union Pacific Railroad, building west, and the Central Pacific Railroad, which was building east, met and joined tracks at Promontory Summit, Utah. Union Pacific and Central Pacific laid 1,086 and 689 miles of track, respectively. The eastern company relied on Irish and second-generation immigrants, while the Central Pacific hired thousands of "coolies," Chinese contract laborers.

The Union Pacific and Central Pacific Railroads meet in Utah, May 10, 1869

Soon after, the Southern Pacific Railroad in California connected to tracks from the East at points on the Colorado River in Arizona. The Denver and Rio Grande Railroad built tracks through the Rockies over precarious mountain gaps, and then connected with the Central Pacific in Ogden. Within years these and other transcontinental routes turned the trip west into routine travel. Just as important, they brought farm produce to all parts of the nation, and drove the demand for new steel tracks, which were more durable than iron.

Railroad companies that took federal land and money were, in general, the least efficient builders, since government policies had the perverse effect of encouraging wasteful spending. The Union Pacific and Central Pacific wasted money by taking routes through the mountains since they were paid more to build there—$48,000 per mile, versus $16,000 per mile in the plains and $32,000 in the foothills. They went on detours to find silver and gold through the Black Hills of Dakota, irritating the Sioux tribes in the process. Once they even refused to connect lines according to the original plans, forcing Congress to step in. In all, the government provided railroads with land worth $500 million ($10.9 billion in 2015). Frustrated with this wasteful spending, in 1874 Congress passed the Thurman Law requiring they repay 25 percent of their earnings to close a $28 million debt.

There were other railroad entrepreneurs who refused government subsidies; and in fact, up until the Civil War all railroads were privately financed, and better managed. Cornelius Vanderbilt's private New York Central had no accidents, while 26 people died travelling Jay Gould's federally supported Erie Railroad. Among the post-war financiers and railroad men was James J. Hill, who built the Great Northern Railroad connecting to Seattle in 1893. Hill was opposed to accepting federal money, and said "the government should not furnish capital to [those] companies, in addition to their enormous land subsidies, to enable them to conduct their business in competition with enterprises that have received no aid from the public treasury."[56] Hill's railroad actually paid $10 to each new settler along his route, and imported 7,000 cattle from England for their farms. He successfully competed with Henry Villard of the Northern Pacific, who received 42 million acres from the government and wasted fortunes building on scenic routes. Hill's more direct routes saved on the costs of construction and on the rates he charged.

Two technical advances also helped the railroads to grow. First was the industry's settling on a standard gauge (width) between the rails, 4 feet and 8 ½ inches between them. Second was George Westinghouse's air brake, which he developed in the late 1860s and perfected with hydraulic power for automatic braking in 1872. Westinghouse thus became one of the first names in a long string of inventor-millionaires whose companies lasted long into the twentieth century.

Transcontinental railroads were also responsible for America's modern time zones. To solve the problem of coordinating train schedules across a 3,000-mile distance, railroad companies acted on their own, drawing the lines between that split America into the four time zones, Eastern, Central, Mountain, and Pacific Time. The transition took place on a single day, November 18, 1883, which became known as the "Day of Two Noons" when cities and stations west of Eastern Time had to set their clocks back.

Through the 1880s the federal government loaned a total of $350 million to railroad companies. Lands granted the railroads included portions of Iowa, Wisconsin, Minnesota, Kansas, North Dakota, Montana, Washington, California, Nevada, and Louisiana. The states also contributed lands for shorter lines and to serve smaller cities. The railroads attracted money from investors in the United States and from Britain and Germany, each of those nations loaning billions of dollars.

You could say the railroads were midwives to industrial America. As historian Paul Johnson puts it: "The transformation of the United States, within five decades, from a primary producer to the world's first industrial superstate was symbolized by the construction of a colossal continental railroad system. The railroad was right at the center of America's industrial revolution. It was more than that: it was the physical means whereby Americans mastered a giant continent and began to exploit it with their customary single-minded thoroughness."[57]

But the big railroads were not the financial successes we might imagine, especially not in their first 30 years of operation. Competition between them got cutthroat, and after the Panic of 1873 many railroads failed for lack of capital. A railroad would charge high rates to a city where they were the sole operator, making up for losses on other lines. Train companies wrangled special deals with cities currently served by another, hoping to undercut their margin. Many historians now believe the "Railroad Baron" was largely a myth, since very few owners made or kept a fortune running the early companies.

Several states, angry at how the chaos in the industry affected its citizens, took the railroads to court and appealed to the US Supreme Court for intervention. For years the government had stayed out of the business and the Supreme Court went back and forth with contradictory decisions. This changed in 1886 when a committee run by Senator Shelby Cullom of Illinois concluded after months of research the railroad industry was three-quarters interstate in nature and was thus eligible for federal regulation.[58]

Even without the burden of government controls, many railroads still went bankrupt during the 1870s. Inefficient and money-losing railroad lines were snapped up by bigger ones with the resources to improve operations and reduce freight charges. In time, train loads and volumes got bigger and labor productivity improved, but not before their rampant growth and widespread financial speculation took its toll on the nation as a whole.

THE PANIC OF 1873

America's first major depression began in 1873, and lasted about five years. Like the Great Depression of the 1930s, it began with a financial crisis in the banks and stock exchanges on Wall Street, the nerve center of the nation. On Thursday, September 18, the banking firm of Jay Cooke and Company closed due to insolvency. Jay Cooke was widely known as a solid and reliable pillar of the banking establishment, and not known for making risky investments. But Cooke had advanced too much money to the Northern Pacific and failed to get financial backing from his regular partners. The partners, including banks in Europe, were already having trouble sorting out bad debt and bonds after the Franco-Prussian War. The banks of Vienna already suffered their own panic in May, 1873.

American stock markets were sliding even before September. Being heavily dependent on burgeoning railroad stocks, Wall Street panicked with the news about Cooke. Financial markets were closed for ten days. Banks started collapsing in a ricochet effect from the panic. Bank loans came to a complete stop. Thousands of factories and other businesses closed, and hundreds of thousands were put out of work. And needless to say, railroad construction, which consumed $1.5 billion in funds every year, was halted.

The Panic of 1873 had a different underlying cause than the Great Depression; and unlike that depression it was not prolonged by government policy. Washington responded by accumulating more gold, thus bolstering the dollar. By 1879 America's banks had stabilized, and the depression ended. While the depression lasted, there was a net outflow of gold from America which caused another round in the national debate over hard money (relying on gold reserves to back up paper currency) and soft money. This debate helped to drive the farmer's revolt, also known as the Grange Movement, which we will discuss below.

EDWARD HARRIMAN AND THE ABSOLUTE VALUE FALLACY

But first, let's discuss one of the first industrial leaders to emerge during this period. Edward Harriman (1848-1909), like many business leaders of the time, started near the bottom, working as an errand boy on Wall Street at age 14. At age 22 he was a member of the New York Stock Exchange.[59] After accumulating some money and plenty of insight, he began investing in what he knew. He owned and sold several small railroads, and made his first fortune selling a small line to the Pennsylvania Railroad. He later became director of the Illinois Central, and in 1895 he bought the Union Pacific. Harriman is remembered as a shrewd operator, but while he "played for keeps," he stayed honest and did not employ the intimidation techniques of the past.

Best for him and for Americans, Harriman knew how to recognize hidden value in a railroad company. He understood the Absolute Value Fallacy, which denies that every business transaction is a zero-sum game, with a winner and a loser.

Harriman could identify the hidden potential of a strong business and develop its full worth. Union Pacific was in bad shape when Harriman bought it. He invested $175 million improving the system and in new equipment, and within a few years the Union Pacific was the best managed and most valuable railroad in America. He said, "A property is only worth what someone is willing to pay for it," and that conviction has been the guideline for growth and prosperity ever since.[60]

THE GRANGE MOVEMENT, THE ICC, AND THE BIRTH OF FREE SILVER

America's farmers as a whole were most injured by the railroads' pricing policies. With just one railroad serving a typical Midwest farming town and communities further west, farmers were at the mercy of whatever charge the railroads set if they wanted to move produce. Predatory pricing often consumed most of the profit the farmers earned; and with American farm produce exported overseas and prices subject to international commodity pressures, even those profits were out of the farmers' control. From the farmers' perspective, the final straw must have been seeing the railroads give rebates to other communities, to compete with other railroads. By the early 1870s the average farmer was enraged at the railroads' abuse of power, and the favors given to them by the federal government.

To oppose the railroads, farmers nationwide organized the Patrons of Husbandry, soon to become known as the Grange Movement.[61] As we have seen, the states enacted their own laws largely to protect the farmers, and took the railroads to court. State battles against the railroads began in Illinois, where the assembly voted to set caps on freight charges per mile, to eliminate special charges for short hauls, and to regulate the railroads via a state commission. On July 4, 1873 Granges across America celebrated the birth of their movement with a "Farmers' Declaration of Independence." Regulatory laws similar to Illinois' were soon enacted in Wisconsin, Minnesota, and Iowa.

American farmers had another dilemma: many were in debt

while America was experiencing monetary deflation. That is, federal policy to strengthen the US dollar had the effect of increasing the expense of existing debt. To understand this, assume you buy a car when inflation starts going up, and you are lucky and get a 3 percent interest rate on your car loan. As inflation rises, maybe up to 10 percent, your loan payment stays the same but you are probably earning more to pay it, and payments seem like less of a burden. People in debt usually benefit from inflation. With deflation, the opposite happens. You need to earn more just to keep even with your payments and they become a larger part of your budget. And so it was with farmers in the decades after the Civil War. With deflation, they had to grow more food in order to keep up with their loan payments.

Naturally, this became a political issue. The Democrats saw an opportunity and displayed more sympathy to the farmers than the Republicans. But neither party would take a strong stand against the banks and other creditors. Undermining the creditor-debtor relationship has always been a dangerous step most politicians are unwilling to take. And like today, politicians get support from major banks and will not act against their interests.

There was no easy solution to the farmers' economic plight. But there were political consequences. The Democrats' rhetoric sided with the farmers, so the party became identified with their cause. This new dynamic, perhaps the first substantial issue separating the parties since the war, was to have long-lasting consequences. From a larger perspective, sectional differences such as North vs South were taking a back seat to the politics of industrial expansion, national growth, and prosperity. Neither party was fully prepared for this transformation. And neither party provided leaders who truly understood how to steer the nation through the era of industrialization, mass markets, and dominance by the big, new cities.

Let's return to the Grange Movement, and how it allied itself to Free Silver. Greenbacker politicians favored inflation by increasing the paper money supply to offset the strong dollar based on gold. Republican presidents including Grant and Rutherford Hayes successfully fought them off, so the Greenbackers' next strategy was to include silver coins as currency and reduce the dominance of gold. This gave rise to the Free Silver movement, which advocated almost unlimited silver coinage, and troubled both Republican and Democratic administrations through the turn of the century.

Money in America was exchanged in both gold and silver coins, called specie, as well as paper bills (greenbacks, starting in the Civil War), and notes issued by banks. As the economy grew, the average person tended to use more paper money, as we do now. Greenbacks could be exchanged at a bank for their face value in gold or silver, and bank notes were mostly exchanged between private banks. In 1873, the US Treasury eliminated the silver coin and would not bring it back, because with western silver mines increasing the supply, the value of silver was falling. But the Grange farmers wanted silver coins back to inflate the dollar by displacing the gold coin. Silver miners from Nevada, Colorado and other parts had obvious reasons to bring silver back in currency, so they joined the farmers and pressed the government for new silver coins.

And they made temporary gains. The Bland-Allison Act of 1878 required Treasury to purchase $2 to $4 million in silver, every month. Silver coins were to be exchanged for gold at a ratio of 16 to 1, but with silver falling in value, silver true worth relative to gold was more like 30 to 1. This would have guaranteed inflation. However, with a maximum of only $48 million in new silver in circulation each year, this was nowhere near enough to cause serious inflation, and gold still supported the dollar. Silver had no chance of being widely circulated. Bland-Allison was only a step in the direction of Free Silver. The Free Silverites became closely associated with the Populist movement in their next push for inflation during the 1890s.

One reason the Republicans stayed on this course was to exploit America's advantages in international trade for as long as possible. For many years, extending into the 1900s, American businesses had the advantage of products that beat the competition abroad, and tariffs protecting them from competition at home. High American productivity overcame much of the competition for farm products and hard goods in

Europe. And in a giant republic with railroads supplying every corner, American business had tremendous free trade inside as well, allowing for a truly national market for all products. And we could still get away with levying tariffs on imported products in order to protect American manufacturers. We had the best of both worlds – economically, we had our cake, and we could eat it too.

The strong US dollar was good for creditors and for strong businesses. The Grange Movement would never fully succeed under these circumstances. The greatest victory for the farmers was establishment of the Interstate Commerce Commission in 1887. This was a case of too little too late, for by this time the railroads were consolidating and learning to "rationalize" operations, i.e. to eliminate waste and improve efficiency, under the influence of men like Edward Harriman. The ICC was established by a Supreme Court decision to standardize rulings enacted by the states into a single code, so it did push the railroads toward fairer treatment and the government brought lawsuit as necessary. However, the ICC Act lacked enforcement provisions, and the railroads, now stronger and better managed, usually won their case when they were taken to court.

RUTHERFORD B. HAYES AND THE ELECTION OF 1876

In 1876, President Grant's scandals toward the end of his second term weakened the Republican Party. (Grant wanted a third term, but Party leaders talked him out of it). The Panic of 1873 had put the nation in severe distress, drying up capital and prosperity for years. In 1874, the Democrats won control of the House of Representatives for the first time since the pre-war years. By 1876, political combat between Radical and Reconstruction Republicans and the resurgent Democrats in the South had created a poisonous environment for the next election.

The Democrats nominated Samuel J. Tilden, governor of New York, and widely admired in the party. The Republicans nominated Governor Rutherford B. Hayes of Ohio, a Union officer who was wounded several times, and seriously in the Battle of South Mountain. Tilden won the popular vote, a point which was seldom in dispute. But as we know, the Electoral College decides who will become president, and presidential campaigns are organized to win electoral votes. It is rare, however, but a loser in the popular vote can still win in the Electoral College.

When the election returns came to Washington, 20 electoral votes from Louisiana, South Carolina, and Florida immediately were disputed, and these 20 votes would determine the winner. Rival vote canvassing boards from these states each announced for their party's nominee.[62] Both sides had committed fraud and tried to intimidate voters. As stated in the Constitution, it was now the responsibility of Congress to resolve the dispute, so Congress created a commission to handle the job.

The commission was politically balanced; however, it was soon shown they had struck a compromise to give the election to Hayes. Underlying the Compromise of 1877 was the concession to Southern states that the federal government would withdraw the troops and stay out of the states' internal affairs, especially regarding their treatment of former slaves. As it was, troops had withdrawn from most Southern states, and in South Carolina and Louisiana, rival governments controlled everything but the statehouses where Republican governments were protected by troops. The Republicans won the presidency, and the Democrats won Jim Crow law for the South. The struggles of the Civil War were to continue for decades.

In spite of the election dispute, President Hayes (1822-1893) was an effective leader. He confided to friends that he intended to act according to principle, not party, and rise above the means by which he won office. Hayes made the first attempt to establish a Civil Service Commission and tame the spoils system, and bring hiring and promotion by merit to federal service. He held to the strong dollar policy, in the face of fierce opposition by the Democrats, and he was vindicated in 1879 when the dollar reached a new peak in purchasing power, backed by $100 million in gold reserves held by the US Treasury. Businesses, employment, and trade recovered under

Hayes' leadership. For years after, the $100 million level was the Treasury's standard for financial stability. But the scandal of 1876 helped the Democrats take back control of both the House and the Senate in the election of 1878, and Hayes declared he would not run for a second term in 1880.

GARFIELD, ARTHUR, AND THE PENDLETON ACT

The next Republican president was James A. Garfield (1831-1881), a Senator from Ohio and another Civil War veteran. In the 1880 election, the Republicans regained control of Congress and Garfield won fairly but by a very narrow majority in the popular vote (less than one percent). Americans had great hopes for Garfield, and by all appearances he was an excellent choice, probably the finest man elected since Abraham Lincoln. Like Rutherford Hayes, President Garfield made civil service reform one of his priorities, motivated in part by the time-consuming problem of interviewing federal office seekers. And on July 2, four months after taking office, Garfield was shot in the city of Washington by Charles Guiteau, a disgruntled office seeker, perhaps a man he had just refused. Garfield lingered for over two months before dying of his wounds on September 19.[63]

Chester A. Arthur

His successor was Vice President Chester A. Arthur (1829-1886). Arthur was a compromise running mate if you ever saw one, a former director of the New York Port Authority fired for mismanagement by President Hayes, but pushed onto Garfield's ticket by New York Republican political bosses to get their support. A one-time abolitionist lawyer, Arthur campaigned for Abraham Lincoln, and during the War he was quartermaster general for New York, where he learned the art of political patronage.

President Arthur surprised his critics by picking up Garfield's commitment to civil service reform, apparently a convert to the cause after Garfield's death. He gained bipartisan support for a new law, the Pendleton Act, named for co-sponsor Senator George Pendleton. The law required that new federal employees pass a standardized test of their practical skills. The Pendleton Act was cleverly designed; at the outset it only applied to the lowest offices in the civil service. But it allowed future presidents to upgrade, and not downgrade, the list of offices requiring the test. This way, a president might protect his appointees once they were in office, but future officeholders needed to pass the test. On the passage of the Pendleton Act, just 14,000 out of 120,000 federal positions were subject to the Civil Service test, and that number steadily climbed to encompass all but the highest offices.[64]

President Arthur should also be remembered for modernizing the US Navy. Most warships of the time were still wooden-hulled, and aging. Arthur pushed Congress to pay for larger, steel-hulled ships easily capable of an ocean voyage. When in 1883 the Supreme Court invalidated parts of the 1875 Civil Rights Act, Arthur appealed for new laws to protect black Americans from discrimination.

TELEGRAPHS, TELEPHONES AND CAMERAS

America is still a young country. We did not invent the art of invention, or to say it better, the work of developing applications based on scientific discovery. In the nineteenth century we still lagged behind Europe in most fields of basic research, so our inventions were largely based on discoveries made by others. For example, Michael Faraday and James Watt were two British pioneers whose work in electricity and engines helped trigger an explosion of American innovation in the mid-nineteenth century. Building on basic science to produce machines and technology that improved the life of the common man was where American inventors really shone— and where fortunes were made.

The growing nation needed a reliable communications system. Thanks to Benjamin Franklin, the United States Post Office had been in existence since the founding of the republic. In 1885 it settled on a 2-cent stamp for first-class mail, a rate that did not increase until 1917. But the future lay in telecommunications.

Telegraphs were in operation long before the Civil War, and they proved invaluable for wartime communications. Thanks to Samuel Morse, inventor of the Morse Code in the 1830s, 32,000 miles of telegraph line went up across America even before the war. Banking, railroads, and other industries now demanded a widespread telegraph network, and the public was accustomed to the telegraph to communicate with family living far away. Telegraph service improved with new devices to amplify signals over distance and with ticker-tape to automatically record messages. The first trans-Atlantic telegraph cable was laid on the ocean floor in 1866. By the 1880s, the Western Union Company was conducting most American telegraph business. Americans were becoming dependent on electronic communications for their most urgent business, and the telegraph met this need, with a message only delayed by the time needed to relay it inside a telegraph office or carry it to its final destination.

Into this environment came the telephone, an even greater leap in communications than the telegraph. In 1876, Alexander Graham Bell (1847-1922) developed the telephone after a series of experiments originally begun to help deaf people hear vibrations. Bell was not the first to study voice transmission over wire; in fact, he successfully fought off hundreds of legal challenges to his patent, but with refinements he succeeded in turning his primitive telephone into a practical device for every day, two-way communication. He formed Bell Telephone Company in 1877, and in 1878 he demonstrated his telephone at the Paris Exposition. Bell retired wealthy and went on to other new inventions, such as a hydrofoil that set the world marine speed record in 1915. Within twenty years his company brought the telephone to almost every American town and city. It was not long before the telephone replaced the telegraph as the primary mode of communication. Telephone switchboards, operated by women, and telephone lines put up by linemen, provided new occupations and employed tens of thousands across the nation. The telephone was the first of several industrial revolutions transforming American life over the next fifty years.

Until George Eastman developed the Kodak camera in 1888, photography was a slow and difficult process. George Eastman lived in Rochester, New York, and grew impatient with having to develop photographs using heavy glass plates coated with three different solutions. His first innovation was a "dry plate" process which allowed the plates to be stored. Next, with the help of other inventors he substituted paper for glass, then celluloid for paper. His crowning achievement was the Kodak, which was small and simple to use. The camera held 100 exposures, sold for $25 ($665 in 2015), and the owner shipped it to Eastman's Rochester factory for developing. It was then returned with the prints, and loaded with new film. In 1900, Eastman developed the Brownie, a $1 camera which the user could load with his own film. The basic system for everyman's photography was established for the next 100 years, when digital prints replaced celluloid film.[65]

THOMAS EDISON, THE LIGHT BULB, AND ELECTRICITY

The pre-eminent inventor of all time must be Thomas Alva Edison (1847-1931). Born in Milan, Ohio, Edison showed an independent streak early on. He left high school after three months, where his teachers considered him dull and unruly. He sold newspapers on the railroads to make a living. At 15,

Edison learned telegraphy and worked as an operator, but he got fired for spending too much time on experiments. Inspired by Faraday's work on batteries and applying a mechanical genius, he went to work for Western Union, inventing scores of devices to improve telegraph operations.

Edison went to work for himself in 1877 and established what must be the world's first research and development center in Menlo Park, New Jersey. He bought the property with $40,000 awarded to him by Western Union for the rights to the quadruplex telegraph, a device which allowed four telegraph signals to transmit simultaneously on a single wire. Edison's research complex grew to cover two city blocks, employing over a hundred scientists and engineers. He worked long hours and often slept in his laboratory and demanded the same of his assistants. His first major achievement was the phonograph, so primitive that we wouldn't recognize it as such, but it could record and play back sound. In 1879 came his greatest breakthrough, the incandescent light bulb. It was developed by a relentless, repetitive series of tests to determine which material filament would glow with an electric current, but without degrading into ash. Edison had the most success with a carbonized filament of bamboo, however his design continued to be refined and improved over the years.[66]

Once word got out about Edison's accomplishment, Americans anticipated the same nationwide advances they were seeing with the telephone. The hunger for light was universal. Edison cannot claim to have invented the first electric light; first came the large arc-light, where a direct current was run across a gap between two electrodes, creating a bright, glaring arc of light. It was very strong and somewhat dangerous, so it was only used outdoors, set on top of towers in city centers. Arc-lights went up in many American cities, but with mixed results; most people complained about the pale light that seemed to permeate everywhere, but was still not bright enough to do anything better than illuminate the streets and sidewalks.

By contrast, Edison's light bulb was perfect for indoors, where people really needed light. They were inexpensive and required a lower electric current than competing bulb designs.

His bulbs were a sensation, rocketing him to fame and fortune. Edison's investors, whom he despised as mere money-men, helped him develop manufacturing facilities and to publicize the light bulb for use in America and abroad. Next, Edison helped pioneer electric dynamos to generate the large amounts of current necessary for city and industrial use. At the Chicago World's Fair of 1893, special exhibits and large illuminated towers showed the light bulb off for all the world to see. Edison had triumphed.

Thomas Edison in his Lab

His next challenge was to power the light. After pursuing a dead end with direct current, which he favored because of its low power requirement and its safety, and facing competition from Westinghouse Electric, Edison realized that alternating electric current was the best power source. His empire expanded with Edison Electric Light Company to include electric generating plants, powered most often by coal, situated in every city with lines connecting the plant to the consumers. Central power generating stations proliferated across America, from just eight stations in 1881 to 2,774 stations in 1898. Edison said, "We will make electricity so cheap that only the rich will burn candles." Over the first twenty years of electrical usage, power lines could be seen everywhere in the cities, and often they were so poorly hung that they were a hazard. A few people died when coming in contact with the power lines, or in the streets when they fell down. It took a new wave of regulation by municipalities to bring this situation under control.

The transition to electric light was even more remarkable than the telephone. Even today, when we await the next iteration of the cell phone or the computer every two years, the pace of change people adjusted to in the late 1800s would be astonishing. After decades of gas street lamps and dimly lit homes, many American homes and offices went electric in just ten years. Street lights in every city, light bulbs in almost every room, theaters and factories illuminated for longer hours—the lighting revolution generated its own momentum.

And once electricity was supplied to the average American home, a horde of electric appliances followed. Electric compressors for refrigerators, electric sewing machines, electric washing machines, and more, became standard items in homes over the coming years.

Edison and other engineers, many working with him and others competing against him, changed American life for the better. Edison later invented the movie camera and the motion picture (though these products failed against competitors' devices) and he registered a record total of 1,093 patents. Of course, new industries did not succeed without the leadership of famous moneymen like J.P. Morgan and the Vanderbilt family who financed the new ventures. Because of their impact on ordinary Americans, the inventors, industrialists, and financiers were the most important leaders of the late nineteenth century, and often the most admired.

CHAPTER NINE—1884 TO 1896: AMERICA GETS INDUSTRIALIZED

We pause here for a word from your American flag. We added seven more stars to the flag, and seven new states to the Union from 1889 to 1896. The 51st Congress (1889 - 1891) wanted to increase the Republican majority so the Dakota Territory was split in two and joined as North Dakota and South Dakota on November 2, 1889. Montana and Washington joined later that month, and Wyoming and Idaho in 1890. The heavily Mormon Utah Territory entered the Union in 1896. This brought the total number of states to 45; the Oklahoma Territory, once exclusively set aside for American Indians, was the next state, and did not join until 1907.[67]

It must be obvious that Bell, Edison, and other inventors were the catalysts for a revolution that overtook America in the last decades of the nineteenth century. In the space of just 50 or 60 years, the United States went from a farming nation to the largest economy on Earth, with booming, heavy industries in every city, the widest transportation system ever built, and industrial exports that dominated the markets they entered. From a set of 13 coastal colonies in 1776 with only four million people, America in 1900 became a world leader where millions thronged to live and work, and a power to be reckoned with in every sphere of activity. From industrial production, to naval power, to invention and innovation, to literature and other arts, America was second to no other nation, and on the path to eventual superiority.

The complete story of these America achievements is too

broad to describe in this book. I hope to at least outline the depth and scope of these changes and give the Average Joe a fuller understanding of the roots of the world we live in now. First we will talk more about the continuing industrial revolution and the important role of steel, then the new wave of immigrants who came to work the fields and the factories. We will briefly examine the new cities that flourished in this era and the quality of urban life. We will take a long look at the American labor movement, the only movement to work successfully in a capitalist economy, after some terrible growing pains. Then it will be time to sort out the role of government and politics during this period. Finally, we will dive into the complex subject of American corporations, oil companies and other trusts, and holding companies, under the leadership of men like John D. Rockefeller and J.P. Morgan.

BIG FARMING, BIG MANUFACTURING, AND BIG STEEL

It's worth repeating – the Civil War transformed American industry with a sudden, huge demand for manufacturing capacity, consumer goods, and a transportation system to bring products where they were needed. It killed off much what was left of local manufacturing; almost everything now was produced for a regional or national market. With the new, large scale of production, more money and financing was necessary, and the corporation was the preferred means of organizing a new or growing company.

Big new corporations were not just running factories in the cities; they spread into the countryside and began consolidating small farms into large farms. They were a double-edged sword however, for while they provided employment for hundreds of thousands of new workers, the average worker gave up much of his independence. If a factory or a farm ran into trouble and had to lay off or close down, the worker was on his own. This was serious trouble in western mining towns, where after a mine was fully spent, the workers had to move out to find new jobs.

History books often talk about the revolution in

manufacturing; it should be remembered there also was innovation on the farm that drove high productivity and created wealth in the late 1800s. Appleby's "wire binder" was developed in 1878, allowing wheat to be harvested eight times more quickly. Farm work that was only powered by horse became more efficient and less expensive when powered by a steam engine. In the 1880s, combines pulled by horses or steam tractors enabled farmers to both reap and thresh grain simultaneously. With only a brief period of time after the grain was ready for harvesting and before it was overripe, the same amount of labor could now harvest a much greater area of land.

Some of the first multi-millionaires made their money servicing, running, and buying from the new farms. The Deere brothers' name is now synonymous with the tractor. Philip Armor, who innovated meat distribution, was first to refrigerate meat from the West and ship it by train to butchers in Chicago and other cities. The Pillsbury family name came from their farms in Minnesota. German immigrant Adolphus Busch of St. Louis had an excellent plan for using the vast quantities of western grain. Another German, Frederick Weyerhauser, developed advanced methods of tree harvesting that balanced forest conservation with demands for paper and wood. In 1885, Weyerhauser was processing over 500 million feet of wood on his 300,000 acres of forest, and had to learn the science of reforestation and soil conservation, or his production would stop. International Paper is another company still in operation today, and after employing Weyerhauser's concepts they were grew four million more cords of wood than they consumed.

The South and its cotton, textile, and tobacco industries also expanded with the new technologies. Before the Civil War, there were 160 cotton mills across the South. The new governments saw the need to change with the times, and applied policies to favor agricultural output. By 1900 Southern cotton mills accounted for half the mills and production in the country. New railroads such as the Louisville and Nashville opened parts of the South that had never been connected. Coal deposits and iron ore discovered in Alabama and Tennessee and brought new capital into the region. With the invention of cigarette making machines, tobacco exploded in popularity around the world and became the predominant crop in eastern Virginia and North Carolina. Northern mills in New York and towns such as Lowell, Massachusetts also reached their peak in production.

This brings us to the big kahuna, the steel industry. The railroads demanded steel for a better railroad track. Steel alloy is more durable and stronger than iron, and new production techniques had brought the cost of steel down. Pittsburgh was the center of the steel industry after the War, since the richest deposits of iron were in the Great Lakes area, and coal for the furnaces was shipped in from nearby mines. Steel refining was a non-stop 24-hour process requiring coal for heat and water for cooling. By the 1890s Pittsburgh, Cleveland, and other steel towns employed tens of thousands of men in sweltering, often dangerous foundries, forging steel that was either shipped out by rail or sent up the Great Lakes to other cities, and down the St. Lawrence River across the Atlantic for export.

Andrew Carnegie in 1876

The steel industry replaced the railroads as the most vital industry in America. Steel grew rapidly with new demands, and with improvements in the refining process. No man was more important to nineteenth century steel than Andrew Carnegie (1835-1919). Carnegie was born in Scotland, and like other business leaders he came from a humble background. But as a businessman he recognized his industry's potential to help America grow into prosperity as a modern nation. Focusing on the chemistry, he recognized and fixed flaws in the old "Bessemer" refining process. Because he trusted in the power of markets for success, Carnegie concentrated first on costs and proper accounting, before revenue or profits. He said, "The price in the market is not your affair—you must meet the price whatever it is." He told Congress, "I was in business to make money....When rails were high, we got the highest prices we could get. When they were low, we met the lowest prices we had to meet." By raising productivity, he slashed steel prices. Consequently, he brought the price of steel rails down from $160 a ton in 1875 to $17 a ton in 1895. His steel plant in Homestead, Pennsylvania produced three times as much steel as per year as a plant in Essen, Germany, nearly four times as large.[68]

Carnegie Steel, which was a partnership and never a corporation, expanded into the production of steel beams for new skyscrapers in American cities. His steel went into the Brooklyn Bridge and into ships for the Navy. In 1900 the profits of Carnegie Steel Corporation were $40 million, of which $25 million was Carnegie's share. His business was by no means untroubled, as we will see when Homestead workers went on strike, but he left a legacy of honesty, charity, and philanthropy that remains the standard for businessmen and women to this day—which we will also see in the pages ahead. In 1901 Carnegie sold his company to J.P. Morgan's United States Steel Corporation for $250 million.

Another industry exploding in the late 1800s was oil production. Oil drilling started years earlier in western Pennsylvania, and by the 1870s oil derricks sprang up to entirely cover rolling hills in what was once farmland. Over

2,000 square miles (equivalent to 1.3 million acres) of land in Pittsburgh, West Virginia and Ohio were devoted to oil production. In fact, Pittsburgh was wealthy first from oil and petroleum, before it became a steel town. Later in the 1800s, more oil was found in the Midwest, the Northwest, and especially Texas.

Gasoline wasn't refined until late in the century. Kerosene was the most important petroleum product, going back to the early 1800s. It was used to light streetlamps in the cities and for simple lamps in homes and businesses. We can thank kerosene for helping to reduce the demand for whale oil, which had been used to light lamps, since it was much cheaper and easier. However, by 1890 kerosene was rendered obsolete by Edison's electric light bulb.

America became a big coal producing nation during these years, and again much of the coal was mined in Pennsylvania, the Virginias, and Ohio. Both coal and oil required the growing railroad network for distribution in North America. Neither oil nor coal were big export products, as Britain and Europe had mines of their own.

Led by steel and oil, big industry transformed America. In 1894 the United States became the world's largest manufacturer. Between 1859 and 1914, there was an 18-fold increase in production, across all industries. Republican Party policies of tariffs and favoring business kept the growth going with only occasional interruption. Prosperity was reaching millions more people than ever before, certainly more than in the semi-monarchical nations of Europe, where hundreds of thousands now boarded boats to come to America. After industrialization, the new immigrants constitute the second great American transformation in the late nineteenth century.

THE NEW WAVE OF IMMIGRANTS

Before the Civil War, America had absorbed a wave of Irish, British, Scandinavian and German immigrants. Anyone living in a major eastern city knows the Irish have long been dominant or powerful in big city politics. They built political machines and enhanced their power with not a small amount of corruption and graft. The reaction of many native citizens to these newcomers ranged from righteous anger to ignorant prejudice. An anti-immigrant movement had developed in the 1840s and nearly gained power as the "Know Nothing" party, before most Americans finally accepted the new immigrants. The Irish and the other groups steadily assimilated, and some of the fiercest soldiers in the Civil War were the Irish. These early immigrants came to America when it was still a risky adventure; most who didn't stay in the cities became farmers in the Midwest.

A huge new wave of immigration started soon after the Civil War and lasted until World War I (1914). The US government, the states, and even the railroads set up immigration bureaus to encourage the new immigrants, publishing pamphlets for people across the Atlantic and selling the promise of the new land in the most inviting terms. They came in large numbers—10 million immigrated between 1865 and 1890. The number arriving rose each year from 250,000 in 1865 to 460,000 in 1873. In 1870, the US Census count of foreign-born Americans was 2,314,000; in 1875 the estimate was 7,500,000, or one out of six in a nation of 45 million. In 1886, the government of France made a sensational gift to America, the Statue of Liberty, which was set on an island in New York harbor where it could be seen by ships arriving from Europe. The Statue bears an inscription from the poem "The Colossus" by poet Emma Lazarus, "Give me your tired, your poor/ Your huddled masses yearning to breathe free." The statue had more than symbolic meaning for the French. By 1894, New York City had a higher population density than Paris (the world's largest city), with 142 people per acre.

This new wave featured increasingly high numbers of immigrants from Southern and Eastern Europe who, culturally, were far removed from earlier immigrants. They came to work in the cities, in factories, plants, and mills, rather than farm the countryside. By the late 1890s immigrants from this region outnumbered the others 3 to 2. One of the largest immigrant groups was the Russian Jews, who were escaping violent pogroms that were nearly eradicating them in western Russia. From 1881 to 1914, Jewish immigration jumped from 9,000 to

76,000 per year. Other large groups in these later years included Italians, Czechs, Slovaks, and Greeks.[69]

Immigrant Neighborhood in New York, 1900

Most of the new immigrants were country folk from villages where they had lived close together, heading to the fields to work and returning at night. Their habits were fixed by centuries of tradition, and the first generation had a hard time adjusting to the pace of American life. Their welcome to America was like a splash of cold water in the face; uprooted from their old ways they now lived far away in a land with few traditions, a new language, and among people too busy to help them. Before they learned the ways of city life, many were cheated of whatever money they brought.

For protection and comfort, they gathered in their own neighborhoods, where they could remain close. Every major city had its own Italian, Jewish, Polish, and Greek quarter, usually with its own newspapers and restaurants. Like the Irish before them, they developed political machines, which led to work on lucrative city contracts. The new groups also gravitated toward the same types of work or labor. Italians took the same unskilled jobs the Irish once had, the Russians and Poles went to the steel mills and the mines. The Jews worked in city sweatshops, and in time many became merchants.[70]

In the countryside, new Scandinavians and Germans joined the earlier settlers, as well as Dutch and Czech immigrants. The plains states of the Dakotas and Minnesota still have plenty of people of Swedish and Norwegian descent. Like the city immigrants, the new farmers needed to adjust to new American farming equipment and methods, and the isolation they felt in farmhouses separated by miles from the nearest family.

The huge influx of city dwellers sparked construction of thousands of tenements to house them. Tenement life at this time was squalid by modern standards, with most apartments housing a family in just one or two rooms. The streets were congested by horse carts and streetcars, and few consumer goods were available a short distance from home.

While America can rightfully boast of being a "melting pot" of different nationalities, there was some resistance against the new, poorer class of immigrants. The Slavs and Greeks spoke strange languages and attended different churches. Even the Irish Catholics looked down on them. Senator Henry Cabot Lodge of Massachusetts advocated restrictions based on a literacy test, which he justified as preserving "…the mental and moral qualities which make what we call our race." (Imagine similar words being spoken today.) Lodge's proposed law was vetoed by President Cleveland, who argued it was misguided and would not test for true ability, only for the immigrant's opportunity. As things turned out the only restriction put into law was on Chinese immigrants, with the Exclusion Act of 1882.[71] The Chinese had long been in California, and in about 1870 sections of San Francisco were zoned as "Chinatowns" to allow them to own property.

The American spirit of growth and mobility inspired the immigrants to adapt, and to assimilate. Most of them viewed their living situations as temporary, a step toward better lives for their children if not themselves. In general, the farming immigrants did better than those who stayed in the city. In spite of the slum conditions and over-crowding, people did move on. The average time for a Jewish immigrant residing in the Lower East Side was only 15 years. Immigrant children of all nations had opportunities unheard of where they came from, going to public schools and many on to college and universities, and most joining the great middle class. By the third generation, most immigrant children had abandoned their Old World traditions, and simply considered themselves Americans.[72]

Make no mistake though, the new immigrants were highly in demand at the new factories, which is where most found work. We will discuss the labor movement they helped inspire, in a little bit. But first it's important to understand the urban transformation happening to America.

BIG NATION, AND BIGGER CITIES

The American population was growing by leaps and bounds, fueled by high birth rates and immigration. The census counted 39,818,449 in 1870, up a quarter since 1860. We passed the 50 million mark in 1880, and 63 million in 1890. The United States was now larger than any European nation except Russia. The birth rate among native-born Americans was beginning to decline during this period to only 30 per thousand each year, but the average life expectancy was climbing from 39 years in 1850 to 50 years in 1900.[73]

Due to immigration, most of the population growth was in the cities. While almost every American city multiplied in size in the years 1870—1900, the most dramatic growth was seen in Chicago and New York.

By the 1870s Chicago was the undisputed queen of the Midwest. Chicago's aggressive building and innovations had overtaken St. Louis, Missouri for the title of greatest city in the region. All the train lines came to Chicago, it was the established center of the meat-packing industry, and it had valuable access to shipping on Lake Michigan. With all the farm produce, meat and livestock passing through or arriving in Chicago, it became the national center of commodities trading.

Ironically, Chicago benefited from a fire that destroyed half the city. As the story goes, a certain Mrs. O'Leary was milking her cow the morning of October 10, 1871. The cow knocked over her kerosene lamp, setting the barn on fire, and it spread out of control. About 250 people died in the Great Chicago Fire. With half the city in ruins, builders and contractors flocked in from across the country and other countries to help rebuild it.

The Chicago Board of Trade (date unknown)

And the result was the first modern city in America. Benefiting from the low prices for steel, companies in Chicago built the first skyscraper in 1885 (ten stories tall), which required the first hydraulic elevator. As more tall buildings were erected, city streets got more congested. Chicago relieved this by building elevated rail lines through the city. Before long, gas lines, running water and electricity in Chicago set the standard for new urban construction in America. Chicago employed the latest building technology, power generation, and transportation. When in the 1880s, city managers realized that Chicago was slowly sinking into the soft soil, they started a city-wide project to jack up every building, four feet higher. They worked so efficiently that most stores and businesses stayed open, even as they were being elevated. By 1895, 3,000 elevators operated in downtown Chicago, and the city boasted fine hotels, theaters, and a concert hall featuring one of America's leading symphony orchestras. Chicago was an innovator in planning its many city parks, and became known for its top-quality furniture craftsmen and interior designers.

Chicago was America's "Second City" in 1900 with a population of 1.7 million, and stayed in that position for 100 years.

Impressive as Chicago was, New York had long been America's number one city, and that has never changed. New York was the center of finance and home of the wealthiest citizens, whether they were financiers, industrialists, or of independent means. Starting after the Revolution, Manhattan Island increasingly urbanized from the south end up to the northern heights overlooking the Bronx River. New York City's population exploded with the second large wave of immigration, from 1.8 million in 1880, to nearly 3.4 million in 1900 (including Brooklyn).

New York had everything Chicago had, and more. It was well planned on a grid of east-west streets and north-south avenues, with several diagonal, intersecting avenues. They allocated a huge space for Central Park, which was still home to cows as late as 1880, before achieving its final distinction as an elegant and peaceful environment in the midst of city hustle and bustle. New York quickly adopted Chicago's elevators for its own building boom; by the end of the century it had achieved its own distinctive skyline, which got more impressive with each passing year into the twentieth century. New York was America's center for fashion, theater, publishing, trade, and finance, and of course, little of that has changed. By 1900 New York was second only to London in international commerce. The wealthiest New Yorkers built magnificent homes, not just in the city but for their summer residences in Newport, Rhode Island, where several are now open to the public.

MASS PRODUCTION AND THE LABOR MOVEMENT

Between 1859 and 1914, American manufacturing rose 18 times, and by 1894 the United States was the world's number one manufacturer. American exports grew with these trends, while imports stayed relatively insignificant. American power and industrial production were closely linked, and both were fueled by the great wave of immigration. After 1880, with the high numbers of unskilled immigrants from southern and eastern Europe, workers were more willing to accept low wages. It's worth noting, there were relatively few immigrants from China. The Exclusion Act of 1882 prohibited further Chinese immigration, out of conviction that only Europeans could assimilate into American society.

The cities were the new power and labor centers driving America's growth. Factories located into the cities to take advantage of immigrant labor as well as Americans moving in from the countryside. The tenements housed the labor, the skies billowed smoke from the furnaces, and city life for most people became a routine of long hours and acceptable pay. As in England and Germany, mass-manufacturing and industrialization ruled how most city-dwellers lived.

These conditions were not what many immigrants expected. While most American workers had it better than their European counterparts, where old social orders condemned most to lives of eternal labor, the new industrial workers had expected more opportunity. By the 1860s they formed workers' unions to demand better pay and hours. The first large American union was the Knights of Labor, formed in 1869.

The Knights relied on individual membership, unlike the modern organization-based union. Their tactics were to agitate for company boycotts, before resorting to a strike. They did not grow to a powerful force until being led by Terence Powerly in 1878. Powerly (1849-1924) eliminated the secrecy that the Knights once used to confuse the public and employers, and forbade strong-arm membership tactics. Consequently, their membership took off, from 28,000 in 1880 to 700,000 in 1886. The Knights won important concessions from the railroads such as 8-hour days and the right to arbitration. They led a major strike against the Missouri Pacific in 1885, forcing them to restore pay cuts, and pay time and a half for overtime. But the Knights' influence was limited by their loose membership and decentralized structure; their skilled workers disliked the anarchistic elements they were seeing among the unskilled. In the 1890s the Knights began to collapse, and they disappeared after a few more years.

The next great union was much more successful. The American Federation of Labor, founded in Pittsburgh in 1881, was organized around existing unions of skilled workers, rather than the Knights' "one big union" idea. Their leader was the great Samuel Gompers (1850-1924), a brilliant organizer and communicator, who understood the need for public respect to achieve labor's goals. The AFL had two clear goals, to protect skilled labor from unfair working conditions, and to get more out of capital, i.e. to gain a larger material share in the overall enterprise. Realizing strength through the talents of their members, they avoided the intimidation techniques that tainted so many earlier unions. The AFL was the first large union to aim for respectability and success through peaceful principles of collective bargaining.

Samuel Gompers in 1894

Samuel Gompers was born in London and moved to New York as a boy. His first job was making cigars, and being a natural leader, he rose through the ranks of unions he joined.

Becoming AFL President in 1895, Gompers usually pushed union pressure as far as possible without permanently alienating corporate employers. He wanted to limit immigration to protect the current work force, and he anticipated the need to relieve workers from technological unemployment when they were replaced by machines. Gompers's greatest successes came from helping the carpenters' union and others win 8-hour days, influencing state governments to pass laws beneficial to labor, and instituting bureaus of labor statistics in nearly every state. He organized the "sympathy strike," where workers would vote to strike at their own company when workers went on strike at a related or similar employer.

America owes a debt to Gompers for defending us from the wave of socialism that was sweeping through European labor. Gompers saw more success for workers through the wage system than in trying to overthrow their employers, companies or governments. During these same years, many socialists (and some communists) tried to infiltrate and influence American labor. Gompers resisted these elements, and American workers themselves were no fans of the socialists' philosophy. With a few exceptions, American workers and the public held fast to the unions to improve their lives. Gompers' success meant AFL membership grew from 150,000 in 1886 to 500,000 in 1900, and 2 million by World War I.

STRIKES, RIOTS, AND SOCIAL CHANGE

But there were many strikes and some were violent. In the summer of 1877, late in the depression lingering from the Panic of 1873, railroads were cutting pay by 10 percent. The Great Railroad Strike of 1877 began on July 14, when workers for the Baltimore and Ohio Railroad in Martinsburg, West Virginia, suffered their third pay cut and struck, stopping movement of all trains. This led to a chain of mostly disorganized strikes in Maryland, cities in Pennsylvania, upstate New York, Illinois, and Missouri. Workers destroyed railroad locomotives, freight and passenger cars, depots, and hundreds of other buildings. Police and state militias were called in to stop the looting and restore service, but they usually refused to fire on the strikers. In Baltimore, crowds attacked National Guard regiments on their way to board trains for Cumberland. Over 100 workers died in the strike, with the worst violence in Pittsburgh on July 21 and 22, where the militia killed 40 strikers. Federal troops including US Marines put down strikes in the cities, some of which went under martial law. In San Francisco, sympathy for the Eastern strikers, unemployment, and resentment at the abundance of Chinese workers caused more labor unrest. Violence was averted when the state Workingmen's Party won concessions to protect labor through changes to the California state Constitution.

There was another wave of railroad strikes in 1886. They were precipitated when a foreman at Texas & Pacific was fired for being a Knight of Labor. Soon, 9,000 workers led by Martin Irons went on strike against all railroads run by financier Jay Gould, and trains across the entire Southwest were frozen. The public supported the strikers until the work stoppage caused shortages of food. State militia broke the strike, and the Knights of Labor suffered a serious loss.

Immediately following the Knights' railroad strike in 1886 was a massive strike for the 8-hour workday. About 340,000 men struck nationwide, and many unions scored gains with their employers. But in Chicago, anarchists were gathering with and encouraging the strikers. On May 3, the police broke up an anarchist's speech and violence erupted, with several strikers killed. On May 4, anarchists and strikers gathered again at Haymarket Square, and they threw a bomb at the police line. When the day was over, seven police and four civilians were dead and over one hundred wounded, counting both sides.

Haymarket's aftermath was just as significant. Eight of the anarchists were put on trial, six convicted, and four hanged. But Illinois Governor John Altgeld, who sympathized with the strikers, pardoned the remaining two men in prison. This act repelled many Americans and earned Altgeld the distrust of authorities and business leaders.

One of the most violent labor disputes happened at the

Homestead steel mill in May 1892. The Homestead plant was a Carnegie Steel plant in the town of Homestead close to Pittsburgh. Andrew Carnegie and the powerful Amalgamated Association of Iron and Steel Workers had agreed to a new contract in 1889, and Carnegie believed he achieved labor peace. In 1892 Carnegie was away in Europe, leaving the plant under the control of his top associate, Henry Clay Frick. In June that year, Amalgamated refused a new arrangement whereby Homestead reduced payments for "piecework," or fabricating end products from steel. Homestead justified the pay cut with the argument that new equipment that made the job go faster, and the workers more productive, and saying the worker would earn the same amount as before.

After hearing Amalgamated's final refusal, Frick locked the workers out of the plant. The workers began constant picketing around the plant, preventing access to anyone, and a committee of strike leaders succeeded in getting support from the towns-people of Homestead. Frick asked the Pinkerton Company to help, and the union saw that Frick was now determined to break them with replacement workers.[74]

The Pinkerton team advised Frick that many of the Homestead workers were being intimidated by the union. On the night of July 6, a small army of 300 Pinkerton men hired by Frick and armed with Winchester rifles came up the Monongahela River on barges to dock at the plant, planning to infiltrate and open the plant by force. But they were met by 600 strikers and townspeople, who fired down on them from the plant and the opposite riverbank. A battle raged for 12 hours, then the Pinkerton agents surrendered. On their way to the jail for protection, the Pinkertons had to walk through a gauntlet of angry strikers. Many were savagely beaten. They were finally evacuated by train to Pittsburgh. The death toll was three Pinkerton agents and seven strikers, but most of the agents came away badly injured.

Strikers occupied the plant at this point, but their triumph was short lived. Sheriff William McCleary prevailed upon Governor Robert Pattison of Pennsylvania to intervene, and Pattison called in 8,500 soldiers of the National Guard to restore order. On July 15, Homestead was back in operation with non-union workers.

Public support for the strikers was undermined by the brutal treatment of the surrendered Pinkertons, and it fell more with an assassination attempt on Frick by Russian anarchist Alexander Berkman, on July 23. In the meantime, Frick lodged criminal charges against scores of union leaders and workers. Although most of the cases ended up in acquittal, the charges kept the union leaders languishing in jail, and out of touch with members as the strikebreaking proceeded. Five months later, members of Amalgamated agreed to return to work, for the lower piece-work rates and alongside many of the replacements.

The next great railroad strike began with the Pullman Palace Car Company, which was created by George Pullman to manufacture sleeper cars for long distance train travel. In 1894, workers for the Pullman Company struck at the company headquarters near Chicago. As with the railroad strikes in 1877, the company was in financial trouble after the Panic of 1893, and it laid off workers and cut wages by 30 to 40 percent. Most Pullman employees lived in a company-owned and managed village, and the worst feature of the cuts was that the Company refused to reduce their rents and expenses to match the wage cuts. The workers went on strike, and Pullman promptly cancelled their credit at company stores. Before long, families ran out of money and many were starving.

Pullman workers were organized under the American Railway Union led by Eugene Debs, the future leader of the American Socialist Party. The ARU brought relief supplies and money for the strikers. On June 26, 1894, Debs and the ARU called on all Western railroads to boycott the company's sleeper cars by detaching them from trains in their railyards. This escalation was met with another, when workers who cooperated with the boycott were fired from their jobs. The ARU strike at length spread into a general strike against all Western railroads.

At this point, anarchists and hoodlums joined the action. Trains were looted and vandalized across America with the worst damage done in Illinois, Ohio, and California. Illinois Governor Altgeld, as we have seen, would take no action against Pullman strikers or any others. Governors in other states were helpless to control the situation, and federal action was necessary. President Cleveland sent 2,000 army regulars along with cavalry and artillery to key stations to intervene. His rationale was to prevent further delays to the US Postal Service, but his purpose was clearly to break the strike. Cleveland and most civic leaders agreed that order had to be restored.

Eugene Debs and other strike leaders were arrested on charges of conspiracy, and soon released. On July 12, they disobeyed a court order not to prolong the strike and called for total, nationwide strikes by all labor. They were arrested again, and sentenced to six months in prison.

CLEVELAND, HARRISON, CLEVELAND, AND THE PANIC OF 1893

In the late 1800s, American government and presidents took a back seat to work and business in people's lives. But that doesn't mean the politicians stayed quiet. The election campaign of 1884 was the ugliest since the Civil War. Republicans nominated James Blaine, a senator from Maine and a former secretary of state, but who was never popular with the public. The Democrats, smelling victory for the first time since 1856, nominated Grover Cleveland, one of the strongest leaders in the nation.

Cleveland had been a corruption-fighting mayor of Buffalo and then governor of New York. Many Republicans switched their allegiance to Cleveland, and were branded "mugwumps" by their former associates (certainly one of the oddest political epithets). Cleveland, who was unmarried, was accused of fathering a child out of wedlock and he refused to either confirm or deny the charge. On Election Day, Cleveland carried the South, New York, and enough of the states west of the Mississippi to win office, though he won only a narrow popular majority—30,000 out of 9.7 million votes cast.

President Grover Cleveland (1837-1908) supported civil service reform, and announced that a Republican doing his job well could keep it. He hired and promoted more on the basis of merit than his predecessors, and reduced the number of federal employees due to their bloated numbers. He also investigated western lands given to railroads by government grants, since many had not extended their lines according to written agreements. As a result, 81 million acres were returned to the government.

Grover Cleveland

Cleveland reversed an executive order by President Arthur allowing white settlement in the Dakota Territory. Just prior to Cleveland's inauguration, Arthur had opened 4 million acres of Winnebago and Crow Creek lands for new settlers, but Cleveland believed it was in violation of treaty and ordered 18 companies of troops to remove the new settlers.

President Cleveland did not faithfully follow the Democrat party line, and he disappointed his supporters most by sticking with the Republicans' "hard money" policy. Like most officials of the time, Cleveland saw government's primary role regarding business interests as setting wide boundaries and only stepping in when a boundary was breached. This was not an age where politicians indulged in economic theory, and government was not so large that its spending, taxes, or internal activities impacted national consumption in any great way, as it does now. Instead, it was the business of Grover Cleveland and the Republicans to keep government apart from the economy, to keep it healthy, and run a tight ship of state.

In one of his first crises, President Cleveland resisted the demands of Civil War veterans for additional benefits. Veterans had long been entitled to pensions for war injuries, but they wanted more compensation, and organized a march on Washington known as The Grand Army of the Potomac. Cleveland stood his ground against their demand for a "paupers" pension, recognizing that it was ripe for abuse. Cleveland did bow to his fellow Democrats and relaxed the high import tariffs from an average of 47% to 40%. The tariffs were raising $100 million in revenues every year, the government's highest source of income.

In the election of 1888, Democrats were disenchanted with Cleveland's hard-money policy, leading many to bolt the party in support of Populists. Businesses and Democrats were both angry with Cleveland's tariff policy. The Republicans used the tariff issue to generate support for their nominee in the election of 1888. Benjamin Harrison was not a political star, and he ran mostly on the strength of his service as a Civil War general, being a Senator from Indiana, and as grandson of President William Henry Harrison. Harrison defeated Cleveland with an electoral map nearly identical to 1884 but where only two states, Indiana and New York, switched from Democrat to Republican.

Once in office, President Harrison (1833 – 1901) proved less courageous on civil service reform, earning the wrath of his own Civil Service Commissioner, Theodore Roosevelt. Roosevelt believed the spoils system was the most enduring source of political corruption in America, but Harrison gave him no support for reform.[75] Harrison was in favor of civil rights for black Americans, and supported a federal elections bill that was defeated in the Senate. But he angered many in Washington by handing too much power to Secretary of State James Blaine and Speaker of the House Thomas "Czar" Reed. Reed got his name by changing rules in the House or Representatives to give himself more control over proceedings, which came to be called "Reed's Rules."[76]

In 1891, the US came close to war with the South American nation of Chile. Chile had just been through a revolution, and the US had been sympathetic to the former government. Ambassador Patrick Egan gave political asylum to officials and others in the American embassy. On October 16, when peace was restored and ships in Chilean ports granted their sailors liberty to go ashore, a crowd of Chileans attacked sailors from the USS Baltimore, killing two and injuring 18. The US Navy made preparations to attack the Chilean fleet and ports while President Harrison sent Chile an ultimatum for reparations. Chile was forced to make a formal apology and send the US $75,000 in gold.

Overall, Harrison was a lackluster president; the people disliked Blaine and Reed, and Harrison was opposed again by Grover Cleveland in the election of 1892. That autumn, Harrison's wife was dying of tuberculosis, and he stopped campaigning weeks before the election, as did Cleveland. Cleveland won office by a greater margin than in 1884.[77]

Grover Cleveland thus became the 21st and 23rd President of the United States, the only man to serve two non-consecutive terms in office. He had to deal immediately with a federal monetary crisis, as gold reserves had slipped far below the $100 million target level. Cleveland took action to restore gold reserves, but the situation still caused fears that the US was about to abandon the gold standard. Wheat prices crashed after a bad year for crops. European investors withdrew their gold, causing a general run on gold. As the economy weakened, people took their money out of banks, starting a bank run. The Panic of 1893 became a general depression. Five hundred banks closed, and 15,000 businesses went under, including several major railroads. Unemployment hit 25 percent or higher in the industrial states of Pennsylvania, New

York and Michigan.

In response, President Cleveland lobbied Congress to repeal the Sherman Silver Purchase Act of 1890, which required the government to purchase 4.5 million ounces of silver every month. Cleveland also borrowed $65 million from financier J.P. Morgan and the Rothschilds of England, giving them favorable terms on Treasury bonds. This deal was heavily criticized and caused a split within the Democratic Party, but it helped rebuild confidence. When the Treasury offered $100 million in four percent bonds, the issue was subscribed five times over. In November 1895 the US Mint stopped production of silver coins. The American economy was on the road to recovery.

The Venezuelan Crisis of 1895 during Cleveland's second term is one of America's more unusual international affairs. Great Britain had long owned the colony of British Guiana, which neighbored Venezuela on the southern Caribbean coast. (British Guiana took the name Guyana on gaining independence in 1966.) Britain and Venezuela disputed the line marking their borders in wild, forested territory between them. Events were heading toward war in the summer of 1895. At Venezuela's request, the US demanded the right to arbitrate the problem, wanting to prevent European meddling according to the Monroe Doctrine of 1824. Britain had a choice of whether to wield its naval power or to acquiesce to American demands, and chose the latter path. Congress approved a fund of $100,000 for a commission to study the border and history of the dispute, and deliver a recommendation. The final result gave British Guiana most of the disputed land but gave Venezuela control over a vital point at the mouth of the Orinoco River.

ROCKEFELLER, THE STANDARD OIL TRUST, AND THE SHERMAN ANTI-TRUST ACT

As mentioned earlier, oil was one of America's first big industries. As drilling techniques improved, oil became so abundant that extracting oil from the earth was the easy part. The hard part was refining it and distributing it cheaply and effectively. One man, John D. Rockefeller (1839-1937) of New York, mastered this business and became the first great oil tycoon, and a force to be reckoned with by both competition and governments.

John D. Rockefeller in 1885

Rockefeller made his first fortune in the produce business before moving into oil. In 1867 he bought five competing refineries and renamed his firm Standard Oil of Ohio. He sought and won special rates to transport oil by rail. His next move was negotiating and forming a company with exclusive control of oil transportation on the Erie, New York Central, and Pennsylvania Railroads. However, this caused a public uproar and the Pennsylvania legislature revoked the company's charter.

Rockefeller continued making aggressive deals, and Standard Oil grew bigger and more powerful. During the

Depression of the 1870s, he spied on railroad records and bullied them into accepting terms that put other refiners out of business. With his growing financial clout he never hesitated to undercut a competitor and buy them out at bargain prices. Rockefeller was also a visionary businessman and saw vertical integration—such as expanding his oil business by adding companies in every aspect of the business cycle, from production through refinement, transportation, and marketing—as the key to eliminating middlemen and cutting overall costs. He built an empire so large and diversified it confused and intimidated his rivals. By 1872 Rockefeller had acquired 20 of the 25 refineries in Cleveland. As of 1879 he controlled 90 percent of all the oil refined and distributed in the US, and had built his own pipeline.

Rockefeller did not drink or smoke, and was a tireless worker and innovator. His firm was first to ship oil by tanker cars on railroads, or in pipelines. His chemists developed uses for by-products and distillates from petroleum refining, naphtha for paints, benzene for cleaning solutions, lubricants, and last but not least, gasoline. Gasoline had previously been burned off during refinement, but was put to work as a fuel for combustion engines.[78]

The company grew so large that in 1882 Rockefeller organized Standard Oil Trust to manage it. The Trust had nine Trustees, each in charge of a phase of operation such as drilling, transportation, refining, and warehousing. The Rockefeller family appointed each of the trustees.

A trust differs from a corporation in being a binding agreement among separate corporations, whose shareholders have deposited controlling amounts of their shares on the understanding that the trust makes decisions in their interests. Several trusts were created to protect an industry from foreign competition when there was no protective tariff, such as the American Sugar Refining Company and the American Tobacco Company. Just 20 years after the Civil War, trusts had spread into nearly every industry, from basic staples and necessities to luxury goods. Inevitably, trust protections were abused by member companies with consumer prices being fixed and producers of raw materials forced to accept what the trusts would pay them. The railroads also formed trusts to circumvent regulations under the Interstate Commerce Act.

A trust may work like a cartel, supporting high prices, but it also eliminates waste and brings costs and prices down with its economies of scale. Trusts prevented companies from undercutting each other on the market. The Standard Oil Trust was different from these industry trusts, since it supported components of a single vertically integrated company, not a group of similar companies; it was not intended for protection from competitors, but to guarantee maximum operating advantage for a single concern.

In combination with his intimidation tactics, Rockefeller's new Trust had devastating effects on other oil producers and refiners. By the late 1880s public opinion of trusts was plummeting, and businesses competing with Standard Oil were crying the loudest. A New York state commission investigating Standard Oil declared that trusts had "spread like disease through the commercial system of the country." Rather than providing protection, they were choking off all new businesses from entering a market independently. Several states enacted laws prohibiting trusts, seeing them as conspiracies to set prices and control local markets. In 1890 Congress passed the Sherman Anti-Trust Act, which was aimed solely at Standard Oil. The Sherman Act tried to limit a trust's control of interstate markets. It branded illegal "every contract, combination, in the form of a trust or otherwise, or conspiracy in restraint of trade or commerce among the several states or foreign nations."[79]

THE HOLDING COMPANIES

The Sherman Act was vaguely worded and difficult to enforce. It quickly started unravelling and was contested in the Ohio Supreme Court. But it did damage the trust as a technical form of business organization. After the Panic of 1893, which businesses blamed on artificial constraints on productivity under the Sherman Act, they responded with a new organization, the holding company, which held all the outstanding stock of another company. American Bell

Telephone, the Oregon and Transcontinental Railroad, and the Southern Pacific and Kentucky Railroads were among the first holding companies. New Jersey was ideal for holding companies, since state laws allowed companies that were purely financial (not producing or manufacturing) operations, so Rockefeller created Standard Oil Company of New Jersey, which held stock in 40 of his previously independent companies, and facilitated his vision of a perfectly integrated oil operation.

In retrospect, Standard Oil's monopoly was never destined to last long. Its success stimulated exploration in Texas and other parts of the country and abroad, for example in Latin America, Romania and Russia, and the Middle East in the mid-1900s. The biggest oil strike ever made was at Spindletop near Beaumont, Texas in 1901. In 1902 there were 1,500 oil companies worldwide. The Sherman Act, never powerful to begin with, could never have cut Standard Oil's market share the way this new exploration did.

More significant to the Average Joe was Standard Oil's part in drastically reducing oil production costs and prices. As with Carnegie Steel, Rockefeller's large refineries produced heating oil and gasoline at much lower costs. For example, Rockefeller knocked $1.50 off the cost of a barrel of oil by bringing refinement in-house. Crude oil plunged in cost to $1 per barrel, gasoline went down from 6 cents to 3 cents per gallon, and these savings were passed on to consumers and industry. He also brought the price of kerosene down by 70 percent—remember that until the 1890s, kerosene was a leading source of home heating and lighting. While his business practices were rough and tumble, a serious case can be made for the benefits of Rockefeller's temporary monopoly on oil.

J.P. MORGAN AND THE FINANCIERS

At this time, American industry and politics were feeling the influence of J. Pierpont Morgan of New York, one of the greatest men in the history of finance. J.P. Morgan (1837-1913) was a financier, not an industrialist, however he had a vision of how an economy should run if it was to be productive and achieve the highest level of prosperity for its citizens. His philosophy can be summarized as the belief that national strength requires a sound monetary system, which in turn results when businesses achieve the optimal degree of concentration, and when money is backed by sufficient gold reserves. Politicians like Presidents Harrison, Cleveland, and McKinley usually agreed with Morgan and followed his advice.

J.P. Morgan

Note above that J.P. Morgan believed in the optimal degree of concentration. In the last hundred years and in his own time, historians have accused Morgan of favoring monopolies. This charge is true when aimed at many industrialists, but Morgan appreciated the need for competition; without competition, companies would rule the economy and banks would shrivel in importance, taking their orders for loans and losing control of the terms of financing. And above all else, J.P. Morgan was a banker. Too much concentration and consolidation meant the death of competition. Too little, and there would be chaos. Morgan said that business concentration was only good when it balanced efficiency with competition and low prices, and that a base of relatively permanent and stable corporations was key to that balance.

J.P. Morgan's extra dimension, which enabled him to have such broad influence, was his emphasis on the good character of the business leader. J.P. Morgan was America's unofficial arbiter of corporate behavior and financial standards. As he once told a Senate panel, "Character determines credit." In his own business, Morgan completed many deals but did not resort to what he called "skullduggery." While he never entered politics, Morgan exerted tremendous personal and political influence. He had an effect on people, and a photographer said of him, "Meeting his eye is like facing the headlight of an express train bearing down on you."

POPULISM AND PROGRESSIVISM

Rockefeller's Standard Oil proved the positive case for a temporary monopoly, where it allowed enough capital to form and create true value and economic savings that benefit society. The railroads, hated as the "Barons" were, had enough capital to make short-distance travel inexpensive and long-distance travel possible for the first time.

But it's also important to understand the counterpoint view, that concentrations of capital were anti-democratic and bad for society. Capital had become a big target of muckraking journalists in city newspapers and magazines. Americans absorbed these attitudes; and by 1890, for the first time the average person was opposed to bigness, especially big business.

Populist demagogues like William Jennings Bryan exploited the anti-business attitude to support his crusade for "free silver." Bryan led the Populist Party but it died when he joined the Democrats in the election of 1896, which we will look at in Chapter Eleven. In the 1898 elections the anti-capital torch passed to Eugene Debs and the Social-Democratic Party (not yet named the Socialist Party). However, the socialists, who only knew what they opposed, lacked a unifying message that could ring true with the public as a whole. They never became a significant force in politics.

On the intellectual front, writer Henry George (1839-1897) articulated much of what was wrong with America with his book *Progress and Poverty*. He stated that economic inequalities almost always stemmed from accumulations of land. But his prescription for the problem, a one-time tax on all land owners to spread the wealth, was unacceptable and impractical. Still, his book was a best seller with two million copies. His arguments were also noticed by the wealthy. Many took to heart his belief that ownership, whether of land or capital, was a human trust to be discharged with responsibility. The political tide turned against monopolies, and by 1888 "planks" in the platforms of both parties featured anti-monopolistic provisions. By 1890, 27 states had enacted anti-monopoly laws and 15 had constitutional provisions.

In the mid-1890s, America's progressive movement was a new ideological force. Progressives essentially picked up the same critique of business and capital as the Populists, with the main difference being their lack of faith in the common man to succeed without help from elites in positions of power. Progressivism was largely born out of Eastern resentment of losing influence to industrialists and business interests in general. Then as now, progressivism was a convergence of several trends and schools of thought: utopian socialism, trust-busting anger, conservationism, and faith in the educated few over the unwashed masses. They were to be guardians of the people.

However, quite a few crackpots helped to birth progressivism, and the movement didn't really hit its stride until well into the 1900s. Rabble rousers like William Harvey, who wrote the mostly ignorant economic pamphlet "Coin's Financial Guide" with advice from a fictitious Professor Coin, condescended to help the little guy with warmed-over free-silver arguments and argued against any monetary controls whatever. Mary E. Lease's *The Problem of Civilization Solved* told farmers to raise "less corn and a lot more hell," but it also advocated for worldwide white supremacy and for the global separation of the races to best facilitate help from white nations.

These were also the early years of the Temperance Movement, which believed alcohol was the underlying cause of most social problems, and was loosely allied with progressive thinking. The Women's Christian Temperance Union formed in Hillsboro, Ohio in 1873 with a program that "linked the religious and the secular through concerted and far-reaching reform strategies based on applied Christianity." Their social reform plan also covered labor, prostitution, and public sanitation. The Union grew rapidly to membership of 158,477 in 1901, and achieved one of its supreme goals with the Eighteenth Amendment, Prohibition, in 1920.

Tycoons like Andrew Carnegie and John D. Rockefeller provided more practical examples than the Progressives of how the wealthy and the elites could benefit others. While still in his 30s, Carnegie knew that he was destined for great wealth, and he resolved on a number that he would give away while he was still alive: $350 million. Even now that is an astounding amount of money, and Carnegie lived to fulfill his promise. His philanthropic works funded hundreds of libraries across America, the Carnegie Institute, Carnegie Hall in New York, and countless other small projects. In 1889 Carnegie wrote an influential article, "The Gospel of Wealth," clearly stating that great wealth means great responsibility, and that the best way to discharge that responsibility was to contribute your money while you could, and not bequeath excessive fortunes to your children.

There are hundreds of examples of nineteenth century multi-millionaires following Carnegie's example. Rockefeller consistently tithed (gave ten percent) to his church and gave $35 million to the University of Chicago. He contributed millions to Baptist and black schools in the South, and financed the eradication of the boll weevil from food crops. Thomas Edison became a venture capitalist and funded small-time inventors who were inspired by him. Henry Phipps, a partner of

Andrew Carnegie, beautified Pittsburgh and founded the Phipps Conservatory. Furniture tycoon William Volker was deeply involved in the civic life of Kansas City; he gave thousands of gifts anonymously, helped expand the city's Research Hospital, and contributed land and money to a new university. Leland Stanford of the Central Pacific Railroad created the endowment for Stanford University, as did Cornelius Vanderbilt for Vanderbilt University in Philadelphia. Julius Rosenwald donated millions to build schools in black neighborhoods in the South. Retail merchant Nathan Straus, co-owner of Macy's and Abraham & Straus, spent millions helping the unemployed and poor New Yorkers during harsh winters. J.P. Morgan was a trustee and contributed both money and art to New York's Metropolitan Museum of Art and Museum of Natural History.

CHAPTER TEN—AMERICAN LIFE IN THE LATE 1800s

The average American in the late 1800s was better educated and more prosperous than in any other nation. American influence overseas was rapidly growing, and word of our achievements was spread through the press, by wealthy visitors to Europe, and through business connections. And American writers, artists, and philosophers were now taking a leading role in world culture.

These advances occurred toward the end of the nineteenth century. In this chapter we will look at the new mass market of American consumerism and the culture called "The Gay '90s," then the widespread reading of newspapers, leading us to the more enduring aspects of American culture, higher education, our great writers and several painters. We will wrap up by looking at women's rights and suffrage.

SEARS, ROEBUCK AND THE REVOLUTION IN MASS MERCHANDISING

As we have seen, by the 1880s the railroads reached every state, city, and nearly every town in America. The trains didn't just haul coal, oil, livestock and farm produce, they delivered new manufactured goods to people in the cities and countryside who were eager to improve their condition. Thanks to massive catalog operations like Sears, Roebuck, the typical farmer's wife could buy ice-boxes, sewing machines, stoves and other appliances that cut their daily chores in half. Mass production brought prices down to fractions of previous levels. For example, a sewing machine from Sears cost $18, less than a third of the price of branded name machines sold in the cities. Sears became the "price maker" for most products and appliances, and the leader in improving quality and reliability.[80]

Sears, Roebuck & Co. was founded by Richard Warren Sears and Alvah Roebuck in Chicago in 1886. Another big catalog name that lasted long into the twentieth century was Montgomery Ward, also based in Chicago. Businessmen Aaron Nussbaum and Julius Rosenwald bought Roebuck's share of the company in 1895, and at this point company growth multiplied. Sears' catalogs and Ward's "Wishbook" were like playgrounds of everyday items for the home, offering merchandise such as sewing machines, sporting goods, musical instruments, saddles, firearms, buggies, bicycles, baby carriages, and men's and children's clothing. Sears added specialty catalogs in 1896 that covered such items as bicycles, books, clothing, groceries, pianos and organs, and sewing machines. They represented American entrepreneurship at its most fruitful stage, bringing regular people convenience and small luxuries unimagined across the oceans.

As markets for consumer goods went nationwide, as telephones and telegraph provided near-instantaneous communication, and as the publishing industry reached readers across the continent, a new and distinctly American culture emerged. Americans identified now more as citizens of the United States, not just as New Yorkers, Missourians, or from any other state. For most Americans, the sectional conflicts of the Civil War were forgotten and people embraced newfound unity and growing prosperity, understanding they were closely intertwined.

THE GAY 90S

The new American culture was so widespread and so thoroughly accepted across social strata that it got a name—the Gay 90s. In these years, Americans could enjoy their free time in parks constructed in every town square to celebrate the Fourth of July and clear summer evenings. Bicycles became the most common way of getting around, cheaper and easier than horses.[81] Popular music celebrating the new life was full of romance. "Daisy" was a favorite song of the period, a carefree ballad sung by a lover who wants to marry his girl and ride off on "a bicycle built for two." In these years before fine audio, amateur singing was the most popular entertainment, and the barbershop quartet one of the finest forms for a local ensemble.

In fashion magazines, and eventually every other magazine, a new ideal of feminine beauty was borne with "The Gibson Girl." She was a fashionably dressed brunette with finely chiseled features, her hair pinned up in a pompadour hairstyle, and a figure that was enticing without looking cheap. The Gibson Girl was reproduced in advertising, stories, and even political cartoons. First created by illustrator Charles Dana Gibson, the Gibson Girl was fictitious, but that didn't stop her from setting standards for women to emulate and men to admire. And, of course, being a mere drawing she didn't ask royalties for her picture.

THE WEAKER SEX

THE YOUNG MAN IMAGINES HIMSELF THE LATEST VICTIM OF SOME FAIR ENTOMOLOGIST.

A Cartoon featuring several Gibson Girls

BASEBALL AND FOOTBALL

Baseball had become the national pastime soon after the Civil War and was a great part of Gay 90s culture. Baseball evolved from the British and colonial-era game of rounders during the 1840s, and in 1848 the New York Knickerbockers baseball club published a rulebook for the game, with rules that were perhaps 80 percent in common with the modern game.[82] In the late 1850s, several teams formed a league in New York City and New Jersey, often playing to crowds of several thousand people.

The Boston Beaneaters in 1888

Team baseball was forced to a halt during the war, but it sprang back with the interest of Southerners and being spread across the country by Union armies. Amateur baseball clubs first formed in St. Louis, Fort Leavenworth, Louisville, and Chattanooga. Dozens of small clubs formed in the Washington, DC area. The Cincinnati Red Stockings were the first professional baseball team in 1869. More professional teams formed in major cities of the North and Midwest, becoming the National League on February 2, 1876, headed by William Hulbert, president of the Chicago White Stockings. The charter member teams were the Boston Red Caps, Chicago White

Stockings, Cincinnati Red Stockings, Hartford Dark Blues, Louisville Grays, New York Mutuals, Philadelphia Athletics and St. Louis Brown Stockings.

There were dozens of leagues in the late 1800's that did not survive long, including the Eastern League, the Union Association, and the Players League. American Association franchises included the Baltimore Orioles, Cincinnati Red Stockings (ejected from the National League), Louisville Eclipse, Philadelphia Athletics, Pittsburgh Alleghenys, and St. Louis Browns. At the conclusion of the 1882 season the National League Champions the Chicago White Stockings played American Association Champions the Cincinnati Red Stockings, in Cincinnati, with each team winning one game, which might be considered the first "World Series." The two leagues would meet each other again in 1884. In 1893 the Western League (in the Midwest) changed its name to the American League.

Baseball was so popular in the late 1800's that there were major leagues in 27 cities across the Northeast and the Midwest, though it didn't expand beyond until the 1940s. The American Association got the nickname "the beer and whiskey league" since they allowed drinking. Ernest Thayer's hilarious "Casey at the Bat" became one of the best-known poems in the country, and a challenge for schoolchildren to recite for decades.

American football has a similar story, but it's more complicated by the various versions of football played at different colleges. The first intercollegiate game of football was played on November 6, 1869 at Rutgers College in New Brunswick, New Jersey, against Princeton College. It probably looked more like rugby than football; throwing or carrying the ball was not allowed, and the ball was round, not even oval like a rugby ball. Harvard and McGill University of Montreal later agreed to a version that involved grounding the ball in the opponent's end-zone, which evolved into a score called a touchdown.

Walter Camp (1859-1925), a star athlete at Yale College, is known as the father of modern football. Beginning in 1878, he instituted changes in the college game establishing a line of scrimmage, reducing the size of the field to its current dimensions, allowing blocking downfield, and revising the point scoring system, although not all the same points used today. Walter Camp's innovations helped football thrive as a college sport, spreading throughout eastern America and west to Kansas and California. The first forward pass was thrown in 1895 in a game between Georgia and North Carolina, though the play didn't become legal until 1905. Professional football evolved from local football clubs in the late 1890s; the first openly professional team was the Latrobe Athletic Association in Pennsylvania.

NEWSPAPERS AND HIGHER EDUCATION

One reason for the Gibson Girl's popularity and for the widespread culture of Americana in the Gay '90s was the predominance of daily newspapers. Americans at this time were the most literate people in the world. In 1870, when many American children were still needed on the farm, the average school year was 78 days and there was 78 percent enrollment in elementary school. Both these numbers grew in spite of high immigration late in the century. Just decades after relying on the one-room schoolhouse, most towns built high schools and grammar schools for lower grades.

Newspapers proliferated across America in the late 1800s. The number of daily newspapers rose from 250 in 1850 to 1,000 in 1880, then 1,600 in 1890, and 2,200 in 1900. Every city had at least one newspaper, and most American homes in the city or the town bought the paper. In the late 1800s, America was most definitely a nation of newspaper readers.

Mark Twain famously said, "If you don't read the newspaper, you are uninformed. If you do read the newspaper, you are misinformed." So it was perhaps inevitable that the news got a political slant. Not just a slant; most newspapers were plainly known to be either Republican or Democrat. They attacked and slandered politicians with no qualms, and reported developments in Washington to fit their agenda or whomever they supported in office.[83]

On a more positive note, newspapers and magazines

established new traditions of investigative reporting, exposing corruption or abuses of power. One of the first important pieces was by Henry Lloyd in *The Atlantic* in 1881, "The Story of A Great Monopoly." *McClure's*, *Collier's*, and other magazines copied this style and became the corporate gadflies of the era. The worst excess of this trend was "yellow journalism," the practice of focusing on reports of cases of violence and sensationalism. Every crime or city fire was reported on the front page in huge letters, highly exaggerated. The most notorious men in this business were Joseph Pulitzer of the New York World, and William Randolph Hearst of the San Francisco Examiner. They earned great fortunes, and in 1917 the Pulitzer family redeemed itself by sponsoring the Pulitzer Prizes for journalism, literature, and musical composition.

America was entering a golden era for higher education. The "ivy league" schools such as Harvard, Princeton, and Yale University had long since expanded from their theological origins and adopted curricula in the arts and sciences. The Morrill Acts of 1862 and 1890 funded education by donating federal land to states to sell or build an institution with a focus on the teaching of practical agriculture, science, military science and engineering ("without excluding ... classical studies"). These were the foundations of our state universities; for example, the formerly private Rutgers College in New Jersey expanded to become a state "land-grant college" in 1864, and is now Rutgers University. Look up "land grant university" at Wikipedia and you will see a map of the many universities founded through the Morrill Acts.

Colleges remained segregated between the races and the sexes past 1900. The first American school of higher learning was the Young Ladies Academy in Philadelphia, founded in 1787. Women's institutions and colleges opened across the eastern half of the country to meet the demand for education. In 1850 the Women's Medical College of Pennsylvania opened in Philadelphia. Between 1837 and 1889, new colleges for women were founded with rigorous educational standards comparable to the men's Ivy League, including Smith, Radcliffe, Bryn Mawr, Mount Holyoke, Vassar, Wellesley, and Barnard. Together they become known as "The Seven Sisters".

Booker T. Washington (1856-1915) of Virginia was born a slave and became a national leader and advisor to Theodore Roosevelt. He called for black progress through education and entrepreneurship, rather than trying to directly challenge Jim Crow segregation laws in the South. Washington founded Tuskegee Institute in Alabama and helped inspire others that we now call historically black colleges. Two of the most prominent schools from these years include Howard University in Washington, DC and Morehouse College in Atlanta (formerly Atlanta Baptist College).

LITERARY PROMINENCE

As mentioned in Chapter Three, American writers first made their mark in the mid-1800s with the great seafaring novels of Herman Melville such as *Moby Dick*, and with Nathaniel Hawthorne's *The Scarlet Letter*. In the last thirty years of the century the production of American writers was so varied and sophisticated as to make it clear they were among the worlds finest.

Mark Twain in 1867

The Average Joe should be familiar with Mark Twain (1835-1910), who was born Samuel Clemens in Florida, Missouri. Mark Twain is best known for *Tom Sawyer* and *The Adventures of Huckleberry Finn*, two books for readers of all ages, with hilarious stories about the typical country boy who is carefree and mischievous but in many ways wiser than his elders. These two books made Twain famous, yet he was also a leading writer and voice for common sense. Twain was cynical but had a gift for sounding like ordinary folks. He wrote for newspapers and magazines and published several books for more mature readers such as *Life on The Mississippi* and *Innocents Abroad*, a memoir about a tour of the Holy Land. Twain traveled several times, and his stories showed his concern for American blacks, and his hatred of European imperialism. His early masterpiece may be *The Gilded Age,* co-written with Charles Dudley Warner in 1873, the story of a hapless Missouri family and their constant hope to strike it rich in a time when it seemed only sheer luck and political connections were any help at all. The Gilded Age became a metaphor for Americans who saw their world being covered with a thin sheen of gold.

Edith Wharton (1862-1937) from New York City wrote very powerful fiction that conveyed the lives of Americans, from the ordinary to the wealthy, from a deeply personal perspective. Her most productive period came after 1900, yet she wrote primarily about life in the last century. Two of her books the Average Joe should know are *Ethan Frome* and *The Age of Innocence*. *Ethan Frome* is a short novel set in a secluded New England village, where Ethan falls in love with his wife's cousin; as the narrowness of their existence closes in on them, they choose a desperate means to burst free; it contains one of the most surprising endings ever written. *The Age of Innocence* is set among the upper middle class of New York City, and again it involves a love triangle. However, the characters this time are all too aware of the limits society sets on their options. In the end, the hero of the story must content himself with the platonic love he has experienced, and the dream of what might have been.

A few more writers to know and explore include O. Henry, who wrote bittersweet short stories of life, struggle, and hope for the middle classes of New York. In "The Gift of the Magi," a young couple needs to buy each other Christmas presents; he sells his watch to buy her a silver comb for her beautiful hair, and she sells her hair to buy him a watch chain. Novelist Henry James was an expatriate writer who wrote often about the experience of wealthy Americans in Europe. James had early successes with *Portrait of a Lady* and the psychological ghost story *The Turn of the Screw*. In our time he might be best known for *The Golden Bowl*, a story set in London about an American financier and his daughter, who is betrothed to an Italian nobleman whose former lover just happens to be the daughter's best friend. The writer Theodore Dreiser began late in the century and used a "naturalistic" style to explore characters caught in ordinary human dilemmas. In 1901 he published *Sister Carrie*, the story of a pretty but directionless young woman in Chicago who allows herself to be manipulated by two different ambitious but irresponsible men.

Two poets from these years are also widely read today. Walt Whitman was an eccentric man, highly patriotic but too frightened to enlist in the Civil War (he served as a nurse to the wounded), and possessed of a colorful and visionary gift to convey emotion. His classic work is the collection *Leaves of Grass* (1871), which initially caused criticism due to its many sexual allusions. And Emily Dickinson was even more eccentric, a woman who almost never left her home of Amherst, Massachusetts, yet who seemed to relate intuitively to the entire world around her. Dickinson wrote nearly 1,800 poems, though less than a dozen were published during her life.

ARTISTS OF THE LATE 1800S

American painters had much greater impact on the culture during this period. Winslow Homer (1836-1910) was a Massachusetts-born painter best known for his ocean scenes and landscapes. He started as a lithographer and commercial illustrator for Harper's Weekly, who sent him to sketch the Civil War. He worked in New York, Paris, and England before settling down on the Maine coast. Homer's early oil paintings depicting childhood scenes and women relaxing in the countryside reflected a mood of nostalgia, but he rejected excess sentimentality. His most successful work, including paintings most likely to be recognized by the Average Joe, were settings of sailors and seashores. Homer often injected tension in his work, as in "The Fog Warning," a fisherman in a small boat struggling to reach his ship as a storm approaches.

The Fog Warning, by Winslow Homer

Portrait painter John Singer Sargent had American parents but he lived and became famous in Europe, before working in America in the late 1880s. Sargent was famous for striking skin tones that added a ghostly elegance to his subjects, especially in the case of "Portrait of Madame X." James Abbott McNeil Whistler was born in America but also spent his career in Europe. Whistler's "Arrangement in Grey and Black Number 1" is better known for its nickname, "Whistler's Mother." It has been parodied for 140 years, but he painted it with no sense of irony, as an homage to his aging mother. Whistler is also known for The Peacock Room, which is an interior decorative ensemble that includes a dramatically romantic painting called "The Princess from the Land of Porcelain." It has been on display at the Freer Gallery of the Smithsonian in Washington, DC.

America's landscape artists painted grand vistas of the western prairies and the wild mountains of the Rockies and Sierra Nevada ranges. Most magnificent of all were the paintings of Albert Bierstadt, huge canvas panoramas of western scenes such as Yosemite Valley in California. Another was Thomas Moran, whose favorite subjects were the Yellowstone Valley of Wyoming, the Snake River and other western scenes. On a smaller scale, and still popular in our day, was the painter and sculptor Frederick Remington, who brought the frontier alive with figures of cowboys and American Indians. One key to success for artists of the frontier was new printing techniques that reproduced their work for magazines and newspapers, in black and white, of course. These men helped popularize Western culture and added to the lore of the lone horseman, the mine prospector, and the Indian warrior.

Partly due to the popularity of Thomas Moran's paintings, 2.2 million acres around the Yellowstone Valley were set aside for protection as America's first National Park in 1872. Years later, President Theodore Roosevelt established the National Park Service including five national parks, four game preserves, 150 national forests and bird sanctuaries, with 230 million acres of federal land.

WOMEN'S RIGHTS

After liberation of the slaves, the biggest social change sweeping America in the late 1800s was the movement for women's rights, especially suffrage, the right to vote. Up until this time, work as a teacher or nurse or maid were about the only jobs available to women. For most women life was still expected to be in the home as wife and mother, or helping on the farm. With the industrial revolution, more women were working for their own living, in mills, at switchboards, and in office clerical work. Many single women came from the country to the cities to make a new life. Contrary to modern misunderstanding, women in America had rights to property, and most state laws granted a widow the right to her husband's estate. In earlier colonial days, only single women, known legally as "femmes soles," could own land, and they lost that right upon marriage. From the early 1800s on, American women had the right to run commercial establishments, and they bought, owned and sold land. They represented their husbands in legal matters. Pre-nuptial agreements first became popular in the 1800s to make clear who had right to what property.

Given these property rights, it's a wonder women did not gain the right to vote soon after black Americans did. Some states led the way; Wyoming first gave women the vote in 1869, followed by Colorado, Utah, and Idaho. In 1869, Elizabeth Stanton and Susan B. Anthony of New York, two women associated with the abolitionist movement, formed the National Woman Suffrage Association to lead the new fight. In 1890 it merged with another organization to form National American Woman Suffrage Association. But NAWSA's proposals faced stiff opposition in the South and from the Democratic Party. Thanks to the agitation of Republican leaders such as Ruth Hannah McCormick, women finally gained the right to vote nationwide in 1920 with passage the 19th Amendment to the Constitution.

CHAPTER ELEVEN—MCKINLEY AND THE SPANISH-AMERICAN WAR

INTRODUCTION TO THE FINAL CHAPTER

America's astonishing growth after the Civil War generated prosperity, industrial strength, and economic power unsurpassed in history. Among Western nations, only Russia had a larger population, and only Germany had manufacturing capability comparable in size and reach to ours. In fifty years, the United States went from being a land of farms, scattered industries, and untamed wilderness, to an interconnected, highly mobile and industrialized powerhouse, with a rapidly expanding middle class and widespread affluence that most Europeans never imagined to be possible.

This fact, America's unexpected and rapid rise to prosperity and world power, overshadows every other development in the late nineteenth century. So why isn't this story better known, and clearly stated? Why don't our histories tell us more about the great advances we made during this period? And why do they seem like a surprise to people who only know our more recent past?

I believe there are three main explanations for this. First, students in American high schools naturally tend to focus more on recent events, not the nineteenth century. They learn a few basic facts about people and dates during the Civil War, perhaps about the struggles for compromise before the war, and even less about Reconstruction after the war, and the rest is largely brushed over. Hopefully by now you realize what students miss when they are taught this way.

Second, America's rise to prominence was aided by geography. We were protected from the other great powers by two huge oceans, and the American people, busy as we were in the new cities and industries, enjoyed the protection that our relative isolation gave us. It took years before the United States was ready to exercise power outside across the oceans. In the larger historical picture, American power isn't truly apparent until we joined World War I, in 1916.

Finally, there's little doubt that for the last fifty years revisionist historians have downplayed any American accomplishment, including those in the nineteenth century. These historians hardly mention how growth and commerce led to unprecedented prosperity. It seems the last thing a revisionist will do is give credit to Americans whose ingenuity or determination gave us innovations and improved our lives. They prefer to emphasize inequalities and injustices concerning either the American Indians or black Americans suffering under Jim Crow laws. Both these perspectives are important, but students lately are only learning one of them. The jaundiced perspectives of such revisionists have been a detriment to secondary and higher education, for they undermine and distort the true story of America over the years.

WILLIAM MCKINLEY

With President Cleveland following Republican policy, populist-minded Democrats in 1896 found a new hero in William Jennings Bryan (1860-1925) of Nebraska, a famously skilled orator and demagogue. Bryan's rallying cause was free silver and the demand to coin it according to the old 16 to 1 ratio proposed 20 years earlier. He was originally in the Populist Party, but he found enough support among Democrats to lead them in the campaign of 1896. Bryan had a magnetic personal presence and a gift for riling up the crowds. Bryan mesmerized the Democratic Convention in Chicago with his "Cross of Gold" speech, the crowd roaring applause with every statement. He delivered his closing line with his arms outstretched and palms pressed against his temples, saying, "You shall not press down upon the brow of labor this crown of thorns; you shall not crucify mankind upon a cross of gold." As he finished, there was a deathly silence, and then twenty thousand men and women went nearly delirious with happiness, and anger.

William Jennings Bryan on the left, on his campaign train car *The Idler*, in Crestline, Ohio

The Republicans nominated William McKinley (1843-1901), a former Congressman and the Governor of Ohio, and another hard-money man. The Democrats staked everything on Free Silver, while Republicans calmly jeered Bryan's Silver Crusade and the absurdity of using "two different yardsticks to measure money." The Republican Convention platform read, "We are unalterably opposed to every measure calculated to debase our currency or impair the credit of our country. We are therefore opposed to the free coinage of silver, except by international agreement with the leading commercial nations of the world...the existing gold standard must be preserved."

The election of 1896 was a pivotal event that turned into

the first real contest between two philosophies since the Civil War. The Republican growth-oriented policies based on a sound national currency were in stark contrast to the Democrats' new populist vision of an inflated currency that, through silver, would scale down and repudiate debt. McKinley ran a sedate campaign, greeting reporters and politicians at his home in Canton, while Bryan went everywhere, raising fire and brimstone against the Eastern establishment. Bryan might have won the election except for an upward turn in the economy in the autumn that benefited Republicans. He won the entire South and much of the West, but California and the North were almost solidly against him. The Democrats also overplayed Bryan's roots among Western farmers, and he failed to win the moderate Midwestern states Minnesota, Iowa, and North Dakota.[84]

William McKinley may be the late nineteenth century president least understood in our time. As a congressman he focused on trade policy, and pressed hard—too hard—for a protective tariff. The tariff was so high it actually reduced federal revenues. McKinley is known for a war with Spain and in the Philippines, but he did not campaign or begin his term as an expansionist. Theodore Roosevelt, who became McKinley's vice president in 1901 and had worked with or witnessed a good deal happening in Washington for over ten years, had mixed opinions about his boss. Roosevelt believed the Republican Party had grown fat, soft, and lazy, and had forgotten its free-market, radical roots under Abraham Lincoln. He thought President McKinley was too fearful to rock the boat and expose petty corruption in the political system, but he gave McKinley great credit in standing for hard money backed by gold, and pressing forward with Civil Service reform.

ANNEXATION OF HAWAII

The Hawaiian Islands and the port of Honolulu were visited by American, European, and other sailors as far back as the late 1700s. Christian missions began work there in the 1820s, and together with the permanent Western settlers they promoted literacy and self-government. The islands were clearly on a path toward white domination and threatening the power of the royalty; in 1893 Hawaiian Queen Lili'uokalani turned against Western modernity, and declared a new Constitution with absolute royal power. A Euro-American "Committee of Safety" declared a revolt, and received special protection from US Marines to complete a coup against the Hawaiian crown.

The new Republic of Hawaii petitioned the United States to be annexed, much as Texas was annexed in 1845. Congress approved annexation in March 1893, but incoming President Cleveland was opposed to it and shelved the bill. Cleveland commissioned the Blount Report to determine what had happened in Hawaii, and the report was the Queen's removal had been illegal. However, the new Republic remained in power.

William McKinley

Most Americans favored the annexation, and strategic thinkers like Theodore Roosevelt were convinced it was the right thing to do, before a large European power snapped the Islands up for themselves. In 1897 it was then up to the new McKinley administration to annex Hawaii. Secretary of State

John Sherman agreed in June 1897 after negotiations with a Hawaiian delegation and expansionists within Congress, though it took a full year for the treaty to be passed by resolution in the House of Representatives.[85]

THE SPANISH-AMERICAN WAR AND THE PHILIPPINE INSURRECTION

War with Spain is where President McKinley faced his real trial. The people of Cuba were in a near-constant state of rebellion against Spain. They had begged for American help during a revolt in the 1870s. Americans later began investing in Cuban farms, and their situation was harder to ignore. The Cubans rebelled again in 1895 and established a "National Junta" in New York to raise bond money for freedom fighters. Many Americans felt an evangelistic urge to expel Spain from Cuba, since Roman Catholic Spain refused Protestant missionaries permission to visit the island.

From this point, business interests influenced American policy with calls for intervention. The first US response was to apply diplomatic pressure on Spain. Presidents Cleveland and McKinley had both resisted the calls for war. McKinley believed he was making progress liberalizing Spanish rule in Cuba, but in early 1898 two events made war all but inevitable.

First, on February 15, there was an explosion in Havana Bay that sank the visiting battleship USS Maine and killed 268 sailors. Spain denied causing the explosion, and in fact it would have been foolish of Spain to do any such thing, given the tensions of the moment. None of that mattered to the "Yellow Press." Hearst's *New York World* blamed the explosion on a Spanish mine, calling it a deliberate provocation. Other newspapers followed suit, inflaming public opinion for war.[86]

Soon afterward was a discovery by US intelligence of a letter written by the Spanish Ambassador to the US, Enrique de Lome, attacking McKinley as a spineless fool.[87] Spanish diplomacy was confused and made matters worse, alternating regrets for the USS Maine with accusations, angry defiance, and defensive statements on their Cuban regime.

President McKinley was now cornered. On April 20,

Congress passed a War Resolution, and McKinley approved it, but only after adding the Teller Amendment which declared that Cuba would be liberated from Spain and become a sovereign nation after the war. By April 25, Spain and the US declared war on each other.

Theodore Roosevelt, in his capacity as Secretary of the Navy, had prepared for war by ordering Commodore George Dewey and the American Pacific Fleet to head immediately for the Spanish colony of the Philippines. On May 1, Dewey's force opened fire on the Spanish fleet in Manila Bay, which was caught by surprise. Dewey stopped for breakfast, then sailed closer and finished the job. The port city of Manila fell later in August without a fight, and war with Spain in the Philippines essentially ended. Dewey did not lose a single man, and his swift victory set the tone for the rest of the war. On June 20, the US captured Guam without a fight, took all Spanish troops prisoner, and sailed away leaving the only American civilian there in charge until the Navy could return.

The American Army was unprepared for the war. The War Department rounded up militias and volunteers for the fight in Cuba. Roosevelt resigned his position in the government and volunteered to help lead a cavalry regiment, who later became known as the Rough Riders. Expeditionary troops including the US Fifth Army Corps landed on June 22 and began an assault on Santiago, on the southern coast of Cuba.

Spanish Army troops were not so easily subdued, however. They made effective use of concealment and their high-powered rifles, and on their retreat to Santiago they managed to ambush an American force in the Battle of Las Guasimas. US troops learned to adapt and only advance in short rushes before finding cover. On July 1, 15,000 American troops, including regular infantry, the Rough Riders and other cavalry, irregular militia, and Cuban rebels, ran direct attacks in the Battles of El Caney and San Juan Hill. Over 200 US soldiers were killed and 1,200 wounded by the higher rate of Spanish rifle fire, but US Gatling guns helped to turn the victory to the Americans. The Spanish left Santiago two days later and the city fell to the American siege.

On July 3, Admiral William Sampson virtually duplicated

Dewey's feat by destroying the Spanish Caribbean fleet, which had been bottled up in Santiago harbor. On July 25, US troops invaded Puerto Rico and relieved an American fleet that had blockaded San Juan Bay in May. They fought a series of inconclusive battles with Spaniards and Puerto Rican loyalists until an armistice ended the fighting on August 13.

On December 10, the US and Spain signed the Treaty of Paris, which the Senate ratified on February 6, 1899. With the treaty, America gained all of Spain's colonies outside of Africa and Cuba became a US protectorate. The Cubans formed a new government and gained independence on May 20, 1902, with a guarantee that they would not form alliances with other countries, and the US reserved the right to intervene if necessary. The US also kept perpetual lease of Guantanamo Bay, on the eastern end of Cuba.

When he seized the Philippines, Admiral Dewey had brought with him the exiled Filipino leader Emilio Aguinaldo to rally his countrymen against the Spanish. In mid-1898 the US had 11,000 troops, and with Aguinaldo's rebels they took control of most of the Philippines outside Manila. The Spanish commander in Manila was unwilling to surrender to Filipino rebels, and made a deal with Admiral Dewey to stage a bloodless, mock battle and surrender to the Americans.

The United States moved to annex the Philippines and make it an American colony, but this was opposed in Congress and by the Anti-Imperialist League. At this juncture, Japan approached the US with a proposal to administer the Philippines, together with a third power. Germany had sent ships to Manila to assert its own influence. Given Japan's wars against China and Germany's intimidation, it became clear the Philippine Islands were the target of a major power play. After long debate in the Senate, on February 6, 1899 the Senate voted to annex the Philippines.

But the war was not yet over. Aguinaldo and the Filipino rebels were ready for independence, and they resented not being allowed to accept the Spanish surrender or to occupy Manila. Filipino-American cooperation thereby ended, and in February, 1899 the Philippine-American Insurrection broke out. It was a brutal and messy counter-insurgency that lasted three years, with atrocities committed by Americans and Filipinos, causing much greater loss of life than the Spanish-American War – 4,200 American lives, 16,000 Filipinos killed in battle, and as many as 200,000 people dead from disease, famine, or cruelty from both sides.[88] As America's first and only war as a colonial power, it stirred opposition at home and had adverse effects on American opinion. After the Philippines, most Americans wanted no more colonies. The Philippines were granted independence in 1946 after the US had reconquered and liberated the islands from Japanese occupation during World War II.

American Artillery in Action near San Juan Bridge, Manila, 1899

MCKINLEY'S SECOND TERM, AND PRESIDENT ROOSEVELT

In 1900, President McKinley was in a very comfortable position for reelection, and his opponent—William Jennings Bryan, again—had trouble re-igniting his free silver crusade. McKinley won without any campaigning. For his vice president, he replaced the deceased Garrett Hobart with Theodore Roosevelt, the brilliant statesman-politician-soldier whose ride up San Juan Hill rocketed him into the public imagination. Roosevelt had been elected governor of New York in 1898, and he suspected that business interests preferred that he go to Washington and leave them alone to run the state. Regardless, Roosevelt gladly accepted his new office and his chance to work with McKinley for further government reform.

As we know, Roosevelt got more than he expected. On September 6, 1901, while visiting the Pan-American Exposition in Buffalo, President McKinley was assassinated by anarchist Leon Czolgosz. Just six months after McKinley's second inauguration, Theodore Roosevelt became America's youngest president at age 42.

Theodore Roosevelt

President Theodore Roosevelt (1858-1919) was America's most successful and popular leader since Abraham Lincoln. Roosevelt is best known for his quote, "Speak softly and carry a big stick." He believed firmly in a strong military, especially the Navy, and expansive foreign policy. Speaking of the Confederacy and other divisive episodes, he said, "The enemies of the Union were the enemies of America and of mankind, whose success would have plunged our nation into an abyss of shame and misery." He championed the Panama Canal, a massive project abandoned by the French. Roosevelt's economic policies blended reliance on traditional American individualism, effective use of authority to maintain order—he despised anarchists and demagogues—and government influence to end abuse of power by corporations. He used federal power to curtail business trusts and to increase market competition. For example, in 1901 Roosevelt's Justice Department sued a large railroad trust called Northern Securities. As he wrote in 1900, "There is great unrest among the laboring classes, who feel bitterly about the wrongs...which are really inherent in the nature of things."[89] Roosevelt would never have bought into notions held by some Americans today, that people don't have full responsibility for their lives, and that the only good things come from government. Roosevelt believed in finding that fine balance that gives men the greatest freedom possible, in a society of which they can be proud.

CONCLUSION

It seems a shame to end at this point. So much American history is just around the corner—the Wright Brothers' first powered flight in 1903, Henry Ford's incredible transformation of the automobile industry, more electrification and convenience in American industry and the home, and President Roosevelt's trust-busting. We have seen how the roots of these changes were planted in the previous thirty years. The Wrights were just bicycle mechanics with no financial backing but a gift for tinkering, an interest in gliders, and a plan for adding an engine. Ford built his first engine in 1892, and spent much of the following years thinking about how his new, inexpensive car could solve the problem of rural isolation. The common thread here is the American drive to create or make things better; geniuses like Edison and Ford, and relentless spirits like the Wrights had visions for the future, long before they were able to make money from them.

America experienced many problems over these hundred years, much of our own making. Labor strife, extremes of wealth and poverty in the cities, and populism all indicated that not everyone thought he or she was getting a fair deal. America's push for manifest destiny too easily carried over into a drive for colonies like our powerful European peers had, though we learned a hard lesson in the process, and faster than the Europeans. Race relations did not progress as hoped after the Civil War, and we remained segregated for too long. Most black Americans were second-class citizens, and in the South they were stuck in poverty and many were lynched for minor crimes, setting the stage for their early twentieth century migration to Northern cities where they hoped to improve their lives.

Most of these problems were to be expected in a nation where freedom, vast natural resources, new technology, and rapid industrialization created and spread wealth as never before, and which had fought a bloody war to end slavery. All these things created a scramble for new opportunity and a new society encompassing both the American-born and millions of immigrants. It's up to the Average Joe or Jo now, to reflect on the incredible, sometimes violent, but always upward course America travelled from 1800 to 1900. Consider our problems with the Old World people left behind in every part of Europe, and with the prosperity, the new civic institutions, the near universal liberty, and the egalitarian spirit most Americans possessed at the end of the century. Think of a world where American power was not strong enough to help our friends and to build democracy, even with our former enemies, as we did in World Wars I and II.[90]

So Dear Joe, what can you conclude about the Nineteenth Century? What stories stick in your mind? Let me offer a few suggestions:

The Nineteenth Century is the story of how a young nation slowly but increasingly grew in power, affluence, and influence, driven by the spirit of liberty that guided most of its relationships with other nations.

The Nineteenth Century is the story of Manifest Destiny, of expansion across an entire continent, of purchasing land from our rivals, of displacing the weak and disordered Mexicans, and of frequent betrayals and subjugation of the American Indians, both friendly and belligerent. In their places, millions of ordinary Americans built thriving farms and towns, and lived lives of freedom and prosperity which, while we would not be content, were tremendous advances over the quality of life known around the world.

The Nineteenth Century is the story of the growing intolerance of slavery's hateful presence in an otherwise civilized land, of how a Democratic Party devoted to slavery forced secession on the states in its voter base, and how the Republican Party was formed to address an issue that previous generations had largely swept under the rug.

The Nineteenth Century is the story of how the inevitable conflict over slavery resulted in the most destructive and deadly war in our history, and how Reconstruction in the war's aftermath could not overcome the bigotry and resentment that spread in the South.

The Nineteenth Century is the story of wild, rough freedom on the frontier where men and women took great gambles with their lives. It is the story of how both the pioneers and millions of immigrants overcame the odds and gave abundance to their children.

The Nineteenth Century is the story of how a new national culture produced some of the world's greatest art and literature, in both the salons of the wealthy and in the books and newspapers bought by its highly literate masses.

The Nineteenth Century is the story of invention that was partly the result of genius and in equal parts fueled by commercial interests and consumer demands. It is the story of the birth of mass production, mass distribution, and the mass market, which standardized goods and services and kept prices down for a flourishing middle class.

The Nineteenth Century is the story of railroads, telecommunications, and the industrial revolution, led by giants and financiers who understood the nation's future better than its elected leaders, and which, after many troubles, resulted in the world's most democratic labor movement.

The Nineteenth Century is the story of our first venture as imperialists in the Philippines which, following a war that was greatly justified, we undertook in a game of global power but which also taught Americans not to take any more colonies.

The Nineteenth Century is all these things and so much more; it is a lesson to Americans today, to understand and respect our history and the sacrifices of previous generations, and not to forget the valuable heritage that in spite of our mistakes has made us the freest and strongest nation on Earth.

AUTHOR'S NOTE

This book is a work of popular history. It is not meant to be comprehensive or scholarly research, rather it is my attempt to make history accessible, understandable and enjoyable to The Average Joe. I am a fan of history, not a professional historian. Living near Washington, DC, I am surrounded by history, which inspired me and made the writing somewhat easier. I have provided notes in the following section to document some of my more detailed statements, and to provide supplemental stories not relevant enough to include in the main text. Much of the detail related herein is a matter of historical fact, and easily verified in a typical textbook or on the internet. Wikipedia was a great source of supporting detail for my book, and I was able to corroborate nearly everything I read there through other sources. Wikipedia was especially helpful in describing the Mexican-American and Civil Wars and the Labor Movement. They are a tremendous resource. (You can believe some things you read on the Internet.) Below you will find suggested reading that I have enjoyed, which will take you deeper into Nineteenth Century America.

I hope you had as much fun reading this book as I had writing it!

— David M. Paine

RECOMMENDED READING

Undaunted Courage: Meriwether Lewis, Thomas Jefferson, and the Opening of the American West, by Stephen E. Ambrose

Founders' Son: A Life of Abraham Lincoln, by Richard Brookhiser

Bury My Heart at Wounded Knee: An Indian History of the American West, by Dee Brown

The Autobiography of Andrew Carnegie and the Gospel of Wealth, by Andrew Carnegie and Gordon Hunter

Titan: The Life and Times of John D. Rockefeller, Sr., by Ron Chernow

Son of the Morning Star: Custer and the Little Bighorn, by Evan S. Connell

The Year of Decision: 1846, by Bernard DeVoto

Narrative of the Life of Frederick Douglass, by Frederick Douglass

American Sphinx: The Character of Thomas Jefferson, by Joseph J. Ellis

Free Soil, Free Labor, Free Men: The Ideology of the Republican Party before the Civil War, by Eric Foner

Reconstruction: America's Unfinished Revolution, 1863-1877, by Eric Foner

Team of Rivals: The Political Genius of Abraham Lincoln, by Doris Kearns Goodwin

Battle Cry of Freedom: The Civil War Era, by James M. McPherson

A Country of Vast Designs: James K. Polk, the Mexican War and the Conquest of the American Continent, Robert W. Merry

The Oregon Trail, by Francis Parkman

Uncle Tom's Cabin, by Harriett Beecher Stowe

Andrew Jackson, by Sean Wilentz

The Great Railroad Revolution: The History of Trains in America, by Christian Wolmar

BIBLIOGRAPHY

Alexander, Bevin. 2005. *How America Got It Right.* New York: Crown Forum.

Daniel Ruddy, Editor. 2010. *Theodore Roosevelt's History of the United States.* New York: Harper Collins.

Freeberg, Ernest. 2013. *The Age of Edison: Electric Light and the Invention of Modern America.* New York: The Penguin Press.

Grant, Ulysses S. 1885, Reprinted in 1999. *Personal Memoirs.* New York: The Modern Library.

Hicks, John D., George E. Mowry, and Robert E. Burke. 1965. *The American Nation.* Boston: Houghton Mifflin Company.

Hughes, Mark. 2009. *The New Civil War Handbook.* New York: Savas Beatie LLC.

Hunt, Michael H. 2009. *The American Ascendancy: How the United States Gained and Wielded Global Dominance.* Chapel Hill: University of North Carolina Press.

Jacksonian America: Society, Personality, and Politics. 1969. *Edward Pessen.* Homewood, Illinois: The Dorsey Press.

James Taranto and Leonard Leo, Editors. 2004. *Presidential Leadership: Rating the Best and the Worst in the White House.* New York: A Wall Street Journal Book.

Johnson, Paul. 1997. *A History of the American People.* New York: Harper Collins.

Miklich, E. 2016. *19C Baseball.* Accessed 2016. www.19cbaseball.com.

Monke, Linda R. 2003. *The Words We Live By.* New York: Hyperion.

Morgan, Robert. 2012. *Lions of the West: Heroes and Villains of the Westward Expansion.* Chapel Hill: Algonquin Books.

Moser, Edward P. 2011. *A Patriot's A to Z of America.* Nashville: Turner Publishing Company.

Schweikart, Larry. 2008. *48 Liberal Lies about American History.* New York: Sentinel.

Schweikart, Larry, and Allen, Michael. 2004. *A Patriot's History of the United States.* New York: Sentinel.

Sears, Stephen W. 1983. *Landscape Turned Red: The Battle of Antietam.* Boston: Ticknor and Fields.

Tipple, John. 1970. *The Capitalist Revolution: A History of American Social Thought, 1890 - 1919.* New York: Pegasus.

NOTES

[1] Schweikart, p. 76

[2] Alexander, p. 16

[3] Alexander, p. 18

[4] Monke, p. 90-91.

[5] Morgan, p. 79. Jackson wrote: "I have long since determined when I die I will leave my reputation untarnished. You have only to act with a little energy for which you will be applauded by your Government. Give me a force for 6 months...and all may be safe. Withhold it, and all is lost and the reputation of the state and [years] with it."

[6] Ruddy, p. 114. Theodore Roosevelt wrote about the Monroe Doctrine about 80 years later: "[It] is not international law, but there is no necessity that it should be...it should continue to be a cardinal feature of American policy on this continent.... To argue that it cannot be recognized as a principle of international law is a mere waste of breath. Nobody cares whether it is or not so recognized, any more than one cares whether the Declaration of Independence and Washington's Farewell Address are so recognized."

[7] Alexander, p. 38

[8] *La Amistad* was a Spanish schooner illegally transporting 49 Africans from Sierra Leone to slavery in Cuba in 1840. The Africans took over the ship, but it came ashore at Long Island, New York. Their fate became a court case, *The United States v. The Amistad*, to decide whether to return them to the ship owners. The Africans won their case and were freed, and most finally returned to Africa with the aid of Northern missionary groups.

[9] Johnson, p. 284, p. 289.

[10] Johnson, p. 355. The First Bank of the United States was chartered from 1791 to 1811, and the Second Bank's charter was from 1816 to 1836.

[11] Hunt, p.43

[12] Jackson's argument followed this statement during

debate over passage of the Act: "Humanity has often wept over the fate of the aborigines of this country and philanthropy has long been busily employed in devising means to avert it, but its progress has never for a moment been arrested, and one by one have many powerful tribes disappeared from the earth.... But true philanthropy reconciles the mind to these vicissitudes as it does to the extinction of one generation to make room for another.... Philanthropy could not wish to see this continent restored to the condition in which it was found by our forefathers. What good man would prefer a country covered with forests and ranged by a few thousand savages to our extensive Republic, studded with cities, towns, and prosperous farms, embellished with all the improvements which art can devise or industry execute, occupied by more than 12,000,000 happy people, and filled with all the blessings of liberty, civilization, and religion?"

[13] Johnson, p. 349

[14] Until passage of the Twentieth Amendment in 1933, Inauguration Day was always, March 4, the anniversary of the date the US Constitution went into effect.

[15] Johnson, p. 390.

[16] Johnson, p. 391

[17] Morgan, Chapter 5. Sam Houston had a long personal and political history before coming to Texas. As Robert Morgan puts it, "Sam Houston's life was a kind of dance between calamity and triumph." As a teenager he ran away from home in Tennessee to live with the Cherokee, and carried a friendship with Chief Ooleteka with him most of his life. He helped Andrew Jackson fight the Red Sticks in the Creek War. After learning and practicing law, he became a district attorney, and then was elected as a Representative to Congress, then returned to serve as Governor of Tennessee. He married a younger woman named Eliza Allen, but the marriage was a miserable failure. They separated, and rumors swirled that he had accused her of infidelity, or committed barbaric acts learned from the Cherokee, or both. He resigned from office and left Tennessee, and went to Arkansas to live with the Chief, and work as an Indian trader. However Chief Ooleteka

hated Houston's heavy drinking and denied him a seat in the tribal council. Houston and the Chief had a terrible falling out, forcing him to leave again, this time returning to Washington. There Houston argued with a Congressman who accused him of fraud, and beat him severely with his cane on Pennsylvania Avenue. Congress put Houston on trial, which was legally dubious as he was not serving at the time, and Houston defended himself with a rousing speech that turned the city in his favor. It is here that President Jackson asked Houston to go to Texas as an Indian agent, and keep an eye on the restless Texans.

[18] Sam Houston first nearly died in the attack at Horseshoe Bend in 1814. He got an arrow in his leg, and was more seriously wounded when another soldier pulled it out. Houston continued to fight, and was hit by two bullets. The field doctor believed he would die and moved on to other casualties. But Houston made it through the night, slowly regaining strength, and survived several more days without proper care before returning home.

[19] Morgan, p. 205. In his inaugural remarks, President Polk said: "Foreign governments do not seem to appreciate the true character of our Government. [The goal of the US was] to enlarge its limits…to extend the dominion of peace over additional territories and increasing millions."

[20] Mexico had six different presidents just between 1840 and the start of the Mexican-American War. Visit en.wikipedia.org/wiki/List_of_heads_of_state_of_Mexico for a bewildering chart of all Mexican Presidents since their independence from Spain.

[21] Morgan p. 236. Historian Bernard DeVoto could only see in Zachary Taylor "total ignorance of the art of war. And an instinct if not for command, as least for leadership. He had been hardened in years of petty frontier duty, he had no nerves and nothing recognizable as intelligence, he was afraid of nothing, and he was too unimaginative to know when he was being licked….The army and even some of the West Pointers worshiped him."

[22] Johnson, p. 381. Captain Fremont was an officer in the

US Topographical Corps, and had already surveyed much of the Mississippi and Missouri River basins. On his third expedition to the west, he changed plans and arrived in California in early 1846 with a party of 60 volunteers, intent on fomenting rebellion among the American settlers. Mexican General Jose Castro drove them out, and Fremont returned to the Oregon desert, until he heard about the outbreak of war.

[23] Moser, p. 200.

[24] Schweikart, p. 21.

[25] I wonder how many Baltimoreans know their NFL team, the Ravens, are named in honor of a poem by Edgar Allen Poe?

[26] Douglass advised President Ulysses Grant, who signed Acts to disrupt the Ku Klux Klan and to protect the voting and legal rights of blacks in the South. In 1877 Douglass settled in Washington, DC and continued speaking, writing, traveling, and working with the Republicans. After his first wife died, Douglass married a white woman, a suffrage activist named Helen Pitts.

[27] Polk did not seek reelection. He entered office with four specific goals, which included California and Oregon, and achieved them all. It is also possible the controversy over the Mexican-American War discouraged him from running for reelection, much as controversy over the Vietnam War discouraged Lyndon Johnson from running in 1968.

[28] In modern times the best example is the Spanish Civil War in 1937-1938. Spanish Loyalists allied with German Nazis fought Spanish Rebels who were armed by the Soviet Union. Three years later, the Nazis and Soviets were fighting each other again in World War II (though Spain stayed neutral).

[29] In Lincoln's First Inaugural, he said: "I am loath to close. We are not enemies but friends. We must not be enemies. Though passion may have strained, it must not break our bonds of affection. The mystic chords of memory, stretching from every battlefield, and patriot grave, to every living heart and hearth-stone, all over this broad land, will yet swell the chorus of the Union, when again touched, as surely they will be, by the better angels of our nature."

[30] Governor Claiborne Jackson of Missouri struggled for

secession and sent the Missouri Militia under Sterling Price to seize the Union Arsenal in St. Louis, but were fought off by General Nathaniel Lyon. After a temporary truce, Lyon again fought the secessionists again in three Missouri battles, and was killed in the Battle of Wilson Creek. Fighting with the Confederate army, Price nearly retook Missouri after the Battle of Lexington. In September 1861, Union General John Fremont pushed the Militia back to southern Missouri, and moved their government to Marshall, Texas in late 1861.

[31] The Confederate flag, nicknamed the Stars and Bars, showed 13 stars to include the governments-in-exile of Missouri and Kentucky. The Union flag never took out the stars of the seceding states, and added stars for Kansas and West Virginia during the war, bringing the total number to 35 stars.

[32] Under Union control, both Missouri and West Virginia emancipated their slaves during the war.

[33] General Lee's beautiful home and estate in Arlington, Virginia overlooked the Potomac River and the city of Washington. The Union seized his property at the beginning of the war and used Lee's hilly estate for Arlington National Cemetery.

[34] The land is still a cornfield. Antietam Battlefield, next to the town of Sharpsburg, Maryland is one of many Civil War sites wonderfully managed by the National Park Service, and features trails, interpretive guides, and many monuments to the war dead at key spots during the fighting.

[35] General Ambrose Burnside had a magnificent set of sideburns, whiskers running from his mustache to his ears.

[36] Moser, p. 14.

[37] Schweikart and Allen, p. 328.

[38] The TriStar Pictures movie "Glory" released in 1989 is an outstanding story of the 54th Massachusetts Infantry.

[39] Union armies tended to be named for rivers, and Confederate armies for states, with only a few exceptions.

[40] President Lincoln's short Gettysburg Address followed a two-hour oration by Harvard President Edward Everett. Lincoln believed his speech had been overshadowed, and

would not be remembered. But it is remembered as the most powerful and concise marriage of idealistic purpose and dedication ever delivered.

[41] En.wikiquote.org: Before leaving Louisiana, Sherman is quoted as telling a Southern friend, "You people of the South don't know what you are doing. This country will be drenched in blood, and God only knows how it will end. It is all folly, madness, a crime against civilization! You people speak so lightly of war; you don't know what you're talking about. War is a terrible thing! You mistake, too, the people of the North. They are a peaceable people but an earnest people, and they will fight, too. They are not going to let this country be destroyed without a mighty effort to save it.... You are bound to fail. Only in your spirit and determination are you prepared for war. In all else you are totally unprepared, with a bad cause to start with. At first you will make headway, but as your limited resources begin to fail, shut out from the markets of Europe as you will be, your cause will begin to wane. If your people will but stop and think, they must see in the end that you will surely fail."

[42] Andersonville, Georgia was the most notorious of all Confederate prison camps. Starvation and disease killed 13,000 Union prisoners, over a third that were sent there. Many survivors were as sick and emaciated as those who survived the Nazi death camps in World War II.

[43] The Hampton Roads Conference was a secret, failed effort to end the war in February 1865. Union emissaries including William Seward sailed to Hampton Roads near Norfolk Bay and met with representatives of the Confederacy, hoping to inspire their help in a possible alliance against France. Union terms showed flexibility on when slaves would be emancipated, and possibly compensating slave-owners with $400 million. The Confederates refused to even admit they were part of the same nation. Seward and company returned to their boat, but sent a black oarsman back to shore with a bottle of champagne as a gift to the Southerners. Seward called out, "keep the champagne, but return the Negro."

[44] Knowla.org/entry/747: Warmoth is quoted as saying "I

don't pretend to be honest. I only pretend to be as honest as anybody in politics...Why damn it, everybody is demoralizing down here. Corruption is the fashion."

[45] Taranto, p. 93.

[46] The *CSS Alabama* was a Confederate warship built in London that sunk or burned 65 Northern merchant ships, without ever docking in a Confederate port. She was destroyed by the *USS Kearsarge* in the Battle of Cherbourg near France in June 1864.

[47] Johnson, p. 543. Congress and the press furiously attacked Gould and Fisk for attempting the gold corner, but each man continued about his business. Fisk later commented on the incident, "Nothing is lost save honor."

[48] Ulysses Grant, p. 611.

[49] Hicks, et al, p. 96-97. "To cheat the government out of land, as long as plenty of it existed, was regarded on the frontier as a very minor offense, if an offense at all."

[50] American History, Barrons, p. 166.

[51] Hicks, et al, p. 80. The Comstock Lode in the Nevada desert yielded at least $15 million per year in silver and gold for over 20 years, before being worked out in 1880.

[52] Bloody Bill Anderson was a pro-Confederate guerilla fighter who with Quantrill's Raiders targeted Union troops and Loyalists in Kansas and Missouri during the Civil War. In August 1863, Anderson was one of the leaders of the Lawrence, Kansas Massacre, and personally executed 14 people. His photographs show the same look of mystique and menace as Che Guevara.

[53] Wild Bill's acting included work with the great showman Buffalo Bill Cody, before Cody started his great Wild West Show.

[54] Thanks to protection inside national parks, the American buffalo herd today is about 4,000 head.

[55] Johnson, p. 539-540. The Battle over the Erie Railroad in 1867 between Daniel Drew, Jay Gould, and Jim Fisk against Cornelius Vanderbilt is one of the great stories of capitalism gone wild. Drew, Gould, and Fisk manipulated Erie stock with sales and purchases, driving the price up and down. Each side

enlisted a crooked judge to support their trading positions. At a high point, Gould threw 100,000 shares into the market, and "Erie went down like a dead heifer." The stock raiders then took their millions in greenbacks and crossed the Hudson in a ferry to Jersey City, where they holed up in a hotel, protected by a small army of thugs and three cannon. Vanderbilt, who had the loudest voice in New York, could be heard roaring from the New York shoreline.

[56] Schweikart p. 281.

[57] Johnson p. 532

[58] Tipple. Historian John Tipple has examined the writings of the 50 most influential analysts who used the robber baron model in the 1865-1914 period. He argues:

The originators of the Robber Baron concept were not the injured, the poor, the faddists, the jealous, or a dispossessed elite, but rather a frustrated group of observers led at last by protracted years of harsh depression to believe that the American dream of abundant prosperity for all was a hopeless myth....Thus the creation of the Robber Baron stereotype seems to have been the product of an impulsive popular attempt to explain the shift in the structure of American society in terms of the obvious. Rather than make the effort to understand the intricate processes of change, most critics appeared to slip into the easy vulgarizations of the "devil-view" of history which ingenuously assumes that all human misfortunes can be traced to the machinations of an easily located set of villains—in this case, the big businessmen of America. This assumption was clearly implicit in almost all of the criticism of the period.

[59] A member of the New York Stock Exchange is a person or firm with the right to buy and sell shares of stocks listed on the exchange. The current price of a member's seat is more than $1 million.

[60] Johnson, p. 546-547.

[61] Originally a grange was a local farmers' association or meeting place in a farming community.

[62] In 1876 the Electoral College was 369 votes. After the Compromise of 1877, Rutherford Hayes won 185 votes, the absolute minimum necessary to win the election.

[63] President Garfield was also a decent mathematician, and developed the geometric proof of the Pythagorean Theorem.

[64] Taranto and Leo, p. 109.

[65] Moser, p. 63.

[66] The filament currently used in incandescent light bulbs is made of tungsten.

[67] The five states joining after 1900 were Oklahoma in 1907, New Mexico in 1912, Arizona in 1912, Alaska in 1959, and Hawaii in 1959.

[68] Johnson, p. 552.

[69] Johnson, p. 513.

[70] The new wave of immigrants did not just congregate in the large cities; for example, there is a population of Hungarian descent in New Brunswick, New Jersey.

[71] Hicks, et al, p. 162-163. In 1868 China and the US signed the Burlingame Treaty, which allowed for unrestricted immigration between the two countries. This made it difficult to start controlling the inflow of Chinese labor in the late 1870s, until China agreed to give the US the right to "regulate, limit or suspend but not absolutely prohibit" immigration, and led to the Chinese Exclusion Act in 1882.

[72] We still recognize some names of Jewish business leaders from around the turn of the century: Julius Rosenwald of Sears and Roebuck Company, Benjamin Bloomingdale, the Strauss Brothers, Arthur Sulzberger of the New York Times, and J. David Stern of the New York Post.

[73] The birthrate in the US has been steadily falling since the post-war Baby Boom, and as of 2015 stands at 12.49 per thousand people.

[74] Johnson, p. 567. Allan Pinkerton (1819-1884) immigrated with a poor family from Scotland. Coming to America, he became a police detective and helped run military intelligence during the Civil War. While Pinkerton generally identified with laborers, he hated bullying and law-breaking. The Pinkerton Company developed tough tactics to break undemocratic strikes and built a nationwide security service.

[75] Ruddy, p. 220. Roosevelt wrote: "The spoils system, which can only be supplanted through the agencies which have

found expression in the act creating the Civil Service Commission, has been for seventy years the most potent of all the forces tending to bring about the degradation of our politics.... It must always be remembered that the prime object of the reform under consideration is to take the Civil Service out of politics."

[76] En.wikipedia.org/wiki/Benjamin_Harrison. Harrison addressed Congress in 1889 and stated: "The colored people did not intrude themselves upon us; they were brought here in chains and held in communities where they are now chiefly bound by a cruel slave code...when and under what conditions is the black man to have a free ballot? When is he in fact to have those full civil rights which have so long been his in law? When is that quality of influence which our form of government was intended to secure to the electors to be restored? ... In many parts of our country where the colored population is large the people of that race are by various devices deprived of any effective exercise of their political rights and of many of their civil rights. The wrong does not expend itself upon those whose votes are suppressed. Every constituency in the Union is wronged."

[77] Hicks, et al, p. 186. The Populist Party nearly cost the Democrats the victory in the 1892 election. Although Grover Cleveland had a solid electoral majority, the 1,041,028 votes cast for Populist James B. Weaver was much higher than the 380,810 advantage Cleveland had over Harrison.

[78] Moser, P. 213.

[79] Hicks, et al, p. 192-194. Senator Sherman's (Republican of Ohio) name is found or associated with several Acts passed by Congress. As Secretary of the Treasury he helped shape the Bland-Allison Act in 1876, which reduced silver's impact on the currency. As senator in 1890 he sponsored the Sherman Anti-trust Act, and the Silver Purchase Act, both described in this book.

[80] Johnson, p. 595.

[81] Automobiles were built in both Europe and the US by small manufacturers, and were a rare luxury until Henry Ford developed methods for mass-production on the assembly line.

Charles and Frank Duryea built the first American gasoline-powered automobile in 1893.

[82] Miklich, at 19CBaseball.com. The story about Abner Doubleday inventing baseball is largely myth. The game's roots go back at least 50 years earlier, as explained in this book.

[83] Actually, very little has changed. Which is better, for papers to openly declare their partisanship as in the 1800s, or for them to hide behind a façade of objectivity, as they do now?

[84] Ruddy, p. 228-230. Roosevelt wrote: "The hatred of the East and the crude ignorance of even elementary finance among such a multitude of well-meaning but puzzle-headed voters, give cause for serious alarm...." Regarding William Jennings Bryan's silver crusade, he wrote: "[Free coinage means] partial repudiation...would shake the country's credit and would damage that reputation for honest dealing which should be as dear to the nation as to a private individual."

[85] Historians agree that Hawaii became a US Territory largely against the will of its people, however they were overwhelmingly in favor of statehood in a referendum held in 1959.

[86] In 1950, Navy divers inspecting the wreck of the *USS Maine* confirmed it was not hit by a mine but sunk when one of the ship's boilers exploded.

[87] Ruddy, p. 238. Concerning President McKinley's hesitation in declaring war on Spain, Roosevelt wrote: "Imagine Washington, or Lincoln, or Andrew Jackson taking such a position! The first duty of a leader is to lead. McKinley has no more backbone than a chocolate éclair."

[88] Alexander p. 70

[89] Ruddy, p. 245.

[90] With the important exception of Germany in 1918. The Treaty of Versailles punished Germany so heavily it bankrupted their economy, and led to fascism and socialism under Adolf Hitler in the 1930s.

Made in the USA
Columbia, SC
27 June 2017